W9-BCV-485

Exhibit Labels

An Interpretive Approach

For Peter and Kathleen

Exhibit Labels

An Interpretive Approach

BEVERLY SERRELL

ALTAMIRA
PRESS

A Division of
ROWMAN & LITTLEFIELD PUBLISHERS, INC.
Walnut Creek • *Lanham* • *New York* • *Oxford*

ALTAMIRA PRESS
A division of Rowman & Littlefield Publishers, Inc.
1630 North Main Street, #367
Walnut Creek, CA 94596
www.altamirapress.com

Rowman & Littlefield Publishers, Inc.
A wholly owned subsidiary of The Rowman & Littlefield Publishing Group, Inc.
4501 Forbes Boulevard, Suite 200
Lanham, MD 20706

PO Box 317
Oxford
OX2 9RU, UK

Copyright © 1996 by AltaMira Press

All rights reserved. No part of this publication may be reproduced,
stored in a retrieval system, or transmitted in any form or by any
means, electronic, mechanical, photocopying, recording, or otherwise,
without the prior permission of the publisher.

British Library Cataloguing in Publication Information Available

Library of Congress Cataloging-in-Publication Data
Serrell, Beverly, 1943–
    Exhibit labels : an interpretive approach / Beverly Serrell.
        p. cm.
    Includes bibliographical references and index.
    ISBN 0-7619-9174-3 (cloth : alk. paper). — ISBN 0-7619-9106-9
(pbk. : alk. paper)
    1. Museum labels—Handbooks, manuals, etc. 2. Museum
    techniques—Handbooks, manuals, etc.   I. Title.
    AM157.S46 1996
    069 '.53—dc20   96-10710
                                                                            CIP

Printed in the United States of America
⊖™ The paper used in this publication meets the minimum requirements of American
National Standard for Information Sciences—Permanence of Paper for Printed Library
Materials, ANSI/NISO Z39.48–1992.

Contents

ABOUT THE AUTHOR

Serrell brings an unusual range of experience as a museum practitioner to *Exhibit Labels: An Interpretive Approach.* Since 1979, she has been an exhibit and evaluation consultant with art, history, natural history, and science museums, as well as zoos and aquariums. Before then, she was head of a museum education department for eight years, and had shorter stints as a high school science teacher and a research lab technician. Serrell holds an MA in science teaching in informal settings and a BS in biology. In 1995, she was a guest scholar at The J. Paul Getty Museum. She has been a frequent museum visitor all her life.

Foreword

Two things about museums make Beverly Serrell's book important. The first has to do with the fact that museums ought to be multi-media experiences, but rarely are. An ideal museum would invite us to engage all of our senses as we try to "know" and "understand" the objects displayed. But most museums do not, in fact, come close to encouraging the full use of our sensorium. We rarely hear anything, and are usually forbidden to touch. Smelling anything is out of the question. And that is why the words that are used to tell us about the objects displayed are of such critical importance. They must carry the burden of making us feel, hear, smell—yes, and even see—what we are looking at. With her considerable experience and sensitivity, Ms. Serrell writes about how to create interpretive labels so that words will compensate for sensory experience denied, so that words will have the texture and resonance to awaken us fully to what is in our presence.

Words can do that, and Ms. Serrell tells us how. But she tells more than that, which leads to the second thing about museums that make this book important.

Museums are, of course, a form of theater. They tell us stories—great and small—about what it means and has meant to be a human being. Without words, the objects displayed cannot tell the whole story, cannot even tell an interesting story. But words in themselves—like a superficial or disorganized script in a stage play—can misdirect our attention or trivialize the action or, even worse, entirely miss the point of what we are seeing. Ms. Serrell knows all the ways in which labels are used to muddle a story. She provides example after example of what should not be done. Even better, she knows how to use words so that the story is revealed with clarity, intensity, and intelligence. To put it plainly, Beverly Serrell is a great literary critic. Her domain is not the novel or the essay. It is the interpretive labels that accompany the artifacts displayed in museums. And I think it is safe to say that

more people spend more time reading such labels than reading any other form of literature, by which I mean to say that
Ms. Serrell's domain is not to be taken lightly. If this book
contributes toward making our museum experiences more
stimulating and profound, then it must take its place among
important works of literary and cultural criticism. As for me,
I have no doubt that the book achieves its aim and will be
given the attention and praise it deserves.

Neil Postman
New York City, 1996

Preface

In 1979, when I wrote the book *Making Exhibit Labels: A Step-by-Step Approach,* I was full of evangelism for making better labels, and, although I had limited experience, I was sure I knew how to do it. Many people took my advice, but I personally had trouble applying what I said to the real world of short schedules, small budgets, resistance to change, and not having as many answers as I thought I did. After several painful learning experiences in the late 1980s, I looked at the book again and thought, "I could never write that book now. I know too much, how hard it is, and why there are so many bad labels out there." Some of them were mine.

The majority of the photographs of labels in the first book were of poor examples, and several of the production methods described are now out of date. Most of the general advice is still valid, but as a field, museum practitioners have learned a lot through visitor research and evaluation that now can help substantiate our earlier intuitions, clarify some assumptions and shed some new light on the process of making exhibit labels.

There are some things that I believed in 1979 that I still believe now; there are things I have learned that I did not know then, and things that I believed then that I do not believe anymore.

What I still believe:
- Labels are really important.
- They can be done right, and it's worth it.
- It takes lots of time and hard work to get them right.
- Labels should be written for the broadest possible audience.

What I have learned that I did not know then:
- Good labels cannot fix a poor exhibition, but they can help.
- There are very few exceptionally good exhibitions.

- Common-sense labeling is surprisingly uncommon.
- Visitors have less time than I thought.
- Orientation is more important than I thought.
- Computers help make editing, design, production, and evaluation faster, cheaper, and easier than I ever dreamed.
- Computers have forever altered the nature of typography.

Things I said then that I do not believe are true anymore, or have changed:

- As recently as 1991, I classified visitors into different types (e.g., "samplers," "studiers") based upon how they supposedly used exhibits. But I no longer believe that it is helpful or productive to prejudge visitors or label them with negative/positive/stereotypic typologies.
- I used the term "the average visitor" and explained that it does not really stand for one person, but I have noticed that just using the term upsets some people.
- Designers and visitors have convinced me that words should not be used alone; visuals are often needed or helpful.
- Many labels these days contain quotations, questions, clever titles, metaphor and humor, but these stylistic techniques are hollow without a clear big idea holding them all together.
- I used to think evaluation was optional. It's not. It is mandatory.

I see a great gulf between what we claim to do educationally for our audiences and what visitors actually do—the disparities between what we say is going to happen in the grant proposal, what we announce in the press release, and what the measurable impacts turn out to be. I want to help narrow that gap and make educational exhibits be just that. I do not believe that we should make exhibitions be the last word or authority on any topic; but conversely, we should not abandon all notions of intent. The museum's mandate to present information must be tempered by a responsiveness to what visitors are interested in and capable of receiving and processing.

In label workshops over the years, I have gone from teaching about words on labels to teaching about words as part of whole exhibitions. Feedback from a recent session at a university museum involved a change of heart by a curator who originally thought my suggestions about writing short labels and writing more concretely was undermining the scholarship of her exhibitions. She later said, "It (the workshop) wasn't just about labels; it was about how visitors use them. We have to face the fact that if the messages are not getting through, it's not working." I certainly agree.

My old book about making labels was more about the basics of writing, editing, and producing labels. It was a step-by-step approach. (In one museum bookstore, they put it on the shelf with other "crafts.") It was directed primarily at small museums, with few staff and scant dollars to spend on exhibitions. This is a different book, still directed at beginning and intermediate label writers, but it contains more details that I hope will be thought-provoking to expert designers, subject specialists, and experienced exhibit planners.

Heartfelt thanks to all the folks who helped with The New Book: to Margaret Menninger, The J. Paul Getty Museum and Getty staff for their help and the Guest Scholarship that gave me the time and place to write; to Kathy McLean, Lisa Roberts, Judy Rand, Britt Raphling, Barbara Becker, Rebecca Mendez, Ian Wardropper, Gary Mechanic, Harris Shettel, Steve Bitgood, Lisa Mackinney, Frank Madsen, Alan Teller, John Bierlein, Richard Riccio, Rachel Hellenga and—last but far from least—Marlene Chambers, for their comments, edits and encouragement. Thanks to Peter Kiar, Nancy Levner and Cliff Abrams for advice on the photographs and to Carlos Morales and Proto Productions, Inc. for fine-tuning the chapter on fabrication. Thanks to my publishers and designers for their interest and support; to the various practitioners and museums who have allowed me to share their examples; and to Shedd Aquarium, Field Museum and Brookfield Zoo for taking risks and allowing me to try out so many different ideas.

Introduction

Notable improvements in interpretive labels have occurred in exhibitions in all types of museums since the 1970s. Scores of articles about labels have been written for museum publi cations. Discussions, workshops, and talks have been offered at professional meetings. We have learned to write shorter labels, use catchy titles, ask questions, and produce text in type large enough to read comfortably, even with bifocals.

There are many good examples we can follow, such as Judy Rand's work and the Monterey Bay Aquarium; Marlene Chambers and the Denver Art Museum's interpretive project. The Field Museum in Chicago, under the guidance of Mike Spock, made significant changes in its approaches to interpretive exhibitions, as has Denver's Natural History Museum. Some institutions have published and shared their manuals of style or label guidelines, such as Philadelphia Zoo, Brooklyn Children's Museum, The Metropolitan Museum of Art, and Minneapolis Institute of Arts. Helpful information about labels is available through the Visitor Studies Association (VSA), the American Association of Museums' Committee on Audience Research and Evaluation (CARE), and the National Association for Museum Exhibition (NAME).

So why do we need another book about labels? Because there are still lots of ways to improve the museum's role of providing interpretation through better labels. We still need to work harder to write labels for visitors, not for ourselves. Apparently some of the advice in the articles and discussions has not reached, or convinced, enough museum practitioners to ensure that more labels are made for visitors, not the curator's thesis advisor.

The 20 chapters in this book can be read in any order, and some information overlaps between chapters. They're meant to be a quick read, with the big idea stated up front in each. Examples of labels and visitor studies are drawn from dozens of different museums, because the principles in this book are meant to apply across the board, from all types of museums—whether they consist of combinations of objects, artifacts, art, culture, animals, music, people, or phenomena.

SIMILARITIES AND DIFFERENCES AMONG TYPES OF MUSEUMS

Among all museums there are many similarities and shared issues about labels, including their sizes and length, the number of ideas presented, visual resonance, design, and intrinsic rewards. Some people naturally resist the notion that what is good for another person's museum could not possibly have any relevance to their museum, because their collection, audience, city, or board of directors makes their case unique. It is the "not-in-my-gallery" mentality. In fact, there are some differences, some of which are specific to museum type:

- Art museums are more concerned with aesthetics and have conflicts about presenting interpretations that might impose on visitors' own impressions and experiences. Art museum practitioners worry about visitors spending too much time reading; all other museums worry that visitors do not read enough.
- Zoos must deal with animals that can move out of view, or sleep in a large lump that obscures the virtues and adaptations interpreted on the label.
- Children's museums, to reach their primary target audience, must appeal to preverbal and developmentally immature learners.
- Science museums have the difficult problem of presenting content that is complicated, abstract, and unseeable. Thus, many science museums rely on computers as exhibit elements themselves instead of as supplements.
- Natural history museums contend with large collections of multiple examples of objects and artifacts that to an untrained eye often look almost identical (e.g., 30 woven baskets, 20 knife handles, 50 stuffed birds).
- History museums see themselves as having a larger interpretive responsibility than science museums (where

knowledge is "relatively certain") or art museums (where knowledge is "a matter of opinion").

There are also differences between museums of the same discipline but of different sizes and different locations. In general, large urban museums share more in common with other large urban museums than they do with suburban or rural museums with small budgets and small staffs, regardless of the topic.

Our patience and empathy with each other's distinctive characteristics will be rewarded with more understanding of the whole field of museum interpretation. There are fewer special problems than ones we have in common. In post-modern thinking, the certainty of knowledge in all fields is challenged. Besides, many people who work at one kind of institution may end up working for another kind at some point.

DEFINITIONS OF TERMS

I recommend that readers begin by reviewing the glossary. As a profession of museum practitioners, we are a relatively young group, with few agreed-upon standards, no basic training manuals, and no clearly shared vocabulary. We need to be more careful in defining our terms and using them consistently. For example, in this book, "exhibits" and "exhibitions" are not the same thing: Exhibits are single exhibit elements, whereas exhibitions are groups of elements that together make up a coherent entity or share a theme.

When I use the word "visitors" I mean casual, free-ranging adults (alone, in social groups with other adults, or with children), not school groups or people in tour groups or with audio-headsets. The primary users of labels are adults.

An interpretive approach to labels means:

- label content is conceived in the context of communication goals and a big idea;
- labels are written with knowledge of the physical context and layout of the exhibition;
- the development of labels requires visitor input through

front-end and formative evaluation;

- labels cannot be thoroughly understood unless visitors read them in the context of the whole exhibition experience.

OBJECTIVES FOR THIS BOOK

When museum practitioners produce labels that are guided by clear goals, and contain accessible content and have words and visuals that work together, more visitors will understand, find meaning in, and enjoy museum exhibitions. This means that in art museums, visitors will spend as much or even more time looking at the art as they spend reading labels. It means that in natural history, science, cultural history museums, and zoos, visitors will be able to trust the labels to contain information meant for them. It means that in children's museums, not just adults, but children will read labels.

The goal for readers of this book should not be to achieve or expect perfection in museum labels, but to be able to recognize quality and make intelligent decisions about how to make better labels and more effective exhibitions.

This is not, I hope, the last book on labels. Museum practitioners, visitors, cultural critics, funders, and researchers will continue to discuss labels because content in the form of text is pivotal to many of the important issues about exhibition effectiveness and a fundamental part of museums' educational mission. The current attempt to reach broader audiences (i.e., more people, with more diverse demographic characteristics) can only be achieved through better communication techniques in exhibitions for people who have no special knowledge, interest, or training in the subject. And, not just those audiences—we also need to reach out to people who do not use museums, or who do find references to themselves there, or have not yet seen what can be gained from visiting them. Only then will museums truly be educationally effective and broadly serve their communities. Good labels are key to this effort.

1

Behind It All: A Big Idea

A powerful exhibition idea will clarify, limit, and focus the nature and scope of an exhibition and provide a well-defined goal against which to rate its success.

Some exhibit developers do not exercise self-control when selecting content for an exhibition. They have no limits and do not resist the temptation to try to tell every story. As one developer admitted proudly, "I'm the one who was responsible for the 450 panels on the wall. I wouldn't give up." But what is most interesting to that expert will not interest, engage, or positively impress most visitors. Faced with those 450, a visitor reported, "My heart sank when I saw all those labels."[1]

Interpretive labels will be easier to write and will make more sense overall to visitors if the exhibition has a single focus that unifies all its parts. Good labels are guided by a strong, cohesive exhibit plan—a theme, story, or communication goal—that sets the tone and limits the content. Not just the labels, but all of the interpretive techniques and the elements designed for the exhibition will be driven by this plan (see figure 1). The best plans are stated concisely as a "big idea."

A big idea is a sentence—a statement—of what the exhibition is about. It is a statement in one sentence, with a subject, an action, and a consequence. It should not be vague or compound. It is one big idea, not four. It also implies what the exhibit is not about. A big idea is big because it has fundamental meaningfulness that is important to human nature. It is not trivial. It is the first thing the team, together, should write for an exhibition.

FIGURE 1
All the media in *Otters and Oil Don't Mix* were integrated to support the big idea—that the damage to otters and the ecosystem caused by the Exxon Valdez oil spill was extensive, expensive, and unforgettable. Media include an open diorama, photographs, documents, text, illustrations, a video, a computer hypercard program, and live animals.

The definition of a big idea, written as a big idea statement, reads like this: The big idea provides an unambiguous focus for the exhibit team throughout the exhibit development process by clearly stating in one noncompound sentence the scope and purpose of an exhibition.

Exhibit developers use the big idea to delineate what will—and will not—be included in the exhibit. It is primarily a tool for the team, not an actual label for visitors, so although it must be clear, it is not necessarily simple. The big idea guides the development of exhibit elements and their labels (e.g., for cases, captions, interactives) that support, exemplify, and illustrate aspects of the big idea. This means that each element must also have a clearly defined objective that supports the big idea. For each exhibit component, the question, What's this got to do with it? should have a clear answer.

Exhibitions with a big idea can be big or small (e.g., 7,000 or 500 square feet). Size is not the determining factor. A small exhibit with a big idea can be very powerful. A big exhibit with a big idea can be very comprehensive and contain many elements that reinforce each other.

Other examples of big ideas:

From a planetarium: "Most of what we know about the Universe comes from messages we read in light." The statement was printed as the introductory panel to the exhibition, shown in figure 2.

From a zoo exhibition about a swamp: "A healthy swamp — an example of a threatened ecosystem—provides many surprising benefits to humans." This means that the exhibits will not be primarily about how animals are adapted to their environment. The statement was rewritten for the beginning of the exhibit as, "What a swamp is good for: clean water, flood control, recreation, habitats for wildlife, natural beauty, cultural traditions. Walk in and find out." The rewrite made the big idea more contextual and specific, for the visitor's sake.

FIGURE 2
A large panel announces the three-word title. It also states the big idea in 15 words (three seconds' worth of reading) and invites visitors to enter the exhibit.

From a science museum: "This exhibit will let visitors try out imaging tools to better understand their world." The statement would be clearer if it did not begin with "This exhibit . . ." but it is clear that the primary experience will be that visitors get to *do* something.

From a historical society: "Manufacturing a Miracle: Brooklyn and the Story of Penicillin." This is an unusual case where the title of the exhibit served as the big idea also. Evaluation showed that visitors easily grasped that the exhibit's title implied that Brooklyn played an important role in the manufacture of penicillin, which made the miracle drug more widely available.

From an aquarium: "Sharks are not what you think." Although this big idea was rather abbreviated (that is, it does not say what about sharks is not what you think), the exhibit developers reported that "an impressive 80% of our visitors left the show with the main message." [2]

From an art museum: "What the artists portrayed about the West in these paintings is largely fiction, which had an impact on perpetuating myths about the West in other media." Viewers could then take their own position to this viewpoint, agreeing or not.

All of the examples above show the difference between a topic and a big idea. Topics, such as swamps, sharks, imaging tools, or Western art, are incomplete thoughts; whereas, a big idea tells you what about sharks, whose myths, or what imaging is good for. A big idea helps exhibit planners share the same vision for what the exhibition is really about.

The examples that follow are flawed big ideas:

A big idea that is too big: This exhibit is about the settlement of the western United States.

A big idea that might be too detailed for a lay audience, depending on how it is done: The exhibit will present the complex historical and scientific information surrounding the questionable authenticity of the sculpture.

Several big ideas strung together, without a single idea to hold them together: Visitors will learn about molecular structure, chemical reactions, and the scientific process of analyzing unknown substances.

Too often, in my experience, museum practitioners, especially those working in children's museums and science museums, do not ask themselves what the big idea is. Instead, they develop the exhibition as a bunch of "neat, affordable devices that visitors will love and not be able to destroy." These neat exhibit elements are often developed with cleverness and creativity, but lack a cohesive or logical relationship to each other and do not always support any exhibit objectives. They also lack soul—the fundamental meaningfulness that answers the question, So what?

Neat exhibit ideas without precision, focus, and soul are not enough. There should be more to exhibit elements than having visitors like them and enjoy themselves. Enjoyment is not the only criterion for success. Especially in exhibitions that claim to be educational, visitors should be able to understand what an element is about, grasp its context in the whole exhibition (i.e., within the big idea), and find it personally meaningful and useful.

As visitors exit an exhibition, if they can easily, unhesitatingly and thoroughly answer the question, What was that exhibition about?, there is strong evidence for immediate impact—comprehension and personal significance. If the majority of them seem hesitant ("Uh, ummm . . ."), uncertain ("I think, maybe, well . . ."), brief and incomplete ("It was about sharks"), or apologetic ("I really wasn't paying attention," "I just breezed through"), there is evidence that the big idea was not clear. Visitors certainly can create their own meanings, in ways unintended by the exhibit developers, but this is not a problem as long as what the majority of them create is not contradictory to the exhibit's purpose, or does not perpetuate misunderstandings that the exhibit was supposed to correct.

Having a big idea does not make visitors' experiences in the exhibition more controlled, constricted, or less open-ended than an exhibition without one, but it does increase the likelihood that visitors will be able to decipher the exhibition's communication goals. A big idea keeps the exhibit team accountable to their educational objectives while allowing visitors to construct their own experiences freely.

The "voice" of an exhibition is linked to the big idea, but is also different from it. The big idea determines what the voice or voices within the exhibit will be like—casual narrator, formal instructor, knowledgeable expert, firsthand experience, or different voices with different points of view.

If the big idea is a controversial one, a balanced viewpoint may or may not be desirable—again, it depends on exactly what the big idea is. The 1995 controversy at the Smithsonian Institution over plans for the *Enola Gay* exhibition was the result of a bad match between the subject (the atomic bombing of Japan in World War II) and the timing (the 50-year celebration of the end of the war, honoring those who fought).[3] Was it supposed to be an academic history-of-war exhibit, or was it a tribute to the United States of America's armed forces? A balance between those two might not have been possible, but a clarification of whose point of view was being communicated and for what purpose would have clearly been a good idea.

A big idea works best when the team writes it down—but does not set it in stone—at the beginning of the exhibition development process and changes it when necessary. The operative words are "written down." If the big idea is not written down, different people on the exhibit team will have their own interpretations for it, and conflicts will develop over what is necessary and appropriate in the exhibition. Even when the big idea is written, it is amazing how differently people will interpret it. Members of the exhibit team should all memorize or post the big-idea label over their desks so that they can refer to it easily.

A big idea can be tried out with visitors early in the planning stages, and visitor response can help developers shape or modify it, or tighten up the exhibit plan. After the exhibition is completed, evaluation can tell you whether or not the visitor's experience successfully reflects or incorporates the big idea.

Exhibitions that lack a big idea are very common. And they show it because they are overwhelming, confusing, intimidating, and too complex. There are too many labels, and the texts do not relate to the objects. The labels contain too many different ideas that do not clearly relate to each other. They are hard to grasp. They are typically underutilized—the majority of visitors move through them quickly, stopping at only one-third of the elements.

Exhibit developers who work in teams will appreciate the power of a big idea. It can unify the efforts of the team members by helping to eliminate arguments over ego and turf. When all members of the team focus on the same objectives, each person's ideas can be considered more fairly. If an idea works, the team embraces it; if it does not fit, the team can reject it without bias by one member. A clear big idea also protects the team from criticism by sources whose support is needed, such as the director or the board. In an exhibition driven by the team's desire to communicate a big idea, there will be less need for the single job of "educator" because the whole team will share that role.

I have given a lot of space to the idea of having a clear big idea in the first place because so many other things depend on it—content research, label writing, image selection, design layout, and size. Without a big idea, the job of the writer is much more difficult: interpretive labels contain fragmented, unrelated facts with emphasis on providing information for the sake of information, not on providing meaningful, useful experiences for the visitor's sake. With a concise statement as the basis for all interpretation, the use of words in the exhibition will have clear direction and defined limits.

In the next chapter, you will see that just as a big idea provides useful limits to the nature and scope of an exhibition, an interpretive approach to label writing gives the exhibition a less authoritative, knowledge-based voice. A big idea defines what the story will be, and an interpretive approach encourages visitors to become part of the story themselves.

NOTES FOR CHAPTER 1:

1. These comments were from the 1995 American Association of Museums' 87th annual meeting panel discussion on "Critiquing Museum Exhibitions: The Sequel," available on tape.

2. Judy Rand, "Building on your ideas," in *Museum visitor studies in the 90s,* ed. Sandra Bicknell and Graham Farmelo (London: Science Museum, 1993).

3. Mike Wallace, "The Battle of the Enola Gay," *Museum News* 74, no. 4 (July/August 1995).

What Are Interpretive Labels?

Interpretive labels tell stories; they are narratives, not lists of facts. Any label that serves to explain, guide, question, inform, or provoke—in a way that invites participation by the reader—is interpretive.

The purpose of interpretive labels is to contribute to the overall visitor experience in a positive, enlightening, provocative, and meaningful way. Interpretive labels address visitors' unspoken concerns: What's in it for me? Why should I care? How will knowing this improve my life? If labels only identify objects, animals, or artwork, they are not interpretive. As one visitor commented about the lack of interpretive labels in a natural history museum's bird halls, "Maybe one out of five birds had a little baseball card thing on them besides the name. 'Hits right, throws left, batted .328.' I guess I was looking for more."[1]

Interpretive labels are part of interpretive exhibitions, which are displays that tell stories, contrast points of view, present challenging issues, or strive to change people's attitudes. Interpretive exhibitions are found in all types of museums where visitors become engaged in the subject of the exhibit toward a particular end result: realizing the communication objectives selected by the exhibit developers.

An exhibition that is a collection of objects, artifacts, art, or mechanisms, with no intended learning objectives—except for the nebulous "visitors will experience it in their own unique way and find their own meanings"—is not a well-developed interpretive exhibition. This vagueness probably traces back to an unfocused underlying theme for the exhibit.

Vague exhibitions do not acknowledge to have, or hold themselves accountable for, any particular impact on visitors. In most institutions that claim to have an educational mission, interpretive exhibitions are the norm, but in many cases they could be much more committed to a particular educational theme or purpose than they are.

But what is "interpretation" itself? It is more than presenting information and more than encouraging participation. It is communication between a knowledgeable guide and an interested listener, where the listener's knowledge and meaning-making is as important as the guide's. It comes to museums (in the United States) from the more oral tradition of educational programming in the National Park Service, and it is far more interactive than traditional, formal educational models of teachers as deliverers and mediators of information.

In the classic *Interpreting Our Heritage,* Freeman Tilden explained his six principles for interpretation, developed from his extensive experience in National Park ranger programs and in writing labels and designing exhibitions at park visitor centers.[2] Although his 1950s-language is noninclusive (e.g., visitors and interpreters are referred to as "he" and "him") and the photographs appear dated, his principles still ring strong and true and are presented in straightforward, down-to-earth style. Tilden's six principles:

1. Any interpretation that does not somehow relate what is being displayed or described to something within the personality or experience of the visitor will be sterile.
2. Information, as such, is not interpretation. Interpretation is revelation based upon information. But they are entirely different things. However, all interpretation includes information.
3. Interpretation is an art, which combines many arts, whether the materials presented are scientific, historical or architectural. Any art is in some degree teachable.
4. The chief aim of interpretation is not instruction, but provocation.
5. Interpretation should aim to present a whole rather than a part, and must address itself to the whole man rather than any phase.

6. Interpretation addressed to children (say, up to the age of 12) should not be a dilution of the presentation to adults, but should follow a fundamentally different approach. To be at its best it will require a separate program.

Tilden proposed these principles in 1957, long before museum educators and other practitioners began using words like "the visitor experience," "meaning-making," and "empowerment." His fifth principle is the most relevant to my point of view in this book: To have a big idea behind it all; to keep everything else focused toward one, overall whole message; and to think about visitors as whole people with many shared needs.

Many other books discuss the importance of and describe the history of interpretive exhibits.[3] And there are several recent books that describe current thinking about serving diverse audiences. Kathleen McLean, in *Planning for People in Museum Exhibitions,* makes the point, "If we want exhibitions to be truly engaging, then all exhibit professionals, not only the educators and evaluators, will have to be communicators and audience advocates."[4] McLean argues for ways to make exhibitions better for the public as well as for many ways to make the exhibition development process function better within museums.

Lisa Roberts, in *From Knowledge to Narrative: Educators and the Changing Museum,* reviews the rise of professionalism of museum educators and its impact on the ways museums present knowledge.[5] She contrasts the curatorial-positivist stance (Here is our knowledge and truth for you to learn) with a multiple-meanings context (Here is what some people believe to be true). This shift of authority—and the acknowledgment of uncertainties and disagreements about what we know—within museums, whether science, history, or art, is part of a larger academic questioning about our assumptions in every major discipline. Roberts credits museum educators for the current trend in making exhibition narratives more inclusive: "It is educators whose sensitivity to visitors has brought them to question the comprehensibility, significance and voice of exhibit messages."

These general notions about interpretation have concrete implications that are important for museum labels. For one, there are some interesting similarities between interpretation, narratives, storytelling, and exhibit texts. Printed words exist as visual and as verbal elements to the reader's eye and mind, and as oral components to the reader's ear (reading silently or hearing someone read aloud). Good interpretation, like good storytelling, carries the listener along with the sound of the words and the images they create, and lets the listener participate by anticipating where the story is going. Good stories don't keep the reader in the dark.

Labels tell very short stories. In figure 3, a caption for an aquarium tank of silvery anchovies captures the immediate essence of their behavior. In figure 4, visitors' first impressions are quickly addressed and altered by the main caption for a diorama. Below are three more examples of interpretive labels that strike a good balance between what the reader might anticipate is coming next and what does:

When the tide ebbs, sandpipers fan out across mudflats and beaches to feed. As the tide rises, they retreat, to preen themselves and wait for the next low tide.

—*from an aquarium, at a seabird exhibit*

These screens were made at the Savonnerie manufactory, which was owned by the French Crown and provided carpets and screens for the royal chateaux. Such screens were known as paravents ("against the wind") and were usually kept folded in the corners of rooms. When the rooms were being used, the screens would be arranged by servants for protection against drafts.

—*from a decorative arts exhibit, as a caption for a pair of textile screens*

The logger needed clothes that were functional and provided freedom of movement. Pants were cut off just below the boot tops to keep the rain out and to prevent snagging. Men working in the woods often had to take off at top speed, and if a pant leg caught it could mean the difference between life and death.

—*from a history museum, as a photo caption in an exhibition about logging*

Anchovies only yawn at mealtime

Watch as these small silvery fish pass in their school, and you'll catch some "yawning." What you see is how they eat. As anchovies swim, they open wide, straining tiny plant and animal plankton from the water.

FIGURE 3
The caption for a large, round fish tank interprets the behaviors of silvery, swimming anchovies. It does a good job of directing visitors to look for the specific behavior discussed in the label.

This is how bison scratch their backs

For bison, there's no better way to stop an itch—or otherwise get comfortable—than by rolling in the dust. Depending on the time of year, they'll dust-bathe to shed old hair, get rid of insects, or just cool off.
During the summer mating season, males roll around to avoid fights. Bulls compete for mates by fighting, but a weaker bull will avoid battle. Instead he'll angrily tear up the ground with his horns and hooves, and hit the dirt.

FIGURE 4
A common first impression—that the bison is dead—is quickly and effectively countered with this caption for a diorama.

These kinds of labels help readers look back and forth between the label and the object, following the details of the narrative. Or, readers can imagine action in their minds and memories, aided by the label's concrete references. You may not see the tide rising, or feel the cold breeze in the chateaux, or witness the logger running for his life, but these quick stories give visitors a "minds-on" moment.

LABELS WITH MEANINGFUL STORIES

Visitors typically refer to labels as blurbs, captions, descriptions, titles, legends, cards, and explanations.[6] What changes would it take to get them to call labels "stories" or "conversations"? One way might be to follow the advice of Joseph M. Williams, in his very handy book called *Style: Ten Lessons in Clarity and Grace.*[7] He gives us some excellent guidelines for how to make prose more clear, less passive, and more engaging. His "First Principle of Clear Writing" states, "When we link the simple point that sentences are stories about characters who act to the way we use the grammar of a sentence to describe those characters and their actions, we get a principle of style more powerful than any other." His principle has two parts:

1. In the subjects of your sentences, name your cast of characters.
2. In the verbs of your sentences, name the crucial actions in which you involve those characters.

Similarly, labels that lack subjects and with unclear action cannot tell clear stories that flow easily. Because many of the stories in museums are about people, labels can be edited to include them as the subjects. In the two examples below, notice the difference between naming who did what, and what information is specific to the visitor's experience.

In the first, the subject "they" refers to the pictographs, not the early people, and pictographs are never defined. The pictographs do not have beliefs, people do, and the second example more actively acknowledges that.

Pictograph

Carvings and paintings on rock are scattered throughout California. They seem to have had magical or religious significance related to the hunting of large game. Other rock paintings were made during girls' coming-of-age ceremonies and boys' initiation rites.

Rock Carvings and Paintings—Pictographs

Early people carved and painted on rocks throughout California. The pictograms they created, such as the one on your left, may signify magical or religious aspects of the large game they hunted. Other rock paintings showed girls' coming-of-age ceremonies and boys' initiation rites.

The nature of storytelling in museum exhibitions and the techniques for doing it well are part of a larger context of issues that surround education, communication and being human. Neil Postman, who writes about modern culture, media, and education, suggests that one of the reasons traditional education in society today is not effective is that we lack commonly accepted stories that give us purpose and meaning. In *The End of Education: Redefining the Value of School*, Postman describes some of the stories that in recent times have failed to give us something to believe in: God and the Bible, Nazism, Marxism, modern science and technology.[8] Instead, he suggests we need stories that tell of origins, envision the future, and give a sense of continuity and purpose. This is especially challenging when we think about the diversity of typical urban communities that museums serve.

Postman proposes five new narratives for redefining the value of schools: the Spaceship Earth, the Fallen Angel, the American Experiment, the Law of Diversity, and the Word Weavers/the World Makers. I believe all of them have immediate relevance for museum interpretation because they help provide a fundamental meaningfulness to what museums are about:

- *The Spaceship Earth story says we are the crew members on this global spaceship and we have a moral obligation to work together to take good care of it.*

In zoos, aquariums, botanic gardens, and natural history museums, the new narrative could be about breaking down the myths and misunderstanding people have about the balance of nature and the preservation of nature. In dioramas and immersion exhibitions, such as rain forests or caves, dynamic processes and the need for global management of disrupted ecosystems could be stressed, rather than messages that reinforce visitors' notions that "everything would be fine, just as God made it, if we just learn to leave it alone." It would make global conservation our responsibility, not His. Currently, there are numerous examples of natural history exhibitions (including those in zoos and aquariums) that stress stewardship.

- *The Fallen Angel story's major theme is that human beings make mistakes, but we are also capable of humbly correcting them.*

In science museums it might mean more stories that show the meaning of the scientific method—its usefulness, its process, its foibles. It would mean putting more emphasis on the process of science—hypothesis making, hypothesis testing—rather than emphasizing science's technological products. It would stress our mistakes, maybe even more than our achievements. It would admit change and uncertainty more openly. In science museums, there are more examples of exhibitions that glorify and astound us with science than those that treat it as a subject fraught with fallibility.

- *The American Experiment is about how to argue and how to discover what questions are worth arguing about, and to recognize that every group has made good arguments and bad ones.*

In cultural history museums, the new stories would use multiple voices and contrasting points of view to stress common needs, questions, and imperfect solutions to problems. They would emphasize the need to argue intelligently, and stories would admit good and bad arguments by every group of people. It is an experiment characterized by change; history museums should encourage and show us how to participate in it.

- *The Law of Diversity tells a constructive and unifying story of diversity, not a divisive, isolating one that stresses differences.*

In art museums, a new sense of narrative and interpretation might mean making art more accessible and recognizing creativity among all people, not just artists. Art has grown and changed in response to multiple influences; it is not static. Of all museums, art museums still have the onus of perpetuating elitism, not inclusiveness. But in most other types of museums as well, the predominant approach to diversity has been divisive and "focusing on each individual piece, while ignoring the whole, thereby alienating visitors who do not identify with the group on exhibit."[9]

- *The Word Weavers/the World Makers is about the story of language and how we use it; how words transform the world, and how we are transformed by them.*

This one cuts to the heart of exhibit labels in all museums, but touches children's museums in a special way. We need to think more self-consciously about the social, moral, and symbolic meanings of words. Maybe we could tell children about this power, and let them investigate words as codes and see the way words work to make our world. There are a couple of examples that touch on this: the Museum of Tolerance in Los Angeles, and the exhibit *Face to Face* at the Chicago Children's Museum about prejudice. Both explore how words make us feel.

The answer to the question, What should label writers

A DIFFERENT KIND OF NARRATIVE

Comparisons: An Exorcise in Looking was a popular exhibition mounted by the Hirshhorn Museum and Sculpture Garden in 1991. It consisted of 15 pairs of objects. Each pair was composed of two works by the same artist in the same medium (oil painting, bronze sculpture, etc.) with similar subjects. It was a narrative exhibition that did not, at first, appear to be one.

The labels with the pairs of objects did not contain the usual paragraphs of text about the objects. Instead, the labels posed several questions that asked visitors to make comparisons, to discover likenesses and differences, and to make judgments. For example, with two Jackson Pollock paintings, the label asked, "Despite the difference in materials, how are these two works alike? Does one area stand out, or do you find yourself looking at the overall pattern in each work? Has Pollock used materials to produce a sense of movement in either of these works?"

While the labels did not tell visitors what the Hirshhorn curators thought about the pairs, or what their answers to the questions were, the exhibition obviously had a focused big idea: it was about the kind of thinking about art that goes into making quality judgments. The fact that the labels were questions, not textual information, created a different kind of narrative dialog between the museum and visitors in the gallery. People spent unusually long amounts of time looking and carrying on extended conversations with each other in front of each pair of art works. Their conversations included arguing about the labels and their answers, validating themselves for what they knew already or found out through the current experiences, and engaging in reveries with the object pairs.

The labels for *Comparisons* met the definition of being interpretive because they clearly helped create a positive, enlightening, provocative, and meaningful experience for visitors. The exhibit experience was about discovering meaning through personal interpretation, not about information given by an expert.

write about? is a complicated one. The general answer is, write about something that will be meaningful and useful to visitors, and write interpretively. Other than that, it depends on the individual museum and its visitors, and the individual exhibition and its big idea.

The question should be reframed as, How do you decide what to write about? The discussions in this chapter, the previous chapter about the big idea, and the next chapter about audiences guide you toward an answer for what the "what" is. The remaining chapters will help you decide the "how."

NOTES FOR CHAPTER 2:

1. From focus group comment in unpublished study by Serrell & Associates, "From Stuffed Birds on Sticks to Vivid Feathers, Gleaming Talons and Sparkling Beaks: A Summative Evaluation of the Bird Halls at Field Museum of Natural History," Chicago, November 1992.

2. Freeman Tilden, *Interpreting Our Heritage,* 3d ed. (Chapel Hill, N.C.: University of North Carolina Press, 1977).

3. Two standard references within the environmental interpretation field are *Environmental Interpretation: A practical guide,* by Sam H. Ham, and *Interpretive Master Planning* by John Veverka.

4. Kathleen McLean, *Planning for People in Museum Exhibitions* (Washington, D.C.: Association of Science-Technology Centers, 1993).

5. Lisa Carrole Roberts, *From Knowledge to Narrative: Educators and the Changing Museum* (Smithsonian Institution, in press). Roberts revised her University of Chicago Ph.D. dissertation (1992) into a book.

6. Lisa Hubbell Mackinney, "What Visitors Want to Know: The Use of Front-end and Formative Evaluation in Determining Label Content in an Art Museum," Master's thesis, John F. Kennedy University, 1993.

7. Joseph M. Williams, *Style: Ten Lessons in Clarity and Grace,* 3d ed. (Chicago: University of Chicago Press, 1990).

8. Neil Postman, *The End of Education: Redefining the Value of School* (New York: Alfred A. Knopf, Borzoi Books, 1995).

9. Eugene Dillenburg, "Turning Multiculturalism on Its Head," *Exhibitionist* 14, no. 2 (Fall 1995).

3

Types of Labels in Exhibitions

Every label in an exhibition has a specific purpose that needs to make sense within the organization of the whole. But given the way visitors encounter them out of order, they also need to function independently.

There is no universal terminology in museums to identify types of labels. Some institutions use function (e.g., orientation, introductory, caption); others use placement (e.g., wall text, case label, free-standing); some have in-house colloquial expressions (chat panels, tombstone labels) and others haven't thought about labels enough to develop standards for an in-house style or vocabulary. Regardless of the names they are given, labels should be developed as an integrated system from the single title to the broadest categories to the one-of-a-kinds. They should all work together.

The most important types of interpretive labels in any exhibition are the title, introduction, group or section labels, and captions. These labels help to organize the information and present the exhibition's rationale for looking the way it does. Although these labels are developed as linear and hierarchical information, they may not be used in the "right" order by visitors. Nevertheless, the labels still should have internal integrity, organization, and design.

Refer again to figure 1 and notice the use of six different types of labels integrated into the design of one small exhibit area. Each kind of label is distinguished and unified by consistent typeface, progressive sizes, and color combinations. The large main title is reversed out in the top bar. Subtitles are screened onto the wall, and smaller subsections are marked with titles reversed out in short bars. Captions are silk-screened on the walls and on the reading rail beneath the diorama next to the photographs and illustrations. The computer program provides an extended electronic label.

Noninterpretive labels include identification labels (ID

labels), donor plaques, wayfinding and prohibitive signs, and credit panels. They will be discussed briefly at the end of this chapter. Labels for interactive exhibits, which have special requirements, will be addressed in chapter 15. Here I will offer a general classification of basic interpretive labels, and expand on the special role of captions.

TYPES OF INTERPRETIVE LABELS

Title labels identify the name of the exhibition. The best titles will arouse interest and curiosity and give enough information to enable visitors to decide whether they are interested enough in the subject matter to enter (see figure 5). Large titles placed high overhead (i.e., more than eight feet from the ground) may be missed by visitors and will need to be repeated somewhere in their line of sight. There should only be one title, and it should be used consistently throughout the museum—the same name on the floor plan, in the guidebook, on the exhibit itself, and in the press release. An example of inconsistency: *Messages from the Wilderness* might get shortened inadvertently to "Wilderness Messages" or be referred to by in-house staff as "Hall 16." Generic gallery numbers or gallery donor names, such as "Webber Hall," do not serve visitors well.

Introductory or orientation labels set up the organization and tone of the exhibition. A large, simple floor plan and a summary statement will help to prepare visitors for the size, sections, and themes of the space, even if it is a small exhibition, and especially if it is large. Quick, clear orientation is a very important feature for visitors, but many people will not stop to read a long introduction because they are being drawn into the exhibit by many competing sights, objects, and sounds. If the entryway is crowded, visitors will not want to stop traffic flow into the exhibition. Dense introductory text with many thoughts all crammed into one paragraph is not inviting or easy to read. For all these reasons, keep orientation information short and the print large so that visitors can get it in a glance without stopping.

Messages from the
Wilderness

What do the messages
from the wilderness tell us?

That all life connects
in nature's puzzle.

Come visit these
American wilderness parks
to see how.

FIGURE 5
Brevity matters.
This example of an
introductory label
is short enough
that visitors can
read it without
stopping.

Visitor research studies have shown that visitors who understand the organization of the exhibition and use it in the intended sequence (if there is one) spend more time and get more out of it. [1]

The prominence and importance of introductory labels make it difficult to get the exhibit team to agree on them. As one label writer put it, "I can write three dozen captions and nobody will take any interest in them. But as soon as I write the introductory label, everybody from the director to the janitor wants to fiddle with the wording."[2]

Section or group labels inform visitors of the rationale behind a subgrouping of objects, paintings, or animals. Why are these things shown together? is a common question in the backs of visitors' minds, and it needs to be answered to help visitors feel comfortable, competent, and in control of their own experiences. Even if there is little cohesiveness in the groupings, inform visitors of that, so they will not wonder if they are missing something. Do not make area or group labels so long that people will want to skip them (see figure 6).

In the exhibition *Darkened Waters: Profile of an Oil Spill* many of the section labels were almost the same as the communication goals for those sections, for example:

Section labels	Communication goals
Recipe For A Disaster	*There were multiple reasons for it.*
We Couldn't Clean It Up	*We couldn't clean it all up.*
Oil and Animals Don't Mix	*It was a huge disaster.*

This unity of concept and design provided a very clear and very strong continuity of messages.

Another type of group label might present alternate points of view to the main thesis of the exhibition or a series of different voices, opinions, or speculations about one particular topic.

Group labels are also called "focus labels" and "chat panels" because they often contain more content than a title or subtitle and are more general than captions.

Captions are specific labels for specific objects (e.g., artifacts, photos, and phenomena), and they are commonly used in all types of museum exhibitions. Captions are the "front-line" form of interpretive labels because many visitors wander around in exhibits, without attending to the linear or hierarchical organization of information (title, introduction, section label). If visitors stop only when something catches their attention, the information in caption labels must make sense independently—as well as work harmoniously with all the other labels.

Sometimes the only labels visitors will read are captions because they are usually short and next to an object. They should refer to the visible specifics—beyond just the obvious—of the objects they discuss. If they are abstract or can be read alone without any reference to the object, they are not doing their job. Labels that support the caption information, such as subgroup or area labels, should be close by, so that visitors can start with the specific caption or ID, then jump to the broader context, and vice versa.

The Civil War

The Civil War is often called the first modern war. For the first time, mass armies confronted each other wielding weapons created by the industrial revolution. The resulting casualties dwarfed anything in the American experience. More than 600,000 men died, the equivalent in today's population of five million.

In population and economic resources, the North far exceeded the South. Yet the Union's task also eclipsed that of the Confederacy. To win, the North had to conquer an area as large as Western Europe, subduing armies defending their own soil. Only after a string of defeats did Lincoln find generals able to bring the North's advantages to bear on the battlefield.

Within days of the firing on Fort Sumter, tens of thousands of volunteers heeded the call of the opposing sides. Later, as enthusiasm for enlistment waned, both sides resorted to the draft, with men able to escape military service if they paid a prescribed amount of money or furnished a substitute.

Each army was a cross section of its society. The Northern forces were mostly farm boys, artisans, and urban workers, supplemented after 1862 by 200,000 black troops; the Southern army was made up of small farmers, with slaveholders dominating the officer corps. Few of these recruits had military experience or were ready for the monotony of life in camp—a constant round of digging ditches and incessant drilling only occasionally interrupted by fierce bursts of battlefield fighting.

Neither side was prepared for modern war. Medical care was primitive; far more men died of disease and inadequate treatment of wounds than in battle. Some 50,000 Americans perished in military prisons, victims of overcrowding and inadequate diet.

Whatever later generations came to believe, there was no romance in the Civil War.

FIGURE 6
A daunting six-paragraph, 36-line, 250-plus word label takes more time to read than most visitors are willing or able to spend. If it were shorter or if there were a separate, short paragraph (three or four lines long) at the top, it would look more approachable.

GUIDELINES FOR EFFECTIVE CAPTIONS

For a good model for caption labels, review some of the old *National Geographic* magazine photograph captions, which they call "legends." As can be seen in these three examples, *National Geographic* legends start with bold lead-in phrases and use active verbs. Content starts by being directly related to the visuals, in present tense, and the vocabulary has a broad reading-level appeal:

With one last look, an entertainer in an Ariguemes brothel checks her costume before going on stage. When her striptease ends, she will change to work clothes and join customers for drinks.

—*the photo shows woman standing in front of mirror*

Lonely at land's end, wild ponies guard a solitary stretch of Assateague Island, a sandy barrier off Maryland's Atlantic coast.

—*the photo shows windswept beach and group of ponies*

Aligned like sleek aircraft, a killer whale family group rests in British Columbia's Johnstone Strait. Here they have turned off the active sonar by which they navigate, staying in close contact instead. These toothed whales belong to pods that have remained permanent for 20 years, each pod with its own dialect of calls.

—*the photo shows row of shiny, black dorsal fins above water*

Legends can be read in any order, and they are not rigidly formatted to a certain number of words. In fact, the number of words for *National Geographic* photo legends is determined by what space the designer lays out for the captions—the writers write to fit. Another good model for active, concrete, clear, and concise captions that work well with visuals can be found in Time-Life books.

Below are some specific guidelines that will help make museum captions work effectively. Many of them are discussed at greater length in other chapters as well:

- Start with visual, concrete information—what visitors can see. Work from the specific to the general, not the other way around.
- Make the vocabulary appropriate for a broad range of ages. (Chapter 8 on reading levels will explain how.)
- Do not cram several ideas into one paragraph. Divide up the sentences into logical chunks.
- Use bullets to make lists easier to read.
- Do not try to make generalizations in captions based on a single object or example. Keep information specific to what visitors are experiencing firsthand.
- Vary the length (number of words), depending on the intrinsic value of the object being captioned. Objects likely to be of more interest (e.g., biggest, most famous) to the majority of visitors or that support the big idea best deserve longer captions. Do not make labels all the same length.
- Make captions short enough so that most visitors, if they choose to read, will be able to read the whole label. Five words per second is an average museum reading speed. Write most of the labels so that they can be read quickly— 10 seconds or less, or about 50 words or less.
- Make caption type large enough for readers' range of visual acuity. Your audience includes senior citizens and children, regardless of the type of institution. A minimum of 20-point type is strongly recommended. (Chapter 17 on typography gives examples.)
- Position captions so they are visible and legible to people in wheelchairs.
- Position captions so they are well lighted and shadows don't fall on them.
- If an object has been removed (e.g., for loan or conservation purposes) and the caption is still there, it is a thoughtful gesture to put up a photograph of the piece that is missing.

The following is an example of a caption that contains several of the above-mentioned characteristics, from an art exhibition about symbolism:

Rain Mask with Reptiles, Figures, and Bats

This powerful object was actually a mask used in a rain-petitioning dance at the Santa Anita settlement in the state of Guerrero, Mexico. It includes several symbols for water and rain:

- blue eyes, the color of water

- twisting, flowing serpents

- a vampire bat's head at the top of the mask, included because bats live in caves, believed to be the home of the rain gods

Another meaning of the mask relates to the notion of transformation and power. Lizards (as half-snake, half-legged animals) were said to be able to whisper secrets to the wearer. By wearing the mask, an individual was transformed into a godlike being with both animal attributes and the power to commune with and control nature.

The "Rain Mask" caption contains numerous references to concrete, visual aspects of the object, encourages visitors to look for details, and think about how it might feel to wear the mask. See figure 7 for another caption label with some similar characteristics.

Captions for interactive exhibits follow the same guidelines as above, but the placement and ordering of information is even more important. Captions that give directions need to be placed where people's hands and eyes naturally go. (See more about this in the section on labels for interactive exhibits.)

NONINTERPRETIVE TYPES OF LABELS

Identification labels contain minimal, short details, such as name, maker, date, material, scientific name, accession number. They are not interpretive, although they are often combined with interpretation or captions.

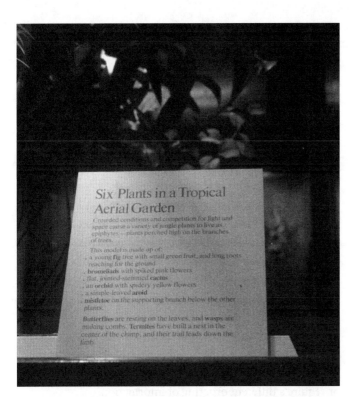

FIGURE 7
Multiple paragraphs, bold words, and bullets are some of the ways to break up a long caption. Because all of the information relates directly to what people can see, reading leads to making discoveries.

Several formats for ID labels are commonly used. The examples below show different arrangements of information and typography, and some work better than others:

The Abduction of the Sabine Women
Painted in Naples, about 1640
Johann Heinrich Schonfeld
Oil on canvas

PIER FRANCESCO
Italian, 1612–1666
Vision of Saint Bruno 1660–1666
Oil on canvas   89.PA.4

PORCELLANIDAE
Petrolisthes maculatus
Anemone Porcelain Crab

DROMEDARY CAMEL
Camelus dromedarius
NORTH AFRICA AND ARABIA
Donated by Hall Foundation

In most cases, what is most important to visitors is what it is—its title, its common name, an identifier that they can relate to. The first sample shows the most sensitivity to the visitors' interests, vocabulary, and priorities. In the second, an unfamiliar artist's name and three sets of numbers present a jumble of details for visitors to sort through. In the third sample, few visitors would even know that the first line was the animal's taxonomic family name and that the second its scientific Latin binomial; the typography and order are in the wrong priority for most visitors. The fourth is functional but somewhat boring.

Identification labels, as long as they are legible, are usually easy for visitors to decode, once a person has seen one or two. While consistency of ID information formats is important within each exhibition, format may vary between exhibitions. Different types of objects, artifacts, or animals might suggest or require a different ordering of information.

Donor information is typically provided last and in the smallest type. These tag lines are not interpretive and they should not be larger than or mixed in with captions, IDs, or other interpretive labels. Labels that acknowledge funders are best dealt with in their own space, near the end of the exhibition, in a discrete, respectful way. Materials, typefaces, and sizes should be sophisticated but not out of character with the rest of the signage. Expensive bronze donor or funder plaques next to dog-eared, paper interpretive labels indicates that visitors are not being considered first. Donor and funder names mixed into titles are ostentatious and confusing, such as "The Webber Hall of Mammals."

Credit panels recognize the contributions and efforts of all the people who worked on the exhibition. A credit panel does not have to be in bronze nor does it have to be big, but somewhere, credit should be given. Visitors should see the many people and different skills it takes to make a good show. Credit panels are also good for staff morale, as well as for reference and accountability.

Wayfinding and orientation signs help visitors find their way around the museum and orient themselves in each new space (such as when they walk in the front door or get off the elevator at an upper floor). These signs are technically not interpretive labels, but the role that orientation and way-finding signs play in satisfying visitors' need to know where they are—and the importance that need has in making people ready and receptive for learning—should not be over-looked. Visitors cannot be ready to receive interpretation if they are lost. A secure and comfortable knowledge of present location—and the subsequent relative locations of exits, bathrooms, or food—are basic to allowing visitors to feel readiness for "higher level" needs that deal with social, creative, or intellectual aspects of being human.

Prohibitive signs tell us not to touch the art or feed the animals. With a little creativity, prohibitive signs can be made friendly, funny, and positive, not threatening (see figure 8).

DIFFERENT TYPES OF LABELS IN ONE EXHIBITION

The number of different types of labels used in any one exhibition will be driven by communication goals, size, bud-get, and other factors, but it is probably a good idea to limit the number of different types of interpretive labels to fewer than 10. More than that, the exhibition design will begin to look cluttered and disorganized, and visitors will have a hard time figuring out what the "system" is and how to follow it. Labels on every available surface—on rails, kiosks, walls, stan-chions, glass, and mounted so that they flip, turn, flow around and over graphics, plus labels that are printed as static, or are scrolling, projected and pixilated—together in one exhibition are too much!

LABEL LENGTHS

All types of labels should be kept as brief as possible. Titles are usually fewer than 10 words. Orientation, introductory, and section labels, which are typically too long—over 300 words—should be edited down and broken into shorter

FIGURE 8
Prohibitive signs
can be friendly
and reflect their
context.

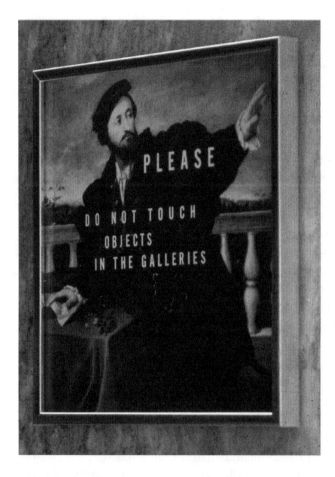

labels (50 words each). Longer introductory labels may be necessary if that is the only type of interpretive label in the exhibition, as might be the case in an art museum. Simple captions (one or two sentences) or extended captions (short paragraphs, plus illustrations) should be visually oriented, concrete, and interrelated.

The next chart reviews typical label lengths and types, but bear in mind that the question, How many words should there be in a label? is better asked as, How many words does this label need to have? And remember: stick to the point or ideas that support the big idea best.

Main types of Interpretive labels	Purpose	Number of words
EXHIBITION TITLES	to attract attention to inform about the theme to identify	1–7
INTRODUCTORY LABELS	to introduce the big idea to orientate visitors to the space	20–300
GROUP LABELS	to interpret a specific group of objects to introduce a subtheme	20–150
CAPTION LABELS	to interpret individual objects, models, phenomena	20–150

The logical order in which visitors encounter different types of labels is important in the flow of information, especially when different types of information are placed on the same label. Interpretive text should be set apart from donor or ID information by space, typeface, or type size.

"RANDOM ACCESS" TO THE TYPES OF LABELS

To test the idea that labels are able to stand alone, or can be read out of order, take all the labels of a certain type (e.g., all the captions, all the section labels) and scramble them up. Pull one out. If this is the first label that a person reads in the exhibition, will it serve as a good entry point? Select a set of three or four at random out of the pile and read them. Do they make sense in that mixed-up order? If you read only one-fifth of the labels, will they still convey the big idea? If labels can pass this test, they will serve visitors well.

BEYOND LABELS

More lengthy exhibit interpretation can be presented in formats other than labels. Besides inexpensive single-page handouts, newsprint, or brochures to use in the museum or take home, there can be books or the catalog to browse through (tables and chairs provided), laminated portable labels to carry around the gallery and put back, and catalogs for purchase. Videos, audio tours, computer databases, and demonstrations by staff can provide other means and modes of presenting information and interpretation. All of these supplementary forms of interpretation will allow interpretive labels on walls or in cases to remain brief, as they should be.

CASE STUDY

ENCOUNTERING LABELS IN A MANUSCRIPTS EXHIBIT

The **title** over the door leading into the room reads *Devotion and Desire,* an unusually sexy title for a manuscripts exhibit, I think.

The **subtitle,** on the same panel, says "Views of Women in the Middle Ages and Renaissance." For a historically challenged visitor like myself, the actual dates would be helpful.

Just inside the door, to the left, at eye level, on a free-standing kiosk, is a 15-inch-by-30-inch **introductory panel** that repeats the title and subtitle. Five paragraphs of text follow, all in the same typographic style. The first paragraph turns out to be a quotation. If it had been printed in italics, it would have been a strong clue or signal of that fact. The next paragraph explains the exhibit's purpose to "investigate different perceptions and actions of medieval and Renaissance women that were considered in some way ideal." I wonder to myself, Does that mean that all women were considered ideal or just some? Are medieval and Middle Ages the same thing? The next three **theme paragraphs,** in a legible, attractive typeface, are each set off with a subhead and numbers: Religious (1–9); Ideals of Love (10–13); Patronage and Piety (14–20). This clearly clues me that the room and the modest collection on view—which is fully in view, with eight free-standing cases containing open books of various sizes inside—are organized around three main topics.

Good exhibitions will skillfully combine several different types of labels, using them in a consistent manner. They need not conform to the exact types described here, but whatever form they take, each type of label should have a recognizable function that is clear to visitors. Size, typeface, color, graphic design, length, placement, and content will all be cues for

Although 20 books does not strike me as an overwhelming number of objects to look at, I want to start with Ideals of Love, but which way do I go? There is no floor plan that relates the topics and numbers on the panel to the room's layout. I take a guess. After glancing at one or two books, I find a caption label that begins with some **ID information** about *A Woman Accused of Breaking Her Betrothal Vow* (so, this must be the "Love" section). The title is followed by words that have little meaning to me, a nonexpert in manuscripts: "Gratian, Decretum (Decretals). Bologna, circa 1300. Ms. Ludwig XIV 3, fols. 277v–278." Perhaps those details could come last, not first? Then comes in small black type against a gray background, under dim illumination, about 60–75 words about the book and the picture in view. The caption begins with some history and background; in the second paragraph, finally, there is information about what I can see. It is detailed and interesting, but not particularly memorable. After glancing at a few more books and caption labels, I leave, picking up the *Devotion and Desire* **handout** from the wall-mounted holder near the door.

These seven types of written material for a small exhibit successfully attracted my attention and engaged me briefly. The labels seemed to cover the topic thoroughly (although I did not use many of them). Could the organization of the types of labels have been better? Only with the minor changes noted above, such as using italics or quotation marks for quotes, having a simple floor plan of the exhibition's layout of the themes, and putting the technical identification information last, not first. Otherwise, the function and label system of this exhibition, including the titles, subtitles, introduction, themes, captions, and IDs were easy to follow.

what the label's purpose is. Multiple cues should be employed to ensure that visitors will easily follow the logic of the exhibition designers' intent and messages.

The exhibition's big idea, the way the stories are told and the system of types of labels, all must take into account the needs, motivations, interests, and knowledge level of the people who come to visit. The next section will discuss popular notions of learning styles, levels of information, label vocabulary and style, and ways to reach audiences of diverse backgrounds.

NOTES FOR CHAPTER 3:

1. There are multiple references in Valerie Crane et al., *Informal Science Learning: What the Research Says about Television, Science, Museums, and Community-based Projects* (Dedham, Mass.: Research Communications Ltd., 1994). See Lankford and see Conroy in bibliography for special issues of *Visitor Behavior* that have focused on orientation issues.

2. Ava Ferguson, personal communication. Ferguson is an exhibit developer and label writer who works with a variety of museums. Her company is called Learning Designs.

Who Is the Audience (and What Do They Want)?

Museum visitors are a diverse group of fairly well-educated, mostly middle-class people seeking a culturally oriented, leisurely, social outing. They come to the museum with a variety of interests, but despite their diversity, they have many expectations and needs in common.

As museums strive to increase attendance and reach new audiences (non-Anglo, non-affluent, non-college educated), the audience for exhibit labels will become even more diverse. Museum practitioners need not, however, become overwhelmed by the diversity of visitors' demographics, interests, and motivations. Although there is no such thing as "the average visitor," we have learned through visitor studies that there are such things as trends and patterns in an otherwise heterogeneous sample of visitors to a particular museum or exhibition.

As a population, museum visitors and their behaviors are fairly predictable. Given a representative sample, there are often many similarities in who they are, what they like, and how they visit at many museums.[1] For example:

- A significant proportion of visitors comes for a social occasion, as a social group. Many of these groups include children.
- Gender ratios (percent males and females) are often not significantly different.
- Teenagers are under-represented in many different types of museums.

- A diverse cross section of visitor types is attracted to the most popular elements in an exhibition. When something "works," it tends to work for many types of people.
- More people read short labels than long labels.
- If visitors cannot understand or personally connect with part of an exhibit, they will skip it.
- Visitors of all ages are attracted to exhibit elements that are more concrete and less abstract.

FIGURE 9
Even though the button is large and obvious, adults probably need an invitation to "Push." Children are typically less inhibited. (A five-second audio plays while visitors read the 45-word label.)

There are also some interesting, but not surprising, differences in types of audiences:

- There are more groups without children in art museums than in most other types of museums.
- Children are more likely to touch and manipulate interactives before adults.
- Children are less likely to read labels than adults are.
- Groups with children allocate their time differently than groups of adults only, but both groups may spend the same amount of time overall.

The most striking differences between types of visitors are age-related, and these differences are primarily associated with children's uninhibited exploratory behavior. Children instinctively investigate things with their hands, but adults may need to be invited to touch and participate (see figure 9). Where adults seek structure or directions, children charge ahead without them.

Audience differences along lines other than age are more difficult to detect, probably because human adults are highly variable. Other than the differences noted above, there are few trends that hold true across many types of museums. Many of the expected differences between subaudiences (e.g., by group size, gender, or visitation patterns) that we think might be significant often turn out to be less so than expected. For example, The Cleveland Museum of Art reported, "We learned that even frequent visitors are not as familiar with the Museum, its art works, and art history as we had assumed them to be."[2]

While every visitor's experience will be unique, experiences of human beings are governed by many factors that most of us have in common. Diverse interests, intellects, and educational and economic backgrounds are all grounded in many fundamental similarities of human drives, such as the need for physical comfort and nonthreatening spaces, feelings of hunger, or fatigue, as well as the desire for self-actualization through our successful dealings with personal challenges, which help us feel competent and confident. Museums must constantly be aware of these factors and integrate visitors' basic drives ("Where's the toilet?") before attempting to help them achieve higher levels of consciousness ("What the heck is that?"). We must keep in mind the visitors' emotions, their yearning for continuity, love of a good story, and natural spirituality. By understanding the way the whole multicultural, multigenerational audience uses exhibitions, exhibit developers can have a more realistic basis for planning displays that will work for more people, and label writers will be gratified because their words will be read.

AN UNEXPECTED UNIFORMITY

This short case study documents how a museum changed its assumptions about its audience, from expecting to find differences to finding similarities.

When the Canadian Museum of Civilization decided to make an exhibition about the life of Samuel de Champlain—one of the best-known and most colorful figures in Canadian history—they anticipated that English Canadians and French Canadians would have different viewpoints about the topic. To help the museum decide how to meet these different audiences' needs, they conducted front-end evaluations with visitors of both groups, including different ages and backgrounds.

They were very surprised by the results of their evaluations. There were no appreciable differences in how Champlain was viewed by the Anglo and Franco populations. People also had a better idea of Champlain's chronological place in history than the exhibit team had expected. They concluded that there was really only one audience to target.

Although it had already been in the planning stages for two years, the exhibition was completely redesigned around the results of the evaluation. It proved to be one of their most popular exhibits ever.

SURVEYING VISITORS

Visitor surveys are a common means of finding out more about who the visitors are. But many of the questions asked do not illuminate the answers in ways that can help exhibitions and labels. Information about the visitor's zip code, income level, educational history, or gender offers the label writer little. More useful are visitors' answers to questions that relate directly to their understanding and self-relevance to the exhibit's topic, such as, "Do you have any special interest, knowledge or training in (the subject of the exhibition)?" Their feedback will reveal information about hobbies and other leisure activities and family history, as well as school or job-related interests. These will give label writers the "hooks" to interest readers. For example, from data gathered in Chicago area museums, we know that the planetarium attracts visitors with interests in telescopes and surveying.[3] Visitors to the natural history museum often have pets, are bird watchers, and have taken courses in biology. Aquarium visitors like to go fishing, eat fish, and keep fish at home. The maritime museum attracts people interested in shipwrecks, boat building and boat operation. There are also specific interests that some visitors to a maritime museum, a planetarium, a natural history museum, and an aquarium have in common, such as antique collecting, scuba diving, navigation, and employment as a teacher. Including references in labels to the interests your visitors are most likely to have in common can make labels more appealing to more people.

Other ways to find out more about your visitors through front-end and formative evaluation strategies will be covered in chapter 13, "Evaluation During Development."

THE TRAP OF VISITOR TYPOLOGIES

Visitor studies have led some people to believe that there are different types of visitors who can be identified by the way they use exhibitions, such as "streakers"—people who go through fast and stop at only a few elements; "samplers" or "browsers"—people who spend some time, and stop at a few things that seem to interest them; and "studiers"—people who spend more than the average time, looking at one thing for a long time, or looking at lots of things.

Much of what we know about visitor behavior in museum exhibitions is based, unfortunately, on poor examples of what effective educational exhibitions should or could be. Visitor typologies, such as "streakers" or "browsers," have evolved based on visitor behavior in exhibitions that encourage streaking, or that make browsing the most viable exploration tactic. The infrequency of "studiers" does not surprise me, given the propensity for displays with numerous, long, technical labels that discourage the reading behavior of adults, not to mention children. I have seen many cases in which children used an interactive device (such as a computer) by themselves—not with their parents—because the exhibit made the adults feel stupid or intimidated. When they cannot quickly understand what is going on and explain things easily to their children, parents hang back.

MISUNDERSTANDINGS ABOUT HOW TO APPEAL TO DIVERSE AUDIENCES

There are several common assumptions about audiences that, I believe, do not enhance the goal of making exhibitions more effective, visitor-oriented, and thoroughly utilized by diverse audiences. Although these ideas may sound good on the surface, further scrutiny reveals some misunderstandings. For example:

1. The assumption, "Exhibit planners should decide which portion of the audience is most important to reach with each exhibit message, and communicate that message using media that appeals to that portion of the audience," can easily lead to an exhibit with too many different messages. A better, more focused exhibit plan reads, "Exhibit planners should decide what the important exhibition messages are and communicate them using whatever media is most suited to that message in a way that will reach the broadest possible audience." While the intent— to appeal to broad audiences—for each of the above statements is the same, the implications for how to do it, and the potential for doing it successfully, are quite different.

According to the first statement, specific media are assumed to be more appealing to certain types of people than others. This has some limited validity in different age groups (children vs. adults), but it does not tend to be true for adults as a group. This assumption encourages too many messages for too many supposedly different people. If the revised assumption guides exhibition planning, media are selected for their appropriateness to deliver the message, and each message is aimed to reach as many people as possible. Thinking about diversity should lead to inclusiveness, not exclusion.

2. The assumption, "All visitors will find something of interest to them if you put lots of information in labels in an exhibition," is misinformed. Instead, it makes for an overwhelming environment dominated by walls covered by words, which will decrease visitors' willingness, ability, and motivation to explore labels carefully. Given that most visitors have a limited amount of time to spend in an exhibition, visitors to a large, dense layout will find it difficult to experience a high proportion of it. Instead of feeling intrigued, satisfied, and energized, many visitors become overwhelmed and worn out. They will feel as if they need to come back again to "do it all." Justifying the addition of labels or exhibit components because you want something for the minority of "more interested visitors" or "studiers" will decrease visitors' overall utilization of the exhibition. When you delete things that do not appeal to the broadest possible range of visitors, utilization of all elements can actually increase (see the case studies in chapter 12, "The Number of Words").

When visitors get to select from a smaller array of elements, each of which is appealing, they spend more time doing something that is interesting to them ("Oh boy, another neat thing") instead of spending time searching for something to connect with ("Nope, not that one; nope, not that one either.")

3. This assumption, "It is difficult to enable visitors to relate the subject to their lives and to examine their attitudes, values, and beliefs because most visitors arrive with limited time and knowledge about the subject," simply passes the buck. More likely, it is difficult for visitors to relate because

the detailed, complex nature of the subject presented in the exhibition is not geared to the limited time and knowledge most visitors bring with them. Should we try to change the visitors (e.g., increase their visual literacy before they arrive), or should we change the exhibitions? To me, the latter seems far more within museum practitioners' area of responsibility.

4. Here's another common one: "We must be careful not to take all exhibits down to the lowest common denominator. Shortening label copy to the point that virtually any visitor will read it denies the more sophisticated or repeat visitor the opportunity to learn more." It is hard for me to believe that some museum practitioners think this is true. Have they ever closely watched visitors in their galleries and seen how hard they try to understand what is going on, and how they typically underutilize what is there? Have they ever surveyed their visitors for their prior visits, or knowledge, interest and training in the subject and seen what percent of them are actually "sophisticated" or repeat visitors? Have they ever observed and listened to a focus group of visitors talking about their feelings of being intimidated, overwhelmed, or lost in museums? Have they ever tried out a mock-up of a label or interactive device with a small sample of visitors and seen that it did not work the first or the second time? Any one of these visitor studies will quickly dispel the notion that there is such a thing as a "lowest common denominator" and will make it clear that all of our visitors are worthy of our best efforts, and that we should always seek to please the *commonest* common denominators.

The key is to include sophisticated concepts as long as they appropriately support the big idea, and to be sure to use a nonexclusionary vocabulary. Chapter 6, on layers of information in exhibitions, will describe how to provide that range of exhibition experiences in a broadly accessible way.

The tendency to subdivide audiences into "types" and pigeonhole them with stereotypic characteristics will not lead, in my opinion, to better, more thoroughly used labels and effective exhibitions overall. Predetermined categories of visitor behavior are not as useful in exhibit design and evaluation as one might like to think.[4] If exhibit developers would think about the whole audience as time-limited, motivated nonexperts, in which almost everyone is a nonsequential "sampler," they would be much closer to the truth (see figure 10). The overarching challenge is to encourage and make possible more and longer sampling by more visitors.

Imagine an exhibition where the majority of visitors use the majority of available exhibit experiences—where children work with other children or adults, where adults talk and read out loud to each other and to their children, where visitors interact with others in different social groups, where people of all ages and learning styles are tempted to linger longer instead of rushing on to the next exhibit or exiting at the first opportunity. It is possible! Good orientation, a clear big idea, and good labels all will help make it happen.

FIGURE 10
Everyone over the age of seven is a potential label reader. Motivated label writers should write so that any one of these motivated readers can understand. Stereotyping people with supposed levels of interest, knowledge or ability is not the most productive way to think about visitors.

BUT WHAT DO THEY WANT?

Given that most exhibit elements and their labels are currently not used by the majority of visitors (Anglo, affluent, college-educated, and otherwise), a radical transformation in label content and form is needed if we expect to enlarge our appeal both to current and broader audiences. This transformation can be guided in part by what visitors say they want, and what to them are the characteristics of ideal exhibitions.

In a study by Alt and Shaw, visitors to the Natural History Museum in London compared old and new exhibitions and, in their own words, described what they thought contributed to the "ideal" one.[5] Of the 13 characteristics of ideal exhibitions listed, more than half are directly related to labels that captivate and communicate quickly, easily, and clearly:

- It makes the subject come to life.
- It gets the message across quickly.
- You can understand the point(s) it is making quickly.
- There's something in it for all ages.
- You can't help noticing it.
- It allows you to test yourself to see if you are right.
- It involves you.
- It deals with the subjects better than textbooks do.
- The information is clearly presented.
- It makes a difficult subject easier.
- It gives just enough information.
- It's clear what you're supposed to do and how to begin.
- Your attention isn't distracted from it by other displays.

In focus groups done at Brookfield Zoo in preparation for renovations of their bird exhibits, visitors discussed the positive factors that contribute to museum learning experience using these expressions and words:[6]

- It is memorable.
- It's an experience that involves your senses.
- You are gently guided to make discoveries.
- It is a personal experience.

- You get lots of opportunities to investigate and make observations.

The opposite experience from what is described above by the zoo visitors would result from an exhibition that visitors never noticed in the first place or forgot about soon afterwards; that did not attract or involve them actively or personally; that was unpleasant, irritating, obnoxious, or crowded; that was authoritative, confusing, and condescending; that did not allow them to exercise their powers of curiosity and scrutiny; that was foreign, strange, boring, obvious, unclear, or overwhelming. While few exhibitions have all these characteristics, these negative qualities exist in too many places. Most negative features, fortunately, can be eliminated through more careful planning (refer back to discussions of big ideas) and testing (discussed in chapters 13 and 19 on evaluation).

The Denver Art Museum's interpretive project looked closely at its audience and what visitors wanted.[7] Researchers found that most visitors were "art novices" with high interest in art but limited art backgrounds. The novices' criteria for liking an object were:

- that it have a pleasing kind of beauty
- that it be very intricate and detailed
- that its message be understandable to them.

For a moment, look at that list and think how it might apply to novices at any type of museum. Change art to history or anthropology or science and think about the pleasing beauty and intricacy of an animal, or a piece of rock, or an electric engine, and then think about the kinds of labels that would work in each case.

The findings from all three studies above have applicability to many other museums and situations. Most visitors are eager to learn, but they do not want to spend much time or effort in trying to figure out things. Good labels can attract, communicate, inspire, and help visitors get what they are seeking.

Visitors vote with their feet as they choose whether or not to spend time in exhibitions. If they find things they like, they stay longer. "What visitors bring to the exhibit determines the template onto which an exhibit can be expressed; but good exhibits can make this template sing!" say John Falk and Lynn Dierking, co-authors of *The Museum Experience.*[8]

Who is the audience? A self-selected group of semi-motivated, time-limited, mostly first-time visitors, who are novices but are curious about the subject matter. What do they want? They are seeking gratification through feelings of competence and an enjoyable social experience. If you select elements and write labels for *them*, chances are you will satisfy the vast majority of your visitors.

Another way to think about audiences is to realize how they, as an entity, are a vital part of the fundamental purpose of museums as places that exhibit and interpret collections and phenomena. We talk about making exhibitions come to life for the visitors; what about the way visitors bring the museum to life? American artist Michael Asher expressed the visitor's role in activating the museum's purpose in an art-work at The Art Institute of Chicago in 1982 for the 74th American Exhibition.[9] Asher hired groups of viewers to stand in front of different paintings in one of the museum's perma-nent collection galleries. Asher's Chicago work was the view-ing process—the intersection of the museum's presentation and the viewer's perception, neither one possible or complete without the other. When museums recognize and fully appre-ciate the audience's vital function, they become more willing to integrate new ways to meet the needs of visitors.

Current notions about diverse audiences stress the differ-ences between people, who they are, what they want and need, and other factors that make the differences between people seem overwhelming. Yet, within the diversity, there are also many similarities—which were the focus of this chapter. Some of the effective ways of satisfying critical differences in visitors' approaches to exhibitions are the subject of more attention in the next two chapters.

NOTES FOR CHAPTER 4:

1. Some of these trends are seen repeatedly in general museum visitor surveys. For more specifics, see articles by Judy Diamond, "The Behavior of Family Groups in Science Museums," and Randi Korn, "An Analysis of Differences Between Visitors at Natural History Museums and Science Centers," and "The Relationship between Exhibit Characteristics and Learning-Associated Behaviors in a Science Museum Discovery Space," by Boisvert and Slex. Also see Steve Bitgood's special issue of *Visitor Behavior* (Vol. 4, 1989) on exhibit labeling.

2. John E. Schloder, Marjorie Williams, and C. Griffith Mann, *The Visitor's Voice: Visitor Studies in the Renaissance-Baroque Galleries of The Cleveland Museum of Art 1990–1993* (Cleveland: The Cleveland Museum of Art, 1993).

3. These data were from unpublished formative evaluation studies collected by Serrell & Associates over a variety of small samples.

4. Jane Marie Litwak, "Another Measurement Tool for Exhibit Evaluators: The Time/Activity Matrix," in *Visitor Studies: Theory, Research, and Practice*, vol. 8, ed. S. Lankford (Jacksonville, Ala.: Visitor Studies Association, in press).

5. M. B. Alt and K. M. Shaw, "Characteristics of Ideal Museum Exhibits," *British Journal of Psychology* 75 (1984).

6. *Be a Bird Focus Group*, videocassette. Brookfield Zoo, June 1986.

7. Melora McDermott-Lewis, *The Denver Art Museum Interpretive Project* (Denver: Denver Art Museum, Winter 1990).

8. John H. Falk and Lynn D. Dierking, *The Museum Experience* (Washington, D.C.: Whalesback Books, 1992).

9. Anne Rorimer, "Michael Asher and James Coleman at Artists Space," in *Michael Asher / James Coleman, June 2 – July 2, 1988* (New York: Artists Space, 1988).

5

Learning Styles

Learning styles, along with other educational models and theories, have some important, but limited, applications for the unconventional, informal, fast-paced nature of learning from museum exhibitions, which takes place in seconds, not semesters.

The previous chapter emphasized appealing to visitors' commonalities. In this chapter we consider ways to make exhibitions appealing to differences—in styles, intelligences, and preferences—by integrating certain conditions and choices in the museum learning environment.

Learning styles are the different strategies people prefer to use in a learning situation: people's preferences for perceiving and processing information. Style categories are based to a large degree on research about how children learn in formal educational settings, particularly how students solve problems.

Learning styles identify qualities, such as "intuitive" or "analytical," that are deduced by watching how learners in classrooms (with a wide variety of resources to use and time to use them) take in and integrate new information, respond to situations, contruct meaning, and devise theories. Styles are also linked to how the right and left hemispheres of our brains process verbal and visual information differently. Museum practitioners find the concept of learning styles useful because it helps them characterize differences between the ways people learn.

A scheme based on a variety of studies about learning style was developed by Bernice McCarthy in which she identified four different types of learners and learning situations.[1] Her model has direct applicability to museum situations. For example, Rose Glennon used McCarthy's four styles to help develop strategies for orientation, interpretation, staff-visitor relations, and formal programs for the Toledo Museum of Art, including these basic ideas:[2]

Imaginative learners learn by listening and sharing ideas and prefer interpretation that encourages social interaction;

Analytical learners prefer interpretation that provides facts and sequential ideas;

Common-sense learners like to try out theories and discover things for themselves; and

Experiential learners learn by imaginative trial and error.

People's preferred learning styles are influenced by their genes, their past experience, and the demands and opportunities of the present environment. It is important to remember, however, that all learners use and need all different kinds of learning experiences. One learning style may be more comfortable for a person in one situtation, but not in another.

Thinking about visitors as having different styles helps exhibit developers honor the diversity of museum audiences and encourages them to provide a variety of ways for visitors to perceive and process information. Thinking about styles also helps all museum practitioners accept the task of motivating people as a primary responsibility.

INCORPORATING LEARNERS' PREFERENCES IN EXHIBITIONS AND INTERPRETATION

Exhibitions can accommodate visitors' different learning styles by providing choices so that visitors can pick and choose exhibit experiences according to their preferences. The three keys to making labels and exhibitions appealing to different learning styles are providing a variety of choices for visitors, making those choices clear and apparent to visitors, and, most importantly, regardless of which choices are made, making the variety of choices available add up to a greater whole when experienced together.

Most of the options for appealing to visitors' different learning preferences are compatible with each other, but a few are somewhat exclusive. Careful planning of options most suited to the exhibition's big idea will help exhibit developers pick the right ones.

Ways of making exhibitions and labels appeal to visitors with different learning styles are generally the same as making exhibitions more accessible for visitors with different personality types as measured with the Myers-Briggs Type Indicator or multiple intelligences as described by Howard Gardner.[3] While these alternate ways of considering the preferences and abilities of learners are worthwhile, they should be used in ways that do not get stuck in simplistic, divisive stereotyping of visitor characteristics or an overload of choices.

The seven subsections that follow are based on my reading and experience with ways of integrating learning style preferences into exhibitions.[4] Each one contrasts people's various preferences and suggest how to deal with them, particularly as they relate to verbal information and approaches to interpretation. They involve the physical and conceptual layout of the exhibition, the environment and experiences, and the social aspects of visiting an exhibition—the informal conditions and choices visitors face in museums.

Sequenced or unsequenced

These choices relate to visitors' preferences for dealing with the physical space of the exhibition and differing psychological comfort levels with orderliness or a more free-form approach.

- Some people like to have the recommended order or pathway laid out for them; they do not want to miss anything, and they want to see things in the "right" order, or at least to be aware of what the suggested order is. People who like sequencing will appreciate having floor plans, introductory labels, numbered exhibits, linear or one-way flow, self-guiding materials, arrows, alternate pathways made clear, and choices apparent, but not forced. In chaotic or confusing exhibition layouts, these people feel uncomfortable.

- Other people do not care what order things come in and want to be surprised or free to do it any way they want.

People who like free-flow will appreciate being able to skip ahead, or backtrack, without a one-way, forced path. There can be a sequence, but they feel free to ignore it.

Exhibitions that have a clear sequence or linear structure and also offer the option to skip around will satisfy the people who want a plan without annoying those who don't. Smaller exhibitions (less than 2,500 square feet) have the advantage of allowing visitors to get a sense of the whole space at a glance as they walk into it and to decide quickly about their own sequence and pace.

Pace-controlled or not controlled

People have different preferences about having control over spending time and the timing of experiences in an exhibition (some of which might also be highly sequenced).

- Some people like exhibit elements that have a built-in structure or pace and a set time limit or duration, such as a video, audio, or a docent-led tour. If an exhibit element has a set time span, it should be clear to the visitor, e.g., "Push button for a three-minute video," or "15-minute tour begins here." (Disneyland rides are examples of extremely pace- and sequence-controlled experiences.)
- Other people like to choose their own pace, to take a brief glance or spend a long time at one thing. These people will also appreciate knowing beforehand what the time limit of an element is, if there is one. These people might feel trapped if they find out—after-the-fact—that, for example, they have to sit through a video before proceeding to the next exhibit area.

Most pace-controlled exhibit experiences will not be a problem for visitors who prefer to control their own pace if they have the option to ignore them.

Peer group or authority-led

People have preferences for acquiring information in different kinds of social situations.

- Some people like to talk to their friends and family about what they see, read, or experience. People who like to talk in their groups will appreciate an exhibition atmosphere where they do not have to whisper or worry about disturbing other visitors when they talk out loud. Labels that are easy to read and sound good when read out loud will help promote social interactions between adults and between children and adults. Interactive devices or phenomena that encourage dialog are appealing to visitors who like to learn in peer groups or casual family groups in which no one is playing "leader" or leadership is fluid and shared.
- Other people prefer to have someone knowledgeable speak to them. Labels written in the voice of an expert will appeal to them. Questions such as, What do you think about this? will not be inviting. People who like to listen to a guided tour or an audio loop, will appreciate having them offered at frequent and convenient times.

If both types of experiences are available, set it up so they do not conflict. For example, tour groups in exhibitions should not hog exhibits and spoil the experience for self-guiding visitors. Exhibit element spaces need to be large enough to allow a family group to interact together. Two chairs instead of one at a computer station says, "Work together on this." In addition, both types of experiences should be timed so that visitors who come in social groups can split up, do their own thing and regroup in a timely manner.

Concrete or abstract experiences

This is a learning style about which we know that the majority of visitors to museums are clearly exercising one dominant preference: to see real stuff.

- Most visitors come to museums to have concrete experiences—seeing, doing, feeling things (e.g., real objects, models, phenonema) directly and literally. Labels that are well integrated with the things that visitors can see and do, that respond to visitors' most immediate questions, or that ask questions visitors can answer through their own observations and experiences appeal to most visitors. Long, detailed, or numerous analytical labels will interfere with the concreteness of an exhibit experience.

- People who enjoy abstract ideas and like to learn through reading and thinking instead of looking and doing are less likely to visit museums in the first place, and, if they do visit, they might find exhibits and labels to be superficial. Even abstract learners, however, will exercise their desire for concrete experiences by coming to museums to see and do things. By providing more lengthy information in forms other than labels, such as brochures, guidebooks, or catalogs, museums can appeal to this minority of people who are "hard-core" abstract learners.

Consider making the amount of abstract information in any exhibition proportional to the number of visitors who are analytical learners—probably less than 30% and maybe more like 5%.[5] Also, consider the idea that when visitors say they want more information, they might be saying that they want more concrete information, not more abstractions.

Active participation or vicarious watching

Both of these preferences also relate to the concrete experiences offered in exhibitions, but show variability in people's level of participation.

- Some people like to do and participate, and hands-on interactive elements appeal to a broad range of ages and abilities.

- Others like to watch someone else try an activity or do a demonstration. Although they might not actively have their own hands on, they can vicariously experience an interactive element by observing from a distance—over the shoulder of a user. Coming to a museum to watch other people whether or not you know them can be an important part of the experience.

Exhibitions can easily provide for both active and passive opportunities and situations, but interactive devices should not be the only opportunites to access interpretation of the exhibition's main themes. Although the people who use interactives are not a separate population from the people who read, there are some people who do not want to have to use an interactive device to understand what the point is. Good labels on interactives allow observer/readers to experience without touching.

Verbal and nonverbal stimuli

In art museums particularly, where nonverbal stimuli offer the dominant experience, there seems to be a dichotomy between people who like to read interpretive labels about the art, and those who do not. Both art novices and experts have opinions for and against reading about what someone else thinks. The degree to which visitors feel that information or interpretation helps or hinders their aesthetic response is an individual preference, but art museum experts know that information is an essential part of having a full aesthetic experience.[6]

- For some art museum visitors, labels are an imposition. If the interpretation is unexpectedly encountered or encountered in a way that feels forced, these visitors are likely to be annoyed. Some people think labels are visually intrusive and the visual clutter makes an aesthetic experience impossible. But those who do not want any information are in the minority.
- Others like finding out why a particular piece is in the museum, what makes it famous, what to notice, or why the artist created it, although they are sensitive to being talked down to or being told what to feel.

Orientation is important for all visitors to make choices: if the art exhibition has a declared didactic purpose and uses obvious, legible labels, visitors can choose to bypass it, or, if they choose to visit, they are still free to use the labels, audio tour, or brochure, or not.

In most museums other than art museums, these verbal-nonverbal preferences are likely to coexist compatibly in most learners.

- Some people like to read more than others, but more people will enjoy reading when the words help enhance their nonverbal concrete experiences, confirm their expectations, anticipations and motivations, and connect with their prior knowledge and feelings.
- Nonverbal communication through graphics (e.g., illustrations, icons, photographs) can reach people who do not want to rely on words. On the other hand, for readers, graphics can serve to reinforce and add new dimensions to verbal and concrete experiences. Changes in mood through lighting, color, texture, and sound can vary the nature of concrete experiences in nonverbal ways.

Appealing to all the senses can add depth and variety to visitors' experiences, although certain situations will call for more or less of one or the other mode.

Concentration and relaxation, noisy or quiet

Different people have different preferences and tolerance levels for the ambiance of exhibition spaces.

- Some people need areas of rest or contemplation to alternate with, or be available in addition to, areas of high-density sensory and mental overload. Some people have trouble concentrating when there are competing sources of noise and distractions. For example, they find it difficult to read a label while a video is playing nearby.
- Some people have no problem focusing on one thing amid a roomful of activity.

Exhibitions that space elements far enough apart to allow for some separation of activities, while still maintaining an overall lively atmosphere, will not drive the first type crazy, and not bother the second type.

We have considered many factors that can enable or discourage various styles, personalities, or intelligences to act. In most cases, the ways to appeal to different learning styles are not mutually exclusive within the whole exhibition context. If an essential exhibit message, however, is embodied in only one element that may have exclusionary appeal, such as a video or a written text, that message will be lost on the person who chooses not to use that element. Therefore, it is important to make essential communication objectives available to visitors through a variety of modes and styles.

Before leaving the discussion of learning styles, we need to look briefly at the question of instructional design, because it is within those designs that the opportunities for appealing to learning styles are embodied. While learning styles focus on personal characteristics that people carry with them, instructional design is a broader way of considering the interaction between educational strategies, learners, the content being communicated, and the contextual relationships between them.

APPROACHES TO INSTRUCTIONAL DESIGN IN EXHIBITIONS

A large body of literature about teaching theory is available. There are theories of learning, educational evaluation, developmental learning, teaching teachers, and communication theory. There are also social, societal and cultural issues that influence teaching and learning. All of this information is useful, to some extent, for museum practitioners.[7] I will deal here only with some contrasting aspects of instructional design that influence the effectiveness of interpretation and the process of developing and evaluating exhibits and exhibitions.

Prevailing learning theories range from models of more traditional, teacher-led, linear, structured activities, to student-directed, open-ended, constructivist activities, to models of the transmission of knowledge through more mutual, shared, group-led, participatory, iterative processes. Exhibition environments for casual visitors, however, are different from conventional educational settings in many ways.

In schools, the learners are usually grouped by age (and sometimes ability), a teacher/facilitator is always present, curricula are defined, and individuals' outcomes are measured by some means. Classroom activities take place over hours and weeks with the same groups of students. Traditional, sequential activities can be planned, offered, and evaluated by performance-based tests. Environments to encourage student-directed, constructivist experiences can be set up with teachers acting as facilitators while students keep a record of their own progress through portfolios. Cooperative learning among social groups with mixed ages focuses on joint tasks and shared decision-making. "Learning communities" can tackle and solve real problems in organized groups with shared leadership. All of these models can incorporate the notion of "scaffolding"—where the learner's readiness is matched with the timing of new experiences.[8]

In museums, the learners are heterogeneous in regard to age, ability, and interest, and are strictly voluntary (free-ranging visitors, that is, not school groups). Teachers or facilitators are largely absent (unless tours or demonstrations are offered), and exposures to exhibits are fleeting and one-time, with multiple entry and exit points. Every hour an exhibition space has a different group in it. Museum learners are under no obligation to learn anything. Nevertheless, many museums have "education" as an explicit part of their mission.

These differences mean that school-based models of instruction—traditional or alternative—have limited applicability in museums, because the museum's intentions to present and teach and the visitors' intentions to have a leisurely, self-rewarding experience are inherently mismatched.

The question of whether exhibits are "controlling" visitors or offering "open-ended" experiences often comes up in discussions with museum practitioners, with heated debates for and against. Some museum staff (especially in science centers) believe that exhibits with one sequence and one outcome (e.g., push a button and watch something happen) are stilted and contrived. They argue for more open-ended exhibits with multiple possible outcomes, and are against being limited by stating narrow objectives for visitors. Others believe that exhibits with no stated or apparent purpose are confusing to visitors, that such exhibits are educationally irresponsible, and that the museum has an obligation to be more explicit. These debates could be channeled more productively if we understood what each other meant. Also, there needs to be a willingness to entertain the possibility, depending on the circumstances, that both positions can be right.

Regardless of which model of instructional design is used in museums (e.g., structured sequences with single "discoveries" or activities with open-ended outcomes), exhibits do not "control" people. Self-selected, casual museum visitors have always been in charge of their own goals, used their own strategies, managed their own tasks and time, arrived at their own conclusions and integrations, and have not worried much about being extrinsically rewarded for learning or punished for failing to learn. Different kinds of exhibits encourage or discourage different aspects of this free-ranging behavior and some visitors will feel more comfortable with one type of exhibit than another. It is the museum's responsibility to present all information and opportunities for experiences in ways that casual visitors can make sense of for themselves by choosing the ones they find attractive and spending whatever amount of time they want to.[9]

The type of approach and degree to which the presentations embody one form of instructional design or another should depend on what ideas are being communicated and what experiences are intended by the museum. Some ideas are best communicated by a linear sequence; others by

multiple examples; others through open-ended experimentation; others through role-playing or mimicking. The design of
exhibitions and their labels should reflect the exhibit developer's intent, and the intent should be explicit: if it is meant to
be open-ended, let visitors know; if it is appropriate to be
pace-controlled or sequential, make that apparent.

THINKING ABOUT MOTIVATION

Besides learning styles or instructional designs, a general
and very useful concept for helping exhibit planners and label
writers to be visitor-centered in their approach to developing
exhibitions is to consider what motivates museum visitors. In
schools, students are motivated by and rewarded with passing
grades for paying attention and understanding concepts: the
rewards for learning are extrinsic. Museums must rely almost
exclusively on intrinsic rewards, which include the learner's
feelings of satisfying curiosity, gaining confidence from using
skills productively, meeting one's own expectations, and getting positive feedback. Regardless of people's learning styles,
the motivation for informal museum learning is self-reward.[10]

Providing for and accommodating people's different
learning styles, personality types, or intelligences is a good
idea because it makes exhibitions more appealing to a broad
range of learners. In the final analysis, however, exhibit effectiveness and impact should be judged by the exhibit's perfor-
mance, not its presentation of opportunities. The question,
How well does the exhibit communicate with visitors and
engage them in finding meaning? should be the driving force
in the actual design process and the summative evaluation,
not the more preliminary question, How will we go about
appealing to visitors' different learning styles? Appealing to
different learning styles is not a goal in itself, but a means to
the end of achieving effective communication.

The next chapter will add to the notions of learning styles,
instructional design and intrinsic motivation by discussing
levels of information in exhibitions and the physical and conceptual modes of presenting them.

NOTES FOR CHAPTER 5:

1. Bernice McCarthy, *The 4MAT System: Teaching to Learning Styles with Right/Left Mode Techniques* (Barrington, Ill.: EXCEL. Inc., 1987).

2. "The Four Basic Learning Styles in Museums" is an unpublished paper by Rose Glennon, The Toledo Museum of Art.

3. I. B. Myers, *Manual: The Myers-Briggs Type Indicator* (Palo Alto, Calif.: Consulting Psychologists Press, 1962). Howard Gardner, *Frames of Mind: The Theory of Multiple Intelligences* (New York: Basic Books, 1985).

4. I have written elsewhere about this in the Introduction to *What Research Says about Learning in Science Museums* and "Learning Styles and Museum Visitors." But that was back in my days when I still believed in visitor types, before I had done a lot of tracking and timing. For my revised viewpoint on styles, see, "The Question of Visitor Styles" in VSA conference papers from 1994. For another person's way of looking at styles without stereotyping visitors in museums, see Otto Kroeger's "Exhibiting Our Differences," *Exhibitionist* 14, no.1 (Spring 1995).

5. McCarthy (see note #1 above) puts the estimate for students in school at 30%, but some museum practitioners' guesses are lower, given the nature of the self-selecting audiences with their social agendas. See Roger Miles' "Museums and Public Culture: A Context for Communicating Science" in *Science Learning in the Informal Setting*, published by the Chicago Academy of Sciences.

6. The art museum issue of the "intrusion" of labels is discussed in *The Denver Art Museum Interpretive Project* by McDermott-Lewis. See also *Insights: Museums, Visitors, Attitudes, Expectations: A Focus Group Experiment* and "What Visitors Want to Know: The Use of Front-end and Formative Evaluation in Determining Label Content in an Art Museum" by Lisa Mackinney.

7. For a very easy to read and brief summary, see Linda A. Black's "Applying Learning Theory in the Development of a Museum Learning Environment," in *What Research Says about Learning in Science Museums* (Association of Science-Technology Centers, 1990).

8. The "learning community" concept is from Barbara Rogoff's "Developing Understanding of the Idea of Communities of Learners," Scribner Award Address, American Educational Research Association, New Orleans, April 1994. "Scaffolding" is based on the writings of L. Vygotsky.

9. D. N. Perkins, "What Constructivism Demands of the Learner," *Educational Technology* 31, no. 9 (September 1991).

10. The concept of intrinsic and extrinsic rewards in school-based learning has been around for decades. More recently, Csiksentmyhalyi and Chambers (see bibliography and discussions in chapter 7 as well) have applied this to informal learning, museums, and exhibit labels, and their research and writings contributed strongly to the thoughts expressed in this book.

6

Levels of Information and Modalities

Creating exhibit experiences through different types of labels and different modes of presenting information will provide for variety and will reinforce ideas throughout the exhibition.

It is a standard cliché these days: *The exhibits are conceived as a series of layers, making information about the objects accessible to visitors with different backgrounds and interests.* The idea of "levels" or "layers" of information is a popular one among museum practitioners because it seems intended to make exhibition concepts appealing to more diverse audiences. People's different "learning styles" or "modalities" are thought of as being served by offering different levels or layers of information. Exhibit planners use these words frequently to describe the organization of information in exhibitions, often without clearly defining what they mean. Thus, confusion reigns about how to design a layered exhibition, and label writers, furthermore, are confused about what it means to write levels of information.

Much of this confusion results from the fact that the interchangeable words "layers" and "levels" have an inherent association with a hierarchy (e.g., high-low, top-bottom, better-worse, first-last, shorter-longer, general-specific). A hierarchy may actually exist among properties and quantities, such as the types of labels (see chapter 3), the complexity of information, and the amount of time visitors may spend with any given exhibit element. Learning styles and modalities, on the other hand, are nonhierarchical and are not interchangeable concepts, although they are related. Both have to do with people's preferences about how they receive (modalities) and process (styles) information. Styles and preferences are not relatively better or worse, they are just different. Similarly, visitors' interests are not a property or quantity that should be thought of as having layers (e.g., more interest, less interest) because of the implied value judgment that relegates "less interested visitors" to a lower status. Levels of interest suggest, consciously or unconsciously, that "more interested visitors" are the favored, desired audience. This notion runs counter to any genuine effort to reach a broader audience. Because visitors self-select to visit an exhibition, we should assume that they are all interested visitors: their interests are based on diverse combinations of experiences—different, but not better or worse.

MODALITIES

Modalities are the forms, or modes, of presenting information or experiences. Different modalities provide choices of ways for learners to receive information, which can, therefore, appeal to a broader range of learners. They provide a useful concept for planning formal educational experiences as well as for informal exhibitions.

Applied to exhibit elements, available modalities include written words (labels, brochures), images (photos, movies), icons (symbols), sounds, touchable objects, devices to manipulate (interactive devices), illustrations and other forms of graphics (charts, maps, diagrams), demonstrations and computers. While individual visitors may have preferences for certain modalities over others, the immediate appeal and context of a well-designed, well-placed exhibit element can override a prior attitude. For example, "I don't usually watch videos, but this one was really interesting," or "I don't like to take docent tours, but I overheard this really good one," or "I don't usually use computer interactives, but I wanted to sit down for a while, and it turned out to be fun."

The best way to develop different modalities is to select the exhibit technology for each element by the content and communication objectives. Instead of saying, "The exhibit should include videos and computers," exhibit developers should be asking, What is the best way to tell this part of the story—a photograph, a video, an interactive device, an object, a group of artifacts, a re-creation of an environment? That way, the variety of modalities evolves naturally and appropriately.

When a variety of modalities carry similar (reinforcing, overlapping) messages, the exhibition as a whole will build toward and support a big idea coherently and completely for the greatest number of visitors. Thinking of modalities as parts of a whole leads to a sense of inclusiveness and inter-connection for the entire exhibition and the total visitor population.

It is less helpful to think of a visitor as preferring only a single, exclusive modality or having only one developmental level or learning style. This narrow thinking tends to encour-age the design of less coherent exhibit elements and ones that will appeal to a smaller fraction of the audience. There are many examples of adults perceiving interactive elements as being only for children, and they feel silly using it, or expect it to be childish and unappealing to them. Often, unfortunately, it is true.[1]

A final thought about a very powerful modality: the real thing. Many museums collect, store, conserve, and display real stuff—and that's why visitors come: to look at it. Forget the label, forget the video, never mind the computer database with a multitude of facts about it—you get to see the real thing, be in its presence, find out how big/small/shiny/awe-some it really is. For many people, their experience with the real thing will always be of primary importance. But other nonreal modalities can function as well, depending on the situation, availability, and purpose, such as a replica, a com-bination of real and fake, a model based on reality, and a model based on conjecture. All of these have the power to fire the imagination, and it is the museum's job to present them in ways that will help that happen.[2]

LAYERS AND LEVELS OF INFORMATION—
RECOMMENDED USES

I have encountered at least six different ways that layering occurs in exhibitions. Some make more sense than others, and some, I believe, are misguided attempts. The best examples of layers and levels of information are where they are defined by some combination of purpose, intrinsic complexity, and the amount of time visitors need to use them. The glue that holds these layers together is an allegiance to a big idea, with content that has focused communication goals. I recommend using levels of information, as defined in these three examples:

Layers defined by purpose: To increase the effectiveness of text-based components, different labels can be given a clear hierarchy by type (e.g., introductory, groupings and themes, object labels, points of view) as the exhibition is developed and designed. Examples of some of these types were discussed in chapter 3. The hierarchy can apply to individual components within the whole exhibition (refer again to figure 1), as well as to the organization of information on individual panels.

The trick, however, is making the organization logical and apparent to visitors. The content, design, and placement of labels enable visitors to figure out quickly which labels go with specific objects (e.g., captions), or which group label interprets a case or area (see figure 11). The typographic design of different labels can reinforce the status of the different levels and purposes. Consistency of typographic and overall design cues is important because it helps signal visitors as to the label's status. Labels that lack these differentiations can be much harder to decipher.

Too often, label levels and purposes cannot be decoded by visitors. For example, labels in a similar design with the same type size and typeface but with different purposes can be confusing. Another big pitfall is the partially developed or incomplete system of levels, where certain label types are clearly defined (e.g., title, introduction, subtheme/area labels)

FIGURE 11
Different levels of information work together harmoniously in this example. The most general information is on the large group label. More specifics are on the captions. The title of the panel captures the action ("Spanning") and resonate nicely with the photos and the model.

and the remainder is a mishmash of one- and two-of-a-kind designs, sizes, color, and purposes thrown into an undefined category called "other."

In the planning process—and in the final realization—the exhibit design and the communication goals (guided and limited by the big idea) need to be clearly defined and tightly structured together. Layers of labels that are defined by their purpose will help exhibit planners agree more readily on the content, and because purposes can be matched to outcomes, it will also be easier to agree on evaluation criteria. Meanwhile, the label writer will have better direction and clear limitations within which to work.

Layers defined by intrinsic complexity: In any exhibition, some elements and labels will naturally be more complex than others, as dictated by the content. All parts of an exhibit story are not equally complicated. If it is a complex idea and it is related to the big idea, it belongs in the exhibition. For example, when trying out mock-ups for an exhibition about forensics, exhibit developers had trouble with an interactive device about a chemical test for antibodies. The activity was frustrating and unclear to visitors. Repeated tests and modifications led to improvements, but the exhibition opened before all the problems were satisfactorily resolved. Exhibit developers decided to keep the exhibit element in, even though it was hard for most visitors to understand, because it was one of the most important and commonly used tests by forensic scientists.

Some labels need to be longer because they label more interesting or complex objects—as defined by what is interesting to the visitors and the nature of the objects. The big idea determines the importance of exhibit information, in the form of layers, and design arranges how visitors encounter the objects in their exhibit environment—as a holistic, multidimensional experience. The organization of information logically comes from and is dictated to a large extent by the exhibit space/experience itself.

Layers defined by intrinsic complexity can be used effectively in combination with layers defined by purpose. Flexibility is key to the success. The system dictated by purpose is modified by and adapted to the intrinsic complexity needs. In other words, the layering system needs to respond to different situations in a flexible way. This will not be possible if the system is too rigid or inappropriate. As one exhibit developer reported, "We had a layered system, but the content kept telling us to do it differently."

Layers defined by time: Architects and designers estimate budgets for huge projects on the basis of size—the number of square feet of a building or room. I believe that exhibit planners could make use of similar time-budget figures based on how much time visitors typically spend in exhibitions.

Visitors use time-budgeting by asking themselves (either consciously or unconsciously), How long do I want to spend in this exhibition? The answer is related to the size of the exhibition, its complexity (e.g., the number of elements, types of activities), and visitors' perceived interest in the subject or activity, as well as the nearness of a restroom or cafe, or when their parking meter will expire.

Rather than making assumptions about visitors' motivations or bladder sizes, I use two types of time—both the *average time* visitors might be expected to stay, and an index for a rate of time per unit space (as visitors walk slowly along, looking around, stopping occasionally), which I have called *sweep rate*. One minute per 300 square feet is a reasonable guideline for sweep rate, based on empirical data from 60 different exhibitions. None of them were "blockbuster" subjects, such as Monet, the gold of Tutankhamen, or the Holocaust, where the subject or objects have unusually strong intrinsic value or dense crowds that limit movement.

Visitors by and large do not spend much time in exhibitions. The average time is 10 minutes or less in many exhibitions ranging from 2,000 to 5,000 square feet, regardless of the topic, type of museum, or modes of presentation. With normal, nonblockbuster subjects, such as astronomical instruments, Native Americans, kelp forests, mammals of North

America, or global warming, it is very likely that most visitors will spend less than 20 minutes.

Each exhibit element in an exhibition can be considered as a unit of potential time, c.g., it takes 5 seconds to look at this; it takes 20 seconds to read that; this video lasts 4 minutes; or, it will take people about 10 seconds to figure this out. Then, the exhibition is planned so an appropriate number of elements can be used and experienced in the amount of time that the majority of visitors are likely to spend.

In exhibitions with an intended educational purpose, communication objectives, and a big idea, every exhibit component or activity needs to be integrated in a realistic time frame. The most logical order in which to use these elements and the amount of time estimated to use each one should be clearly understood and defined by the exhibit developers. Time-budget planning by the team will help make exhibitions that are not overwhelming to the majority of visitors. Instead of giving visitors dozens of choices and activities or labels that take a long time to use, try giving them fewer choices or activities that take less time.

People appreciate being given information that will help them make intelligent choices. If an exhibit element has a set time span, it should be clear to visitors, for example, "Push button for a three-minute video," or "15-minute tour begins here," or "This activity takes four minutes."

Writing and designing exhibit text in "chunks" of information can lead to exhibitions that are more accessible in a non-linear, time-limited way. Chunks are typically text blocks and illustrations—functioning at the caption level and purpose—that can be read in any order and in any quantity. The images alone tell part of the story, and all of the text is written at the same level of detail (see figure 12). Visitors who choose to use more chunks will spend more time. Visitors who have more time to spend can use it by using more chunks. Chunks do not have a hierarchy, and thus are less structured than levels.

Time-use categories are more practical, empirical, value-free, clear, and objective for planning and evaluating exhibits

Down on the
Catfish Farm

FIGURE 12
Next to a large tank of catfish, this back-lit label shows a good example of "chunking." Text blocks and illustrations can be read in any order and in any amount. They are all the same "level" of information as defined by complexity, vocabulary, and purpose.

than the negative, elitist, or bovine images ("grazers" and "browsers") evoked by most typologies or style names.

Before leaving the good examples of layering, there is one other definition of levels that should be mentioned: levels in terms of physical height from the floor. Some examples of this are large labels with text at eye level for adults and large graphics at a child's eye level (see figure 13); small, simple interactives or touchable objects at a child's height; and viewing levels, such as ramps in an exhibition that take visitors up to a different level to look over into an area or ramps down to look up at something from underneath. This definition of levels in exhibitions applies to physical properties and is quite different from the conceptual definitions I have discussed above.

FIGURE 13
"Levels" can
refer to physical
heights of labels
or elements in
exhibitions. Here,
large, colorful
graphics are at
eye level for
children.

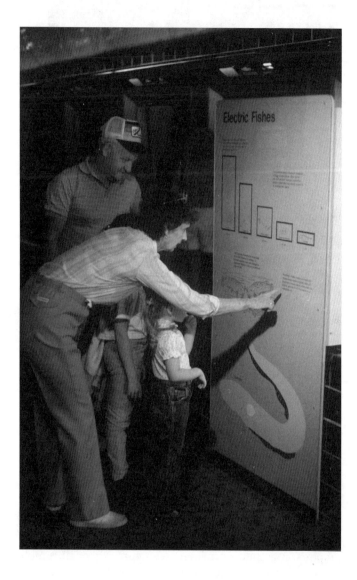

LAYERS AND LEVELS OF INFORMATION—
NOT RECOMMENDED

The next three types of layering of information are common, but I believe they have some serious faults—mainly because they encourage information overload in exhibitions, but also because any levels based on differences in the quality or amount of interest, ability, or intelligence among visitors implies a hierarchy in which those possessing more have some priority or favor over visitors with less.

The something-for-every-special-audience layering system: The worst example of layering or levels comes into play when exhibition planners (often large teams of staff and exhibit consultants) try to accommodate every different learning style, gender difference, developmental category, intelligence type, interest and experience level. It's easy to agree to do this in order to avoid telling members of the team that they are trying to put too many ideas into the exhibition. Every addition can be defended by the rationale, This part is for young children, or the scholars, or the women, or intuitive learners, or families . . . or whomever. What they really mean is, "Someone, somewhere, sometime is bound to find this interesting because I do, and I don't want to leave it out." Their evaluation criterion is, "If one person in 1,000 gets turned on by this, it's worth it to me, so put it in." The something-different-for-each-audience mistake is commonly made by today's educators. The result is unwittingly equivalent to the age-old curator's mistake of writing primarily for their peers—an exhibition that is overwhelming and underused.

The notion of adding information "for the visitors who want more" is a well-intentioned idea that is rarely realized successfully (see figures 14 and 15). If that information is too dense or too specialized, it will not be used by enough people to justify the time it took to research, write, edit, design, fabricate, install, and light it. More importantly, there seems to be no good way to signal those few "serious" visitors which levels make higher intellectual demands without being demeaning,

FIGURE 14
This label from an exhibition about jade uses different levels of information. Even though the second paragraph is quite long, all of the information refers to what the visitor can see, explore, and verify in the objects themselves. The label writer stuck to the principle "If you can't see it, don't write about it."

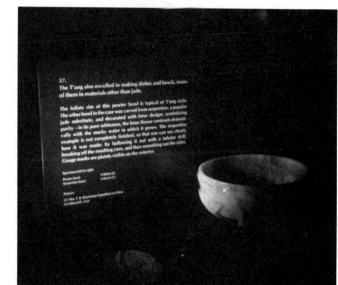

FIGURE 15
Panels about the lifesaving service contain three levels of text, defined by content, purpose and typography. But the long paragraph—a reprint of a historical newspaper article—is not tied directly to what visitors can see.

overwhelming, or confusing to the rest of the visitors. For example, after attempting a multilayered approach to match a variety of visitors' knowledge and interests in the *Human Biology* exhibition at the Natural History Museum in London, Roger Miles concluded, "It is better to concentrate on communicating some basic ideas than to fail to get anything over at all, and we feel that it is better to concentrate on succeeding at one level than to risk failure at two or more."[3] Perhaps the signaling devices needed to be less subtle. For example, on an element that requires a sophisticated understanding of DNA, put a big sign that announces "Genetic engineers love this one!"

In the exhibition *Prehistoric Journey* at the Denver Museum of Natural History, planners organized the information according to three audience levels of interest—discovery, exploration, and study—and signaled the levels with graphic design cues. For example, the signal for study level information is a panel shaped like a large open book. A magnifying glass signals the discovery level. Summative evaluation will reveal to what extent these assumptions and predictions about levels of interest in exhibit design work successfully.

Sometimes layers are hidden by a system of multiple flip labels. This design structure has the advantage of keeping words out of sight and off the walls. In the exhibition *Beyond Numbers* at the Maryland Science Center, little tabs that say "solution" or "more about math" signal users about the nature of the information contained on layers below. Some exhibit developers felt, however, that some of the layers were added to appeal more to the advisory group of mathematicians than to the visitors.

The disadvantages of these layers are the same—presenting overloads of information that lead to underuse by visitors. Something for almost everyone can be achieved in exhibitions by striving for inclusive, broad appeal, not by segmenting experiences into mutually exclusive audience categories.

THE "LAYERED" APPROACH—A CASE STUDY

In creating new exhibitions for two of the main galleries at the National Postal Museum, the exhibit developers used a layered approach to the interpretive information provided. They identified specific interpretive techniques for six exhibit components: large panel texts, quotes on walls (sometimes two quotes with different viewpoints), object label copy, mechanical and computer interactives, videos, and special interpretive panels. After the exhibition was open and had been evaluated, they revised their understanding of levels to a more inclusive, rather than exclusive definition.

The summative evaluation of visitor response to the exhibits, as well as a critical review by an evaluator, found that the layered components functioned differently than originally defined and expected:

- The **introductory panel** graphics were intended to introduce and summarize the key ideas within a gallery area, but the panels' design (color, type size, use of graphics) and placement were neither unique nor consistent, which made them difficult to be recognized as conveying one particular type of message.

- The **special interpretive panels** were planned to be more intellectually challenging than other reading materials in the exhibit and to offer "a deeper, analytical experience," connecting historic themes to the present. As it turned out, the challenge for visitors lay less in the panels' content than in their design. Text length (more than 300 words) and muted colors with low-contrast typography made them less attractive and less legible than the surrounding elements. In addition, although the panels were supposed to be related to each gallery's main theme, their content served as a counterpoint or critical analysis rather than a more detailed "layer" of the basic information.

- The **computer interactives** were meant to introduce or review a key idea in the exhibit and were directed at children. The number of visitors of all ages who used the interactive components exceeded expectations, a pleasant surprise. But the computer's intended introductory role was confounded by the considerable time necessary to complete a sequence or loop (e.g., two to 10 minutes).

- **Videos** were meant to offer more detailed information. Visitor data showed that the videos attracted a wide variety of visitors, but it was not possible to tell if that was due to the video's highly visual mode and ease of communication (and, perhaps, a desire to sit down), rather than the visitor's search for more depth or detailed information.

The assumption that interactives are a "layer" for visitors who do not read is a common one in museums, but the National Postal Museum's summative evaluation found that people who use interactives and those who read labels did not represent two distinct groups. Ninety-three percent of visitors who used two or more interactives also were observed to read in at least three instances. Interactives, it appeared, were attractive because they communicated information in a form that was different from, but not a substitute for, text.

Another assumption made by the exhibit planners was that some components would be used by visitors who were more interested and motivated than others. Using time as an indicator of motivation or interest, the data from this study showed that only about 10% of the exhibition's audience were at least "20-minute visitors." However, more of the exhibit elements (e.g., intricate reproductions of detailed letters, individual labels containing more than 50 words, videos lasting more than two minutes, and complex computer programs) were geared to that 10% than to the other 90% of the visitors who budgeted less time. The clarity and brevity of the thematic object labels (captions) throughout the exhibit, however, appeared to provide an accessible way for the majority of visitors to enjoy and understand the exhibit quickly.

One of the explicit tasks of the summative evaluation had been to evaluate the effectiveness of the layering system itself. Given that the exhibition's design did not fully express the original intentions of the layers, however, it was unrealistic to expect visitors to be able to figure out which elements were meant to be used first; which were meant to be optional and less integral to the storyline; which elements contributed most strongly to the themes; which were suitable to a particular age group. (This situation is far from unique among museum exhibit planning scenarios.) Nevertheless, many of the components were very effective—as evidenced by visitors' time spent and the attraction rates

→

in the tracking and timing data. The attractiveness of the individual elements in National Postal Museum galleries seemed to be more due to their context and content than to their intended function or place in a layering system.

Fortunately, there is a happy ending to this case study. Money was allotted for some remedial changes to improve the communication effectiveness of the different types of text interpretive elements, such as making the group labels recognizable through the use of similar size, colors, location, or placement and repetitive use of graphics.

In addition, museum staff's notion of layering was modified to conform more with how visitors actually used the exhibit. Rather than expecting visitors to do some things first, or assuming that some visitors will seek out only one type of modality over another, the exhibit designers realized that they had provided several different types of experiences—modalities (interactive, video, text)—with no actual hierarchy, which offered many different opportunities for communication of the main messages to a wide range of visitors. Instead of thinking of this as a "layering of information," they began to think of it more as a "buffet of opportunities." The buffet metaphor suggests a variety of opportunities *that all fall within one theme, for one general audience*. Visitors are free to pick and choose which elements appeal to them, and any of their choices will be likely to add up to an experience that is within range of the exhibit developers' intended goals.

The I.Q. layering system: Another unfortunate example of layering and levels is based on visitors' supposed intelligence, for example, "This label is for the dummies," or "This label is for smart people who are knowledgeable about the subject." The result can be an insulting, underutilized exhibit, where levels of labels either pander or baffle. Labels without humility are pompous and insulting. Although there is a range of visitor intelligence, for the developers to make decisions based on assumptions about I.Q. is unnecessary and degrading to visitors.

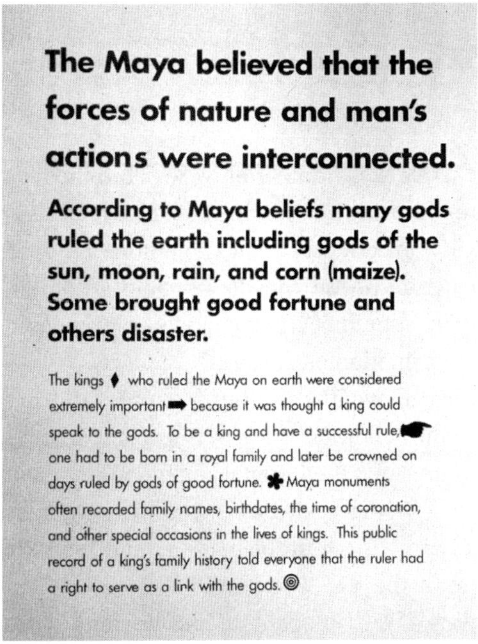

The Maya believed that the forces of nature and man's actions were interconnected.

According to Maya beliefs many gods ruled the earth including gods of the sun, moon, rain, and corn (maize). Some brought good fortune and others disaster.

The kings ♦ who ruled the Maya on earth were considered extremely important ➡ because it was thought a king could speak to the gods. To be a king and have a successful rule, ☞ one had to be born in a royal family and later be crowned on days ruled by gods of good fortune. ✽ Maya monuments often recorded family names, birthdates, the time of coronation, and other special occasions in the lives of kings. This public record of a king's family history told everyone that the ruler had a right to serve as a link with the gods. ◎

FIGURE 16
The three levels of information and the icons in this label have little to do with the visitors' experience in the exhibit. "Multiple levels of information" are not effective when they lack context.

The expert's layering system: A third example of layers or levels that works *against* making exhibitions more appealing and thoroughly utilized is one in which label information is organized from simple to complex, or from general to specific.

The expert's hierarchy of knowledge gives rise to tri-level labels with the most general information first in the largest type, more details next, and minutia in the third paragraph in smallest type (see figure 16). This hierarchy is based on conceptual, abstract knowledge, where "simple" or "general" may have nothing to do with visitors' primary questions prompted by the exhibition context. Similarly, "complex" may take visitors far beyond anything suggested by the exhibition itself. The notion of simple-to-complex often lacks sensitivity to the immediate, contextual needs of visitors and their curiosity and information priorities.

The assumption that visitors who are in a hurry or are not very interested will read only the first, top, or large-type text part of a three-tiered label is a largely untested assumption that, I suspect, is false. Most visitors in a fast-browsing mode are looking for concrete, specific tidbits of information, not paragraphs of general or abstract concepts. Thus, it is not the sheer amount of information that is important to consider in creating layers of levels (i.e., number of words), but the type of information and how far it strays from the concrete, visually based, immediate experiences in the exhibition.

The logical structure of the knowledge about an object, defined by the expert, should never be the only criterion used to select layers of information on labels.

In the case study above, the exhibit developers did not clearly agree about the definition of layers, learning styles, and modalities at the outset, and their original intentions were not thoroughly realized in the final design. Fortunately, they figured out what many of the problems were and took the time and money to fix them.

Notions of levels, layers, modalities, and learning styles have great appeal to exhibit developers because they offer the promise of something for everyone in exhibitions. But they often are poorly defined and don't provide easy answers. To solve the complicated problems of how to use labels to communicate content, we have to understand the multiple guidelines, possibilities, and limitations of the written word in exhibitions. As we have seen in this chapter, some types of layering of information work better than others. The next four chapters deal with elements of style to increase the appeal and accessibility of labels for broad audiences.

NOTES FOR CHAPTER 6:

1. Obviously we are not talking here about children's museums, but I would venture to suggest that children's museums' exhibitions targeted for anyone over the age of six would benefit from the same kinds of conceptual integrity, intellectual clarity, and personal meaningfulness as is appropriate to any and all other exhibitions.

2. For a good discussion about "Objects: Real or Not Real," see Carolyn P. Blackmon, Teresa K. LaMaster, Lisa C. Roberts, and Beverly Serrell, *Open Conversations: Strategies for Professional Development in Museums* (Chicago: Field Museum of Natural History, 1988).

3. Roger S. Miles, "Lessons in 'Human Biology': Testing a Theory of Exhibition Design," *The International Journal of Museum Management and Curatorship* 5 (1986).

Writing Visitor-Friendly Labels

The overall goals for a visitor-friendly label style are to appeal to a broad audience, to be used by the majority of visitors, and to create positive experiences for them.

Interpretive labels speak to visitors in an appealing voice—not preachy or pedantic, but not simplistic or condescending. They encourage visitors to start to read, to read aloud to others, to read all the way to the end, and to remember what they read. The best kind of interpretive labels will also be useful and meaningful to visitors.

Marlene Chambers, editor and label writer *extraordinaire* at The Denver Art Museum, encourages us not just to write well, but to make messages useful to visitors.[1] She believes we must offer messages that give visitors something to do—such as agree with the ideas, disagree, use them as building blocks in making conclusions, or make discoveries of their own. She believes that most of the messages in museum labels, even friendly ones, are of no personal use and have no relevance to visitors' lives because they are one-way communications of information from curators to visitors. Her advice and philosophy resonate with the idea of open-ended interpretation and of exhibitions that not only encourage but actually present multiple meanings. This emphasis on usefulness and meaningfulness is a large part of the current efforts toward making museums more visitor-centered.

I believe that a museum's goal of offering visitors important, appropriate messages, and the visitors' goals of creating personal meaning and enjoying themselves are not incompatible. It just takes more work, because museum practitioners first must find out what visitors know and want; then, figure out how to design and present what the museum has to offer in ways that will make useful sense to them; and finally to evaluate all along the way to make sure that both sets of goals are achieved. This is not a quick or easy task.

No book about exhibit labels can tell you *what* to say because that depends on the museum, its collection, its mission, its visitors, and the exhibition's big idea. But we can identify guidelines for *how* to say it, and how to write more user-friendly labels.

Start with information directly related to what visitors can see, feel, do, smell, or experience from where they are standing. You do not know the age, gender, race, or educational background of your reader, but you do know the exhibit's setting and context. Take full advantage of that fact: Use words that are keyed to the most noticeable size, shape, color, position, content, question, or directions to get readers started. What will visitors be likely to notice or do first? Start with that.

Vary the length of the sentences. The longest ones can be around 25 words; the shortest, two or three; the average, 10 to 15 words long. Sentences that are longer than 30 words make it difficult for visitors to follow the train of thought or keep track of the points. A variety of lengths will keep visitors from becoming bored and help them stay alert for the unexpected.

Use short paragraphs and small chunks, not large blocks of information. A common mistake in label writing is to put too many ideas into a single paragraph. Paragraphing serves to separate thoughts and give readers a brief rest between ideas or a chance to look at the thing being written about—actively using the information or judging the interpretation. Write so that visitors can read a little, look a moment, read a little more, look again—all in less than a minute. If space is limited and separating paragraphs is eating up too much space, try two things: either cut down on the number of words, or insert paragraph icons to signal readers of the change of thoughts, like this:

Lorem ipsum dolor sit amer, consectetur adipscing elit, sed diam nonumy eius-mod tempor incidunt ut labore et dolore magna aliquam erat volupat. ?◆ Ut enim ad minimum venimami quis nostrdu exercitiatiion ullam coropor sucipit lobir nis ut aliqui es ea commodo consequat. ?◆ Duis autem vel eum irure lolor din erte-henderit in voluptate velit esse molestaie son consequia, vel illu dolore ue fugiat mylla pariatur. ?◆ At vero eos et addusam et justo ioi dignissim quie blandit pras-esent luptatumm delenit augue duos dolor et moletsa.

A paragraph longer than 5o to 6o words will look longer on a wall label in large type than it does on a page of draft text or in a book in small type. Labels that look too long discour-age, overwhelm, and frustrate readers. How many visitors walk into a text-heavy exhibit and say, "Oh goody, look at all those neat words"?

Metaphors are better for other forms of narrative, not labels. Label readers must contend with far more distractions than readers at home in the comfort and familiarity of their own easy chairs. Metaphors—in which one thing is likened to the properties of another—add other visual ideas to the already complex environment of an exhibition. Three-dimensional metaphors, on the other hand, can add intrigu-ing visual richness. See figure 17 for a good example of the kind of visual metaphor that exhibitions do well.

Alliteration is a easy device to overuse. It is series of words starting with the same letter or sound. For example:

Sea stars use suction to pry open their prey.
Pulling on a shell for hours with its small
hydraulic tubefeet, a sea star will exhaust
even the most clammed-up clam.

—from aquarium exhibit about starfish

FIGURE 17
In an exhibit about
the feeding habits of
two different kinds
of whales, the visual
metaphors are cre-
ative, clear, and fun
to look at.

When editing, make sure alliteration is really necessary, not just a gimmick.

Exclamation points in labels shout at readers and force emphasis on them. Let visitors discover and exclaim on their own (e.g., "Look at that!" "That's neat!" "I never knew that!"). If you are tempted to use an exclamation point, think about what it adds to the label's voice. Some people find them overly forceful!

Humor should also be used sparingly. Humor is one aspect to label style that should definitely be tried out on a sample of visitors (in context, if possible) to make sure that what is supposed to be a joke really is (see figure 18). If visitors seem misled, or confused, or if they don't laugh, drop it. Humor is often an indulgence for the writer's benefit, not the reader's. Puns that do not interfere with readers who don't get them are allowable, but with restraint. What percent of the audience is likely to find these examples funny, too cute, or obscure?

FIGURE 18
Humor makes the
point in this cartoon
which demonstrates
a possible explana-
tion for a zebra's
stripes: "Zebras
are attracted to any-
thing with stripes.
The pattern seems
restful to them
and may promote
'togetherness' in
the herd."

Womb with a View

—from a panel on marsupial development at a zoo

The Wharf—Pier pressure is heavy
where animals compete for space.

—title and subtitle on a panel at an aquarium

Pixel this.

—on a science museum exhibit on digitizing

Go lightly on the use of metaphor, alliteration, exclamation points and humor. While you might want to use these
techniques of writing style to spice up your labels, they can
also be distracting by overpowering the point you want to
make. Use them sparingly. Humor is subjective, and it can be
hard to find universal standards.

Use quotations when they advance the narrative and are necessary. They can add color and another voice to the exhibition. Or just fill space. Unnecessary, irrelevant, or obscure quotes are worse than no quotes because they will quickly teach your readers not to pay attention to them. The following are two examples of well-integrated quotes in a contemporary exhibition at The Denver Art Museum:

JENNIFER BARTLETT
Plaid House, 1989

Jennifer Bartlett explained how the museum building inspired this special commission: "I find plaid extremely eccentric. This piece relates strongly to the museum building. It's an extraordinary building, completely eccentric, and wonderful. I was concerned that they have a painting and sculpture that they could use anywhere in the building."

Plaid House is a study of contrasts. It is painting and sculpture, singular and plural, mechanically precise and expressively freehand, serious in intent and humorous in appearance.

JEAN DUBUFFET
Effigie Erratique, 1972

"Art should always make us laugh a little and frighten us a little, but never bore us." Following his own advice, Dubuffet transforms a familiar form of art—the dignified portrait bust—by modeling it roughly from an untraditional material, resin, and covering the surface with bold patterns derived from his ball-point pen doodles.

Dubuffet despised bland, undemanding art. He found inspiration in the raw, direct painting of children and the mentally ill. Though he claimed that the most truthful art was anonymous, his distinctive style says "Dubuffet" more clearly than any signature.

Quotations give strong emotional content a first-person voice, as seen in the label with the burned Northwest Coast Indian mask in figure 19.

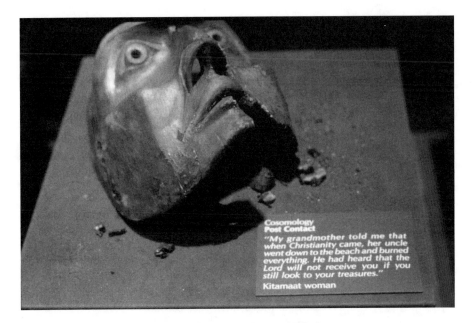

Cosomology
Post Contact
"My grandmother told me that when Christianity came, her uncle went down to the beach and burned everything. He had heard that the Lord will not receive you if you still look to your treasures."
Kitamaat woman

Expect visitors to want to read. Make labels short enough and interesting enough so you can be confident that the majority of visitors will want to read them. Do not put information into the exhibit unless you expect it to be read. "Tertiary information" with technical and abstract details meant for a few visitors just adds clutter and confusion. What if a highly detailed label is the first label a person reads? Will the visitor want to keep reading more, or conclude that all the labels will be like that? The assumption that visitors who are not interested in this level of information can just skip it is probably the most significant factor contributing to poor labels in museums for the past century. As long as museum practitioners use that excuse for adding labels, we will be stuck with too many labels, too much information, and information not used by or useful to the majority of visitors.

Use informative paragraph titles and subtitles. These stylistic devices help break up labels and introduce ideas quickly. They also help transitions between thoughts. A common mistake, however, is to make titles and subtitles that are clever and catchy but that do not advance the narrative. Titles

FIGURE 19
First person quotations can express emotions effectively. Next to a burned, charred Northwest Coast Indian mask, the quote tells a poignant story.

and subtitles should be submessages, not isolated, unrelated
thought fragments. They have to have meaning on their own,
add up to a complete idea when read with each other, and be
able to stand alone.

Have a snappy ending. Just as most of your visitors self-
select to come to the exhibit in the first place, readers choose
to pay attention to the words. Give readers a reward for reading it all. Rewards can be in the form of closure, reinforce-
ment, or new insight. When finished, visitors should feel glad
they took the time to read through to the end. This example is
from a hand-written label in a history museum:

In 1847 this bell hung in the cupola of the congregational
church. It was later used as the village fire alarm. It also
sounded the 9 o'clock curfew when every kid was off the
streets or had a good excuse why he wasn't home. I know,
I was one of those kids.   *Les Schrader*

Newspaper journalism is not a good model. It is a bad
model because newspaper articles are written with the
assumption that most readers will not read the whole thing.
After the headline or subhead that communicates a short
teaser or summary, the body of the article that follows has the
most important information up front, then goes into more
detail, often repeating information. The length of newspaper
articles is often not dictated by need, but by space available,
and newspaper editors assume that their readers are sitting
down. Labels, on the contrary, should be written to be read in
total, all the way through to the snappy end (see above).
Labels are for standing, time-limited readers and should
begin with an informative headline or subhead, follow with
body copy that sparingly covers the essential information,
and then stop. If there is more to say in detail for "the more
interested readers," put it in a brochure or handout, if the cost
can be justified.

Stay flexible within the label system. Types of labels usually have recommended word lengths, but some flexibility should be allowed. Caption labels that all have *the same number of words* make for boring design and dull writing style. Don't be afraid to leave some white space occasionally. *Area labels* that all contain two paragraphs of four to six lines each will be easy to design space for, but what if there is not two paragraphs' worth of something to say about each area? *Catchy titles* used on every label can be annoying and uninformative. Overusing *question labels* gets to be insulting (see the section on using questions in labels below).

Interrelate labels and their settings. Most of all, do not get locked into a system that does not allow label content and design to be responsive to its setting and context. Information on labels works best when it reflects, enhances, and echoes its environment/placement/setting. Labels that need their context in order to make sense are going to be more integrated with it. Labels written to be read and be comprehensible anywhere will lack integration with their context. This means that it is very difficult to show examples of good labels in a photograph in this book—the context is missing. It is easy to show examples of poor labels because they are bad regardless of their context.

Set up a conversation. Let visitors have some of the time to do the talking. Labels should tell stories that encourage a four-way conversation, between the absent label writer's voice and viewpoint, and the reader and the reader's companions, and the museum's collection. Labels can help do this by being short and by encouraging participation. Let the labels be an easy jumping-off point for visitors to talk to each other in their social groups.[2] For example, in a science museum, next to x-rays of human bones, the short labels giving only the person's age and the bone's name prompted many comments like, "Remember when Grandma. . . ."

VISITOR-FRIENDLY LABELS PUT FOREMOST VALUE ON VISITORS' EXPERIENCES

Visitor-friendly style, in the overall analysis, means that museum practitioners learn to put visitors first—respecting and valuing their concerns, wishes, desires, and perceptions. When label writers indulge themselves with catchy phrases and clever style, or curators indulge themselves in more, more, more words on the wall, or designers indulge themselves in award-winning new graphic styles, they are not being visitor friendly. The whole exhibit team must agree and care about what the primary impact on the visitors will be.

Being visitor friendly means putting visitors' experiences and dialog before communicating new knowledge. The Denver Art Museum's interpretive project report expands on the definition of what those experiences might be like. Based to a large extent on the work of University of Chicago psychology professor Mihaly Csikszentmihalyi, the project included experimental labels in the galleries to help novice visitors expand their aesthetic experiences, explore color, make comparisons, and make value judgments.[3] The intent was to encourage novice visitors to move beyond their primarily emotional criteria for liking a painting—that it be pleasingly beautiful, detailed, understandable. Figure 20 shows a mockup of an interactive label that asked visitors to consider why they liked or did not like a painting by Bouguereau and use that information to think about the way they look at art.

Another one of the label experiments at The Denver Art Museum was intended to integrate Csikszentmihalyi's concept of "flow experience." Flow involves a focusing of attention, a challenge equal to a person's current skills, and a discovery (positive feedback and a sense of being in control).[4] A paradigmatic model for an experience-driven label that set up conditions that lead visitors to making discoveries of their own was created and compared to an information-driven label that passed on discoveries made by art experts. Although it was not evaluated to see if it actually worked, it remains one of the truly new ways to be visitor-friendly that anyone has tried.

In a 1995 *Museum News* article, Csikszentmihalyi summarized some of his thoughts about motivating visitors to learn in informal settings where intrinsic rewards are important and flow experiences are motivating.[5] He does not say exactly what it would take to create a 30-minute flow experience for the non-expert visitor in a museum exhibition, but, based on his writing and the characteristics of "ideal" exhibitions detailed by Alt and Shaw (described earlier on pages 46–47), I will venture a guess:[6]

> A museum flow experience involves immersion in an aesthetically pleasing, physically comfortable space; with well-organized, clear, enticing information. Visitors would have a feeling of being in control (self-paced, not confused, exercising free choice). A variety of experiences (many senses used) would be available, as would new challenges appropriate to the learner's knowledge level. Visitors would not feel overwhelmed or apathetic.

From the above description, labels play an important, but probably minor role in creating flow experiences in museum exhibitions. Factors involving the entire environment

FIGURE 20
Using artist Bouguereau's well-loved *Two Girls,* this prototype for an interactive label invites visitors to explore their reactions to the painting and discover the roles of emotion and knowledge in art experiences.

working together, with labels as just one part, create flow.[7] Labels probably cannot do it on their own.

Labels that contain information and interpretation aimed at the right place between boredom and anxiety for the majority of visitors will be very visitor-friendly and will help provide optimal conditions to facilitate museum flow experiences. A clear big idea and good orientation are also essential for facilitating flow. Selecting the right reading level and providing bilingual labels contributes to the optimal conditions as well, as we will see in the next two chapters.

NOTES FOR CHAPTER 7:

1. For provocative discussions, see Marlene Chambers's articles "Is Anyone Out There? Audience and Communication," "Beyond 'Aha!': Motivating Museum Visitors," and "After Legibility, What?" which are referenced in the bibliography.

2. Paulette M. McManus in "Watch Your Language! People Do Read Labels" and Lois H. Silverman in "Of Us and Other 'Things': The Content and Functions of Talk by Adult Visitor Pairs in an Art and a History Museum" point out some socially determined patterns of visitor conversations in museums.

3. See Csikszentmihalyi's *Beyond Boredom and Anxiety: The Experience of Play in Work and Games* and *The Art of Seeing: An Interpretation of the Aesthetic Encounter* for interesting ways to think about weaving motivation and prior knowledge together in visitor experiences.

4. See article by Chambers in "Improving the Esthetic Experience for Art Novices: A New Paradigm for Interpretive Labels" in McDermott-Lewis.

5. Mihaly Csikszentmihalyi and Kim Hermanson, "Intrinsic Motivation in Museums: What Makes Visitors Want to Learn?" *Museum News* 74, no. 3 (May/June 1995).

6. See "Characteristics of a Positive Museum Experience" for my attempts to weave motivation and prior knowledge together in visitor experiences.

7. Part of Mark Harvey's Colorado State University dissertation, "The Influence of Exhibit Space Design Features on Visitor Attention" (1996) attempts to define and measure visitors' sense of immersion and flow.

Selecting the Right Reading Level

Writing clearly does not mean writing simplistically, but it does mean writing for people who are not experts in the subject.

All labels should strive to be appealing and suited to as many visitors as possible: the casual tourist, the layperson interested in the subject as a hobby, the person whose job is related, the family group visiting to entertain the children, the foreign guests with limited English, the new immigrant in the city. That is a diverse group.

Try this quiz: What is the best way to make sure you are writing at the right reading level for your audience?

A. Aim for the lowest common denominator
B. Use a sixth-grade vocabulary
C. Write different labels at different levels
D. Write for your peers
E. None of the above

The correct answer is "E," but before discussing some different alternatives, let's review the misconceptions or difficulties presented by the answers A, B, C, and D.

A. *Don't* aim for the lowest common denominator. There is no point in writing for the so-called lowest common denominator because they are the people who are unable or unwilling to read labels. Nor should you aim for the highest common denominator. Give the companions and families of those uncommon visitors a break ("Norbert, come on. The rest of us want to get going!").

Instead, select the content and style that will work for the commonest common denominator. Aim for the majority. Appeal to the would-be readers—people who will read if the label is short enough, if it looks easy to read, if it is legible, and if they have time. Visitors are more likely to take the time to read if a label looks like it is written for them.

B. *Don't* use a sixth-grade vocabulary, unless your museum is only for sixth-graders. Sticking only to words that sixth-graders know will help make labels have a broad appeal, but it makes them less interesting, less colorful and less interpretive than if that rule could be broken. It is all right to aim for a sixth-grade level, but do not be a slave to it. The basic idea is never to write for a twelfth-grade level, because that puts text out of reach for a large portion of the audience, especially younger children, non-English speakers, and less educated viewers.

C. *Don't* write different labels at different levels. Writing for different vocabulary or developmental levels—labels for kids, labels for adults—makes labels twice as hard to write, more expensive to produce, and it creates visual clutter in the exhibit. Most visitors, given a choice, will choose to read labels that look easier, are shorter, and have larger print.[1] Keep it simple: write one-level labels.

Children's museums are a special case. Labels for children's exhibitions should be crafted for their developmental levels, not a watered-down childish version of an adult label. They should stick to vocabulary words that are familiar to children, especially avoiding geographical proper nouns and words related to geologic time. Children exist in the here-and-now and have a poor sense of extended time (past and future) and of world space (far away is down the block). If children's museums want to fully realize their goals for their primary target audience, they should not attempt to write for adults. Children will read labels written for children. Adults also will often choose to read labels directed at children, because they know the labels will be easier to read and understand than most other museum labels.

D. *Don't* write for your peers. The label writer who writes for her peers claims, "I'm writing for the more interested readers, and I don't care if people don't read them. Besides, it is our scholarly obligation to present these concepts." This attitude sends a counterproductive message to the majority of visitors: the labels are not meant for them and the words are not important or essential to their experience in the exhibit. Exhibits displaying this attitude cannot be called visitor-centered. Institutions that keep label writers on their staffs who have this attitude are not sincere about seeking to reach a broader audience.

THE BEST GUIDELINES FOR SELECTING VOCABULARY LEVELS

So what is the right reading level? There is no single right level, but a good guideline is not to write below a sixth-grade level or above the eighth-grade level. Beyond that rule of thumb, here are three other ideas:

1. **Test your text.** Many computer word-processing programs have built-in tests for analyzing text. You can check the reading level occasionally as you write, to stay on track. Microsoft Word, for instance, does a grammar check that tells the average number of words per sentence, the percent of passive sentences, and text grade-level analysis by Flesch, Coleman and Bormuth formulas.

But there are other ways than using rigid reading-level formulas to guide your use of colorful, descriptive language and still make labels comprehensible for children and novice adults. Two of these are by using front-end evaluation and by editing for "core" meaning.

2. **Use front-end evaluation.** After drafting a good plan, objectives, and a big idea, but before writing labels or fully developing all the exhibition components, do a simple front-end evaluation with a small, representative sample of potential visitors (20–25 people). Read the exhibition concept, title, or key ideas to them and ask, "What would you expect to see, do, and find out about in this exhibit?" Or, show them (one at a time) the technical words associated with the exhibit concept and ask, "What do you think of when you see this word?"

Common sense and relatively quick, open-ended evaluations can give you qualitative feedback from visitors about what vocabulary, experience, and expectations they have with your planned exhibition. Front-end studies often come to the same conclusion: while visitors may be superficially familiar with many of the terms, they do not have thorough understanding of what they mean. The implications for this are that exhibit developers can use familiar technical terms in labels, but they must not assume that visitors will understand them well. This underscores the need for labels to be written clearly and simply for readers who do not have sophisticated knowledge of the subject, whether it is microbiology, French impressionism, or the Civil War. Visitors may know the words "germ," "Monet," and "Yankee," but they probably have limited and fragmentary knowledge about them.

3. **Do "core" editing.** An editing technique that can help make reading levels broadly based is to review the text and cross out words that are above a fifth- or sixth-grade vocabulary. See if the sentences still make sense without those words. In label-writing workshops I have sometimes told the story of the first label I remember reading. While riding in the car with my parents, we passed a sign on a lawn in front of a house that had three words. I could read the first and the last words: "Free xxxxxxx kittens." The middle word, "Persian," was not in my vocabulary, but certainly added to the meaning of the sign for someone who could understand it, yet did not interfere with my comprehension and subsequent question: "Can we stop the car?"

Higher-level vocabulary words that are used as adjectives, not nouns, will add more information to a label without obscuring its core meaning. For example:

The ~~anti-malarial~~ drug comes from the bark of a ~~tropical~~ tree.
These ~~ritual~~ bowls were made from ~~exotic~~ materials like copper and ~~marine~~ shells.
The sea star uses its ~~hydraulic~~ tubefeet to open a clam.

These labels are certainly more informative with the additional words, but they still make sense without them to readers with unsophisticated vocabularies. If the label is clear with the words crossed out, leave them in. If it does not continue to make sense, as in this example from the first sentence in figure 21, consider dropping those words, defining them, or rewriting.

The ~~alleged perpetrators~~ of the Chicago Fire look ~~sublimely~~ innocent in Norman Rockwell's *Mrs. Catherine O'Leary Milking Daisy,* painted during the 1930s.

—original version does not make sense without crossed out words

Mrs. O'Leary and her cow, who ~~allegedly~~ started the Chicago Fire, look ~~sublimely~~ innocent in Norman Rockwell's painting *Mrs. Catherine O'Leary Milking Daisy,* from the 1930s.

—edited version still makes sense without the crossed out words

---

FIGURE 21
Colorful language, sentences of varying length, and a snappy finish make reading this caption easy and fun for adults. The subject would also be of interest to many children (readers aged 7 to 12 years old), but the vocabulary reading level is too advanced for them.

The alleged perpetrators of the Chicago Fire look sublimely innocent in Norman Rockwell's *Mrs. Catherine O'Leary Milking Daisy* painted during the 1930s. Other artists were not as charitable. Mrs. O'Leary was often depicted as a crazed hag and her cow as a demonic beast.
Gift of the Office of the Mayor of Chicago   1949.28

Another type of core editing is to eliminate words that are used interchangeably as nouns, verbs, or adjectives. Images created in the reader's mind by words should match what they see, so using the right words is important. Readability and comprehension can be slowed or impeded by words with more than one function and meaning, such as: cement, project, concrete, fly, minute, envelope, scales. This goes for spoken words in audio labels as well. Words that sound the same should be avoided, such as: maze, maize; coarse, course; paws, pause; sales, sails. Good editing eliminates these trickster words.

Appropriate reading levels are best governed by guidelines that are based on the assumption that the majority of the readers, regardless of age, are not conversant in the vocabulary of the subject. Visitors who are experts are not the target audience for the label copy, and experts (unless they are really snobs) will not be insulted by clear, concise labels written with enthusiasm for the subject and a respect for novice visitors.

There are other considerations to keep in mind about reading level when visitors' reading ability is in another language. This raises the issue of bilingual labels, dealt with in the next brief chapter.

NOTES FOR CHAPTER 8:

1. Stephen Bitgood et al., *Effects of Label Characteristics on Visitor Behavior*, Technical Report No. 86-55 (Jacksonville, Ala.: Jacksonville State University, Psychology Institute, 1986).

Bilingual Labels

Bilingual labels help a museum to be politically correct, but they are not easy, quick, or cheap to produce.

Bilingual labels should not be considered casually, because they add twice the number of words to an exhibition. Bilingual labels are also costly to write, design, and produce. They can double the lead-time needed for developing an exhibition. Creating two sets of labels in two different languages is most warranted when a large proportion of the audience speaks a language different than the local tongue, or when it is the law (as in parts of Canada). If there are significant numbers of visitors representing several different languages, bilingual signs will not suffice.

There are several alternate ways to provide bilingual or multilingual interpretation without two complete sets of labels on view. Laminated, portable, reusable labels can provide two or more languages, as can free handouts, brochures, or audio tours. Museums in large urban centers, or with heavy foreign tourism, make use of these devices routinely.

When translating labels from one language to another, it is best to use a translator who is very fluent in both languages because interpretation involves subtle forms of communication that cannot be translated word for word, such as metaphors or colloquial expressions. The person who is translating must actually reinterpret the messages using the style and manner of the given language. The draft of the labels being translated should already be edited carefully for appropriate reading levels and clarity of thought.

If two sets of labels on the wall are the only solution to meeting a need for bilingual labels, keep label copy short so that words do not dominate the exhibition. Make the design (colors, typefaces) of the two sets readily different from each other to cue visitors quickly into the bilingual system, but be careful not to make one more legible than the other: the sizes should be the same and choices of contrasting colors should be balanced equally (see figure 22). Their placement together (right, left, top, bottom) have implications for importance and priority. In regional or local ethnic museums, the given language will probably have priority.

For traveling exhibits, separate panels provided for each language can be rearranged to meet the needs of each venue. For example, in one location, the French panels could be placed to the left, English on the right; while in another location, the social/political climate might call for the reverse.

Another alternative is not to make two sets for every label, but to select only a few, based on the nature of the audience and the communication objectives for the exhibition, or for special occasions. For example, one zoo made labels in Spanish for a temporary interpretation of animals from Mexico and Central and South America. Another zoo put Swahili titles on buildings and services in the exhibition that featured animals from Africa. Besides using words, the addition of flags, graphic motifs, music, even food (smells), and other multiethnic elements can help create a mood or atmosphere appropriate for special and diverse audiences.

Another word of caution for museums before getting started with bilingual labels, especially if they have never used them before: creating an institutional system or set of guidelines will take lots of time, because many people (e.g., museum staff, board of directors, community members) will have a stake in the decisions. "Allow three or four times as much time to accomplish this task as you might first estimate," is the advice of exhibition designer Merritt Price, who went through the process at the Art Gallery of Ontario.

In a primarily English-speaking community, another alternative to bilingual labels is to write label text in a way that people who speak English as a second language would be able to understand the basic ideas.

FIGURE 22
These two examples of bilingual labels show the English text first and the non-English second. In "Glacial Goop" (above) the type sizes are the same. In "Sam Nail Ranch" (left) the Spanish version is in same typeface and color as the English, but in a slightly smaller type size. Equal balance is best.

10

Labels That Ask Questions

The best questions in labels are the ones visitors themselves would ask.

You have probably heard that it is a good idea to ask questions in exhibit labels to stimulate visitors to think, look, get involved with, and learn from your exhibits. While asking questions may be a good idea, it is important to recognize that there are good and bad questions. Some work better than others.

The best questions are those that visitors themselves ask. Two ways to learn what those questions will be are by watching and listening to what visitors say to each other when they look at exhibits in existing situations, or by doing front-end evaluation or testing mock-ups with visitors during the development of exhibits before final design. The first is the most natural way, because visitors are acting spontaneously and the exhibit is in context with all its parts. For example, "Is he dead?" visitors ask at the snapping turtle's tank, as they observe the huge, mossy turtle who rarely moves.

Unfortunately, most questions asked in labels are not really questions at all. They are mock queries, because the asker (the writer, curator, exhibit developer, designer) is simply disguising the delivery of *more information* in a superficially user-friendly form. These questions are gimmicks, and are not good pedagogy, especially when they are used on labels that accompany static displays of objects, artifacts, animals, or photographs. A question that does not flow easily from the visitors' interest can feel like an imposition. A question that cannot be easily answered by looking at the objects can be frustrating. And one with an obvious answer is offensive.

The nebulous "Why?" question is a particularly obnoxious form of the mock query. For example:

- Why is Japanese armor lightweight?

- Why are insects commonly found in virtually every environment except the oceans?
- Why did volcanoes occur in Missouri during the Precambrian?

These questions imply one right answer, known by the expert, that is not visible or apparent to the visitor. These are not visitors' questions, and their answers might rightly be, "I don't know," "Who cares?" or "Because God made it that way."

All of the examples listed above could be rewritten into different questions or made into statements that more honestly reveal the asker's intentions or values, such as:

- Japanese armor is lightweight, because . . .
- Are insects commonly found in the oceans?
- What factors made volcanoes possible in Missouri?

If the point of asking the question is to make visitors see a comparison, think about an issue or explanation, or understand the purpose of a structure or design, just say so, "Three factors that made volcanoes possible in Missouri were. . . ."

There are two conditions that make "why" questions appropriate: when you are sure that visitors would phrase the question that way on their own, and when discordant, easily seen factors are present that cause the "why" to occur. Usually those two conditions occur together. For example:

Why don't the sharks eat the fish living with them in the tank?

—*visitors at an aquarium see predators swimming with prey*

Why don't the birds fly out?

—*visitors at a zoo see free-flight area with birds and no door separating area*

Why were these [dinosaur bone jackets] never opened?

—*visitors in natural history museum see large, white, plaster-of-Paris, unopened bundles with numbers painted on the outside*

Why do they call this art?

—*visitors in art museum see a room full of gaudy looking chairs, clocks, tables, and tapestries of the decorative arts collection*

Those are real questions asked by real visitors.

Being able to anticipate what visitors want to know and in what order they want to know it—that is, which questions need to be answered first—can be achieved through a combination of experience, intuition, common sense, and trying it out and fixing it if it doesn't work right the first time.

If you decide that you have to use a "why" question, or any other question, it's usually a good idea to *answer it* in the first sentence of next paragraph of the label, in one short statement. It is very frustrating to visitors to have their curiosity aroused and then not be able to find or confirm the answer because it is not there, or it is difficult to find because it is buried in the text somewhere 12 lines later.

The information in this chapter refers mainly to questions asked on labels in static or nonparticipatory exhibits. Questioning techniques used for labels on interactive exhibits present a different challenge, which is described in the next chapter. Before going on to that discussion, we need to look at a type of label that often shares characteristics of static and interactive elements—flip labels.

QUESTIONS ON FLIP LABELS

Flip labels (text and/or images on a hinged or sliding panel, covering a panel beneath with more words and/or images) are common, inexpensive, popular devices in museum exhibitions (figure 23). Also called "flappers," they offer visitors something to do—the overt, physical action of lifting or sliding the panel—and thus, are referred to as interactive or hands-on labels, although the amount of interaction is typically minimal. Depending on what information is on the flips and what visitors can do with them, there can be more interaction. If all they are doing is asking "Did You Know?" and covering up more information, they indeed require a very low level of involvement.

Integrated, engaging flip labels will give visitors a logical sense of anticipation, a more compelling reason to look under the label, and an intrinsic reward for doing it, such as:

FIGURE 23
These lift-up labels
reveal more than
just a bunch of
words, making
them more reward-
ing to use. Words
under a flap should
be kept to a mini-
mum, because it
can be an effort to
hold the flap up.

- To peek at something hidden, such as a graphic of a desert with flip labels hiding pictures underneath that show "What lives underground?"
- To confirm an answer to a question and find something else, too. For example, the flip label asks, "How heavy is a hippo?" and underneath is not just the number of pounds, but also a cartoon of kids piled on one end of a seesaw, with a caption that says, "As heavy as eighty 12-year-olds."
- To go beyond answering, What is it? to encourage open-ended thinking, such as, How are these things used? with the flip-label clues: "It was buried with an Egyptian mummy" and "It held the mummy's guts" (for a ancient Egyptian canopic jar, without ever naming it) and "This is used for carrying things" and "It helps a woman balance and hold things on her head" (for a woven African head ring).

- To convey different points of view, such as having a question with two different answers, e.g., "Yes, because . . . " and "No, because . . .," neither one the "right" answer.

In the earlier chapter on levels of information, we mentioned flip labels as a way to layer information. Often this is done with questions, overtly as above, or implied as in the

CASE STUDY

ANSWERING A COMMON VISITOR QUESTION

The Getty Kouros was a 500-square-foot exhibition at The J. Paul Getty Museum named after the Getty's "kouros"—a large white statue of a standing Greek male youth. The majority of the visitors (78%) to the museum saw the exhibit, but of them, less than half (42%) had heard or read about its topic beforehand—the authenticity of this particular kouros. In addition to the Getty kouros, the exhibit contained two other sculptures (replicas of two other kouroi) and six large interpretive panels on the walls, plus one large photo of the kouros pieces. Together, the exhibition consisted of 11 elements.

The Getty Kouros stood in the center of the rectangular room, the introductory panel was on the wall to the left, and beyond it, a label titled "What is a Kouros?" Observations of visitor behavior in the kouros exhibition showed that some of the elements had very high attracting power. Eighty-four percent of the visitors stopped at the central kouros figure, and 80% of the visitors read the "What is a Kouros?" panel. But 42% of the visitors skipped the introductory panel.

Since most of the visitors did not know what a kouros was, perhaps the word "kouros" should not have been used in the exhibit's title in the first place. Also, if that question had been asked and answered in the first part of the introductory label, more visitors probably would have stopped there first.

Knowing what your visitors know and what their top-of-mind questions are can help plan the best order and emphasis of information.

following example. In an exhibition about AIDS, the lymphatic system and its role in the immune system is shown and described in short texts. On a large panel, a silhouette of a muscular male is partially covered by three labels that say "THYMUS GLAND," "BONE MARROW," and "LYMPH NODES" in large comicbook-style letters on labels that are flip-doors. The implied question is, What is behind this door? The door opens to reveal, underneath, EEK!—a real (preserved) human (?) thymus gland. And EEK!—a real leg bone, and, . . . well, I was afraid what I'd find under the lymph nodes label, so I didn't look.

Flip labels are very seductive. Visitors can hardly resist peeking under a flap to see what is there. With children, the activity of lifting is satisfying by itself. For adults, the manipulation is time-consuming and requires effort. Is it worth it, the adult visitor might ask? A question or statement posed on the outside of a flip label that seems difficult to an adult can make them feel stupid. For example, on the outside the label says, "When you are done comparing the two, lift the sheet for more information." As one visitor rephrased it, "Lift the sheet and find out how dumb you are."[1] If you're going to take advantage of visitors' natural investigative behavior, make sure the payback is commensurate—useful, interesting, enjoyable, memorable discoveries underneath, not just more words.

Questions on interactive exhibits present a different challenge that is described in more detail in chapter 15. But first, let's consider some of the more nitty-gritty questions such as Who should write the labels? How many words should there be?

NOTES FOR CHAPTER 10:

1. John E. Schloder, Marjorie Williams, and C. Griffith Mann, *The Visitor's Voice: Visitor Studies in the Renaissance-Baroque Galleries of The Cleveland Museum of Art 1990–1993* (Cleveland: The Cleveland Museum of Art, 1993), p. 31.

11

Getting Started
(and Getting It Done)

Resist the temptation to begin writing actual label copy until all of the other front-end exhibition tasks have been done. Getting finished is easier when you can see the way to the end from the beginning.

Once you have the big idea formulated, the front-end evaluations conducted, the floor plans roughly laid out, and the modalities chosen for the different types of exhibition elements, you are ready to start writing. Those are a lot of things to have in place before ever putting pen to paper (an archaic notion in this age of computers, though some writers still prefer to begin this way), but the more you know about what you want to say, to whom, and for what purpose, before you write, the faster and easier the actual writing will be.

Some writers recommend writing a general overall narrative or walk-through of the exhibit experience before writing labels. This can be helpful, especially for giving funders or marketing people an idea of what the exhibit will be like. But the narrative walk-through should not be set in stone. It will become out of date very easily, and trying to keep the narrative and the actual label copy both in agreement is difficult once label drafts are started.

WHO SHOULD DO THE WRITING?

Who, in the first place, should write the labels? The answer I give is the person who has the most time and the most enthusiasm for the project. The person can be a content or subject expert, or a nonexpert. The subject specialist might need help in making labels speak in visitors' language and in remembering the most basic questions a novice visitor has about the topic. Writers who are not intimately familiar with the topic, on the other hand, will need a little help in making labels accurate and comprehensive and in not trivializing important points. Enthusiasm is necessary in either case because it gets the writer through many drafts and repeated rounds of criticism from the team. Time is absolutely necessary for the editing and evaluation that will be needed to improve the label's effectiveness.

More and more museums are contracting out the writing to freelancers, because there is no one on staff who has the time or label-writing expertise—which inspires enthusiasm—to do the labels. Sometimes the writer is a guest curator who is an expert in the subject, but not a staff member. Sometimes it is a person skilled in writing. Even when an outside person is hired, the museum still has the ultimate responsibility for the voice and the content, and the writer needs clear guidelines for what those are. Furthermore, it takes time to get a new person up to speed with the rest of the project, if they are brought into it in the middle.

SELECTING A VOICE FOR THE LABELS

The "voice" means who is speaking to visitors in the labels. Is it a knowledgeable expert? A close friend? An experienced docent? Is it an institutional voice or a personal voice? Should more than one voice be heard?

If the voice of the labels is unique to a specific individual, it should be identified as such to the readers. Visitors should be aware, from the outset, that the labels were written with a personal viewpoint, if that is the case. Otherwise, visitors will assume that (by default) the institution's view, values, or opinions are being expressed, and that can lead to confusion. For example, labels for an exhibition of historical photographs of African Americans were written by a descendant of slaves of the period who used colloquial expressions, such as "mammie" and "boy." Some visitors took offense, thinking that the museum was speaking in a derogatory way. The author of the labels had actually been identified in the introduction, at the bottom of the panel, where most visitors missed it. If the name and a photograph of the writer had been obvious, this misunderstanding could have been avoided.

In an exhibition about an environmental crisis caused by industry, should visitors be allowed to hear the industry's side of the story? This decision should be driven by the definition of the exhibition's big idea, but whichever voices are chosen to express it, they should be clearly identified. In *Darkened Waters: Profile of an Oil Spill* the credit/introductory panel stated that the "we" speaking in the exhibition was the staff of the Pratt Museum in Homer, Alaska, who originally developed it. Throughout the exhibition, other voices were heard as well: industry professionals, spill workers, Native Americans, other residents of the spill zone—and their points of view often provided interesting contrasts. It was clear that there was not one simple explanation for the spill, no clear or easy solution to the problem, and no foolproof way to avoid another spill. The various voices gave visitors a variety of perspectives from which to think more deeply about their own prejudices and points of view.

Some museums give their voice a personality. The San Diego Wild Animal Park identifies the fictitious person who speaks in their educational signs as "an eloquent and succinct host who is visionary about wildlife."

Whether the voice is institutional, personal, or multiple, it should be discussed and decided *before* the labels are drafted. It is difficult to put one in or change it after the fact.

VISITORS' VIEWS ON POINTS OF VIEW

On two separate occasions I have had the chance to evaluate attempts to portray specifically different voices and points of view in exhibitions. In one case, in a front-end evaluation, we asked visitors if they believed that the institution could make an "unbiased, objective exhibit about controversial marine mammal conservation issues." Most visitors said "yes" or "probably," because they trusted the institution to be fair and reasoned—as an educational institution interested in preserving the environment and "not run by a business or corporation with specially funded interests." They expected to be given more than one side of the issue so that they could make up their own minds. Visitors who said "no," said so because they expected the museum to have a strong point of view and to express it convincingly. As one visitor put it, "It is the nature of the work you do here to be in favor of some things and not sympathetic to others."

In the other case, involving a summative evaluation, we wanted to know if the exhibition successfully communicated different points of view through different voices as the exhibit developers had intended and how visitors felt about it for future exhibit plans. We asked, "What do you think about the idea of including other viewpoints and voices in future exhibits?" Because this question was not linked to any specific subject, as it was in the case above, it was more difficult for visitors to answer (some responded, "What do you mean?"), but most people said "yes." Their reasons included: It makes the exhibit more educational; it helps people make up their own minds; it is more interesting.

It seems to me that unless told otherwise, most visitors will assume that the exhibit voice or voices represent the institution, are factual and, while not unbiased, are at least reasonable. In both cases above, visitors wanted and expected to hear more than one side of a story or issue, but wanted the museum to be clear in terms of whose voices and viewpoints are intended. As one visitor put it, "If they're not factual, they should be labeled so that they're not taken as the gospel. If they are contentious or someone's opinion, we should know that."

The clarification of an exhibition's point of view and making clear whose voice is speaking to visitors is particularly important in exhibitions that present some form of debate, issue, or strongly held different views. Some exhibitions have been picketed, shut down, or never even allowed to open because of criticisms over the points of view portrayed in them. Neil Harris, a professor of history at the University of Chicago who writes and speaks often about museums, calls what is happening to museums in the last 30 years "a blurring of cherished artifacts and social contexts, scholarly research and exhibition venues, aesthetic values and cultural meanings."[1] Whereas museums used to be more about objects and authoritative points of view, they are now more about interpretation, and whose interpretation it is should be stated. In interpretive exhibitions where museums present multiple meanings and "right" or "factual" are matters of opinion, visitors will have to adjust to a new, unexpected, nonauthoritative stance, and it is the museum's responsibilty to help them see the difference and make that adjustment.

SCHEDULING THE TIME

How long will it take to write the labels? This is a loaded question and a difficult one to answer. "Everyone is in denial about how long it takes and how much it costs," says Judy Rand, an experienced and well-known museum label writer and exhibit planner who has managed many writing projects.[2] Many museums have unrealistic expectations for the number of labels that a writer can crank out in a week, uninformed conceptions about how long the editing and review process can take, and naive notions about what is involved in transforming words into a well-integrated typographic presentation in exhibition design.

GETTING ORGANIZED

When it is time to write, I have found that it is helpful to have the following items handy to look at as I write: my research notes, the exhibition floor plan and elevations, and pictures of the objects or other visuals of what the "stuff" of the exhibit looks like. I try to imagine I am a visitor, with limited time and no special vocabulary to understand the topic. What would I want to know first? What would probably catch my eye first?

Even in a first draft of label copy, before any room layouts have been designed, label writers should be imagining what visuals would work well with their words. "But I'm a writer, not a designer," a label writer might say. You need to be a bit of both if you are writing for exhibitions, because words in exhibits cannot, do not, and should not stand alone. You should write with the verbal and visual in mind.

When making the first draft, use a two-column set up: words that describe possible visuals on one side, words for label text on the other. The visuals list should be thought of as an aid to visual thinking at this point. The designer can use the suggestions or not, or come up with a better idea, as designers often do. The writer is not dictating anything, only suggesting and thinking visually. The following is an example of the two-column set up from a zoo exhibit plan:

Possible Visuals	Draft Text
photo of a mass of crawfish in a healthy swamp	Pound for pound, there are more cooked red crawfish than all other animals combined.
people eating crawfish	Crawfishing in Louisiana swamps contributes greatly to the local economy. Each year, people
photo or illustration of crawfish harvesting	throughout the U.S. eat about 40 million pounds of crawfish caught in swamps.

In the first draft, there does not have to be close agreement between the suggested visuals and the text. Beginning with more visuals than you will need will allow for more flexibility and choices later on; whereas if only one image is specified, and it turns out to be unobtainable, it will leave a hole in the layout.

DOCUMENTATION

As you write, and as you research images, be sure to keep good records. Documentation of authors, titles, sources, and dates will be valuable pieces of information when you have to go back and look something up, verify a fact, defend an argument, relocate the source of a photograph or illustration, or remember when and why you decided to do something a particular way.

Keeping track of drafts by date and number will aid the writer, editor, designer, and other team members to stay in sync. Electronic copies of drafts can become hopelessly mixed up and errors that got corrected once can reappear when disks and files are shared, modified, and not updated. One person needs to be responsible for knowing where the text is and what stage it is in. Ways of keeping track should be established before you start writing, not halfway through.

GETTING THROUGH THE EDITING PROCESS

The place to spend the most time is in the draft text stages. Refining stylistic subtleties, responding to editorial suggestions from advisors, matching words to visuals, honing down text so that it expresses the communication goals with economy, efficiency, and effectiveness, evaluating text with visitors, putting the copy away for a week and coming back to it for a fresh look—all of these things take time. Schedule it in.

It is not uncommon to have five to seven drafts between the first and the final, often with very minor edits, sometimes major ones due to changes in emphasis, new information, disagreements about style, or getting the actual photograph, object, or artifact in hand. By doing all the right things before you start writing (e.g., consensus on the big idea, types of labels to use, voice), the editing can be relatively quick and painless, even though many drafts may be necessary. Editing is much easier when it involves polishing, not major overhauls or redirections.

The differences between a first and subsequent draft will involve editing for style, content, and matching words with visuals. Below is an example of a first draft for a label with a photograph to go on a concrete post outside a maritime museum's lifesaving station (see figure 24):

Key Clock

Before radio communication, regular beach patrols were made to look for mariners in distress. Surfmen walked the patrol 2.5 miles in opposite directions from Life Saving Service/Coast Guard stations to a key post.

To prove a surfman did his job, he took a key from the post and inserted it in a clock he was carrying making an impression on its dial and recording his arrival.

FIGURE 24
A picture is worth a lot of words, but only when the image works well with the words. Here it does. In addition, both the photograph and the text are directly related to the object, the U.S. Coast Guard post itself.

Key Clock Post

Key posts were located 2 miles in opposite directions from Life Saving Service or Coast Guard stations. Surfmen patrolled the beach on foot carrying a time clock.

On arriving at the post, the surfman used the key to make an impression on his clock, proving that he did his job.

In the original draft, notice how there is no visually related subject in the first sentence: radio communication is abstract history; patrolling the beach is not shown in the photo; mariners are not shown. The photo shows a surfman with a key clock and the post. An edited draft matched the photo and the label on the post better:

Key Clock Post

Key posts were located 2 miles in opposite directions from Life Saving Service or Coast Guard stations. Surfmen patrolled the beach on foot carrying a time clock.

On arriving at the post, the surfman used the key to make an impression on his clock, proving that he did his job.

In the edited example above, how would the editing be different if the label was just with the photograph and not on the post itself? If so, the subject should be the surfman, not the post. Always edit for more concreteness.

In the next example, the first version contains too much subjective interpretation, which gives the impression that the label writer is trying to dominate the visitor's experience. The second version was shortened to make the text more specific and subtle. The label is for one photo, *Industrial Detail,* from an exhibition of black-and-white prints by German photographer Albert Renger-Patzsch.

Renger-Patzsch always photographed his subjects with an objective eye, yet his photographs often transcend the literal and present a magical transfiguration of the object. Here his subject was a row of freshly milled metal castings that had just been planed smooth, their residual filings still accumulated in the crevices. He angled his lights to cast a silvery sheen over the surface of the castings and the filings which punctuate the composition with tiny specks of luminosity. The factory assembly line has been transformed into a hypnotic maze of interlocking abstract forms.

—*original version*

A row of freshly milled metal castings had just been planed smooth, with residual filings still accumulated in the crevices. Renger-Patzsch angled his lights to cast a silvery sheen over the surface of the castings and the filings which punctuate the composition with tiny specks of luminosity. The literal factory assembly line has been transformed into a hypnotic maze of interlocking abstract forms.

—*edited, shortened version*

The person who has been designated as the label writer should be given the responsibility for seeing the draft texts through the editing and design process. The writer needs to have control over what happens to the copy, to keep the process on track, and to keep one, clear vision of where it has been and where it is going. This also helps the writer retain enthusiasm and "ownership" of the labels. If the writer writes and hands label copy over to editors, who make changes and hand it over to designers, who mark it up and add illustrations, the end product may lack the cohesiveness and consistency that can only come from having one person in charge.

There are several things that can slow down the editing process:

- Working with inaccurate, incomplete, or out-of-date materials in the first place.
- Editors or reviewers rewriting or retyping your text instead of editing directly on the draft provided for comment.
- Failing to provide comments within the designated time schedule.

Reviewers should be asked to respond by hand on the draft copy and return it to the writer on time. The team of reviewers should be large enough (five or six) so that if one person is out of town or cannot perform the job in the allotted time there will be enough other comments to cover the task adequately. The team should also be small enough (less than 10), so that integrating comments does not become a herculean job. The person who has the last word (usually the director, curator, or project manager) should be identified early in the process, and should be available to provide reviews in a timely manner.

Tricks that can speed up the editing process include:

- Spread all the returned drafts out on a table and go over all of the comments from all of the reviewers for each page or label, slowly, one by one, at the same time.
- Go through all the labels at once, and only once, incorporating all of the comments in a single, new draft.
- Circulate revised drafts as soon as possible, before the reviewers forget what they last saw.
- Save and date all previous drafts.

Tell reviewers that you will not respond to or incorporate all their edits and that they should keep a copy of their own comments. If the reviewers understand that their edits are suggestions, not the law, the label writer will be able to function in a more professional manner. Reviewers should review, not write.

A smooth editing process is most likely to happen when the reviewers know and trust the label writer. But that is not always the case. Sometimes it is necessary for writers to respond individually to a reviewer's comment—to show why they are not taking the suggestion and to argue for their choices. This is a time-consuming mentoring process, and it can add significantly to the editing turnaround schedule. If the reviewers are not going to be comfortable with allowing the writer some amount of freedom, the review process should be factored in with a longer timeline. When everyone on the team wants to be intimately part of the label creation, it takes a very long time to produce a finished product.

CASE STUDY

A HYPOTHETICAL LABEL PROJECT TIME BUDGET

Depending on the purpose and length of the label (function, number of words) and the complexity of the content (subject matter, big idea) and the amount of background research required, it can take from 15 minutes to 2 hours per label to research and write—the first draft. It can take another 15 minutes to 2 hours to get through various editorial and review stages. It can take another 15 minutes to 2 hours per label to integrate the words with the images in the design process. This gives a range of 45 minutes to 6 hours per label to get from research to final, integrated copy. If there are 25 objects needing caption labels, an introduction, three group or section labels, and a credits panel, that's approximately 30 labels. Thirty labels multiplied by four hours each (a rough and low estimate), gives us a total of 120 hours.

But that 120 hours is deceiving, because it is not 120 continuous hours. It is not a three-week job at 40 hours a week. It actually takes much longer. There are many hours "lost" in between, including the time it takes to:

- get references from the library;

- get calls back from information and image sources;

- submit rough drafts and hear back from reviewers (weeks!);

- make appointments with busy designers to hash out layouts, images, communication goals, and a host of other design decisions that must be made jointly by the writer and the designer;

- review (more weeks) rough layouts, revisions, and "final" camera-ready images and type in place.

A rough rule of thumb: Multiply the number of labels by 3 hours each for how long it will take, then triple that figure. "Yikes!" you say, "That's unreasonable, impossible; we don't have that kind of time!" Well, I was speaking ideally. This hypothetical scenario was to make you think again about allowing more time for labels. There is no denying that good ones take longer to make.

GETTING FINISHED

There is no such thing as "final" copy. Even after it has been silkscreened on the wall and the exhibit is open, changes can be made, if necessary. There has to be some flexibility and graciousness in letting things go even though they are not perfect. You do the best you can, in the time you have, within the budget you have. "Don't get it right, get it written" can be watchwords to avoid getting bogged down. Again, a clear vision of the communication goals, shared by the exhibit team, is invaluable.

The question of how many words each type of label should contain was touched upon in chapter 3, "Types of Labels," and it was not discussed here because it is such an important question that it deserves its own chapter—coming up.

NOTES FOR CHAPTER 11:

1. Neil Harris, "Exhibiting Controversy," *Museum News* 74, no. 5 (September/October, 1995).

2. Judy Rand, personal communication. Rand headed the label-writing team at the Monterey Bay Aquarium until 1995. She now has her own exhibition planning business, Rand and Associates. See Rand's paper, *Fish Stories that Hook Readers* (Technical Report No. 90-30. Jacksonville, Ala.: Center for Social Design, 1985).

12

The Number of Words

It is a museum exhibition, not an encyclopedia, not a library, and visitors should be allowed to feel they are there primarily to look and do, not to read. Select the number of words accordingly.

How many words should there be in a label? How long should a caption be? How much text can there be before visitors get overwhelmed? These are common questions that exhibit planners always deal with.

An average reading speed for adult visitors, who speak the language, who are on their feet, with many distractions, is about 250 words per minute. If the exhibition space is about 2,000 square feet, and they spend the typical short time—a total of between six and 10 minutes, average for an exhibition of that size—that is enough time to read 2,500 words, but only if they spend the whole time reading. If they spend half the time looking and half reading, that allows for about 1,250 words. If they spend three-quarters of the time looking, talking to the other people in their group, sitting down to rest briefly, that leaves enough time for about 625 words.

What kind of experience is the exhibit developer trying to create? If the 2,000-square-foot exhibition space contains 20 different things to look at or do, and each one has a label containing only the most important information, and the exhibit planners hope that most visitors will read the labels and use the information to enhance their experiences with the objects or phenomena, then the average number of words per label should be about 30. That is not many, but it is a realistic way to think about it.

There is a positive correlation between the amount of time visitors spend and the number of different things they do in an exhibition.[1] This means that there is a tendency for longer-time visitors to spend their time doing more things cursorily, not doing a few things in greater depth. Overall, when they

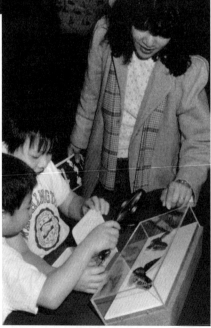

FIGURE 25
In a wildlife
forensic science
exhibition, the
information at
each interactive
station is broken
up into doable
chunks in a consis-
tent, yet flexible,
format. The back-
ground story
and directions are
large and short.
Visitors can read
from a distance
and choose
whether to do
the hands-on part.

linger longer, they stop at more of the available materials, e.g., 70% of the exhibit elements, instead of only 30%. The time that it would take to read all the words in a single exhibition should probably not exceed some humanly reasonable possibility, such as one or two hours, rather than six or 10. The argument that more reading opportunities will make more visitors come back more often is based on wishful thinking, not reality.

When a caption or group label has more than 200 words, in several paragraphs, visitors may appear to be reading that long label as they scan it, looking for the most interesting pieces—most likely the interpretations relevant to the objects nearby. If the number of words in such a label is cut down to include only those relevant, visually based bits of information, the overall result is that more people will be able to find what they are looking for quickly and easily. You'll be giving them a reward for reading the label. When each label gives them satisfaction, enjoyment, and intrinsic rewards, they will linger longer. They will be thinking, "I'm hungry, my feet hurt, and the parking meter is about to run out, but I want to look and read just a couple more things in here."

Some exhibit planners like to put 5,000 words into a 2,000-square-foot exhibit and do not care whether visitors read them or not ("We put them there; visitors will read what they want"). This attitude does not serve the visitor well. Of all the opinionated, prescriptive advice there is about label writing, this is one area where we do have the studies to show that shorter labels increase visitors' reading behavior.[2] More copy might please directors, donors, funders, founders, or curators who think that more is better, but they are not the primary users of the exhibition.

CASE STUDY

TWO CASES OF SELECTING THE AMOUNT OF TEXT FOR AN EXHIBITION

The animal halls at Field Museum of Natural History were being renovated. The first phase was complete and summative evaluations had been done. Observations of visitor behavior showed that the average time spent by visitors in the three halls completed thus far, which were more than 5,000 square feet each, was about 10 minutes each. Exit questionnaires and interviews with visitors revealed that although most of the visitors enjoyed the new exhibits and found many interesting things, the majority of them did not grasp some of the themes that the exhibit developers had believed were important communication goals.

In planning the next phase of diorama renovations, the exhibit developers decided it was important to narrow the focus of the theme in order to communicate the overall message to more visitors than before. They asked themselves, "If visitors spend only 10 minutes in this hall, and they visit only six of the 18 dioramas, will they be able to get the message (the big idea)?" They also knew, from their earlier evaluations, that many visitors had skipped the 75-word introductory message in the halls, so they asked themselves, "How do we make an introductory label readable without requiring visitors to stop?"

Solutions to their questions were to limit all of the chunks of label copy to approximately 50 words or less and make the concepts for each diorama reinforce and complement the main themes, instead of introducing many separate themes or levels. In addition, they made sure that the messages at each diorama contained direct, visually reinforceable, uniquely suited interpretation—which was guided by front-end evaluation data from visitors' impressions of the prerenovated dioramas. They also wrote an introductory panel that had only 25 words and designed it to communicate quickly and visually what the hall was about (refer again to figure 5).

After the hall opened, summative evaluation showed that visitors moved more slowly through this hall than the other renovated or old halls, and used a higher percent of available elements. In addition, more visitors grasped the main message. *Less of the right kind of information equaled more.*

In another case study at Shedd Aquarium, a temporary exhibit about wildlife forensic science was planned for the 2,300-square-foot special gallery. Concerned that their visitors might not want to spend much time in a science exhibit that contained no live animals, the exhibit developers were very conservative about the number of words planned for each label in the exhibit. The first part of the exhibition contained artifacts and photographs, and the second section had 10 interactive stations.

At each of the 10 interactive stations, all label copy was written in chunks of fewer than 35 words, and the ordering of the information was kept consistent among seven different parts: 1) title; 2) introductory scenario; 3) "what forensic scientists know"; 4) directions for what to do and notice (usually in fewer than 20 words); 5) a question for visitors to answer by comparing two specimens; and 6) the answer under the flap; plus 7) a sentence about a consequence or result based on the introductory scenario. Each chunk could be read and understood independently of the others, and they could be read in any order. See figure 25.

All of the interactive stations were mocked up and tried out with nonexpert adults and revised before the final versions were produced. Some were more difficult for visitors than others, depending on the type of forensic test being demonstrated. For example, the morphological characteristics of a feather are easier to see and compare than antibody gel plate tests. In response to visitors' obvious struggles, some copy was edited several times by cutting down the number of words, clarifying concepts, simplifying the messages, and eliminating confusing terms. In the end, the text turned out to be accessible to children as well.

NOTES FOR CHAPTER 12:

1. This tendency applies to the way visitors spend time and use interpretive exhibitions and may not apply to nonthematic groups of exhibits, or whole-museum visits.

2. Empirical studies have repeatedly verified this. See the special issue on the review of the literature on label research in *Visitor Behavior* 4, no. 3 (Fall 1989).

Evaluation During Development

*Getting feedback from visitors at all stages of exhibit development
and label writing—before you start, during rough drafts, and at the
"final" text stage—can help you produce better exhibit labels.*

Reading this chapter cannot be a substitute for learning about
evaluation from other resources where the philosophies,
rationales, methods of collecting, processing, and reporting
data are covered more thoroughly. A good place to start is by
attending a Visitor Studies Association conference workshop
for beginners. Many other resources are listed at the end of
the book. My hope is that this discussion will make readers
who have not tried evaluation want to try it and give more
useful examples and ideas to those who already have. You
cannot learn how to be a good evaluator just by reading this
chapter or imitating some of the methods described, but you
might want to become one—and learn where to get help.

WHY WE SHOULD DO EVALUATION

One of the biggest mistakes writers make, especially writers who are subject experts in what they are writing about, is
to assume that "people will know that—it's obvious." Equally
dangerous, however, is to assume that the audience is stupid
and the only way to reach the majority is to simplify text to a
childish level. Neither assumption is true. Evaluation can help
sort out what visitors know, what is or is not obvious, and
whether the assumptions the exhibit developers are making
about the audience are grounded in some form of shared
reality.

Before I ever did any kind of evaluation, I knew a person
who spent his summer on a research project to analyze family
group behavior at Brookfield Zoo.[1] When the summer was
over, I asked him what he thought of visitors, after spending
many hours following them around the park in the noisy

crowds and the sticky heat. I expected him to be glad that he never would have to watch another one, but instead he replied, "Oh, they are really very nice. They work very hard to find their way around the zoo and to understand the labels near the animals. They seem to really appreciate what the zoo is trying to do for them." I later found the same thing to be true in many other museum settings: by carefully watching visitors you get a much better perspective on several things— what is good about visitors, the problems they encounter, and solid clues about how to make improvements.

Museum practitioners who have not spent time systematically watching visitors may tend to remember only the people who are acting rudely, breaking the rules, or not paying attention. After watching visitors more objectively and carefully, you lose the typical condescending attitudes of "lowest common denominator" or "dumbing down." As art educator Danielle Rice put it, "It is possible to fall in love with one's visitors and to respect and value their wishes, desires, and perceptions."[2] You get to the point where you thoroughly appreciate what they can teach you about exhibits and labels.

When visitors cannot figure out what labels and exhibits mean—when people fail to understand or make a connection—many will blame themselves by saying, "I didn't have enough time to look carefully," or "I don't have any background in art," or "I'm just here because my friend wanted to come." The fact that they are so willing to blame themselves as opposed to the museum shows what respect they have for the institution. We, in turn, should be more respectful of them.

Evaluation can help exhibit developers encourage and enable their visitors to feel competent and confident. Visitors will enjoy their visit more and leave the museum feeling that it was a place for them. In the new paradigm of visitor-centered museums with narrative interpretive exhibitions, evaluation is essential to making museums inclusive, equitable and socially responsive to their communities. Labels play a very large role in creating positive feelings for visitors. When visitors do not have successful learning experiences, the failure to communicate may lie to a large extent with the labels. Harris Shettel, who has been evaluating exhibits for many years, says, "In every exhibit we evaluate, labels are key to the problems."[3]

WHAT EVALUATION CAN TELL YOU

There are many ways that exhibit evaluation can be used and many benefits for using it. The types and benefits are often broken down into three major groups, depending on when they are done:

Front-end evaluation—Before an exhibit project gets under way in detail, studying the current state of the potential audience. Developers can find out what visitors know, what their expectations are, and to what extent their vocabulary describes a particular exhibit topic.

Formative evaluation—During exhibit development and draft label writing, evaluations can fine-tune texts to make sure that directions, information, and vocabulary levels are being expressed appropriately for the audiences that will be using them.

Summative evaluation—Once the exhibition is open to the public, evaluations of the whole context can reveal areas that need further refinements that could not have been anticipated earlier. Evaluations after opening also give researchers the opportunity to test hypotheses about visitor use and impacts and make comparisons of exhibition success.

Evaluation is about making improvements. If all you want is praise, skip evaluation, and do a peer review by hand-selected people who will only tell you what you want to hear: "Beautiful installation," "Stunning presentation," "Best collection west of the Mississippi." But if you want to do a better job, and you can face a little constructive criticism, evaluation can lead to making a better match between what you want to achieve and what actually might happen.

PLANNING FOR "A MIRACLE"

Findings from brief front-end evaluation interviews at the Brooklyn Historical Museum gave exhibit planners a wealth of data about visitors' experiences, emotions, and expectations to help them plan a new exhibition on the history of the development of penicillin in Brooklyn. To find out what visitors knew about the topic, a sample of visitors was told that the museum was making a new exhibit called *Manufacturing a Miracle: Brooklyn and the Story of Penicillin,* and then they were asked one open-ended question, "What would you expect to see, do, find out about, and how would you feel in an exhibit about that?" The question was a mouthful, and visitors were allowed to choose which aspect to answer first. Then the evaluator followed up by probing for responses from the other categories, until the visitor had said all he or she had to say.

Visitors' comments formed the basis for many planning recommendations for the exhibition's content and design. Most interesting were their responses to how the exhibit might make them feel. Many people said they would feel pride in Brooklyn for being important in the story of penicillin. Many said they expected to feel more knowledgeable, interested, and "more confident about what I know about penicillin." Stronger emotions were also reported: "I'd feel very emotional because it saved my dad's life." "I'd feel sad, for the people who have suffered illness." "I'd feel anger—I wish they knew then what we know now about preventive measures." Appreciation for the drug's success; fascination with the scientific investigation process; hopefulness for future cures (such as for AIDS); and surprise that such a topic was being dealt with at a historical museum were among the other feelings visitors expressed.

These rich, affective expressions provided by visitors gave concrete direction to the text and images for the exhibit development process, as developers could ask themselves: Where in the exhibit will visitors see, find out about, and feel sadness, anger, hope, and surprise? Where could the exhibit design present the fascinating process of penicillin discovery and refinement? Where will the question about the difference between finding a cure for a bacterial disease and a viral disease be discussed? The front-end interviews revealed visitors' basic emotions and questions to which the exhibition narrative and label writing could be tied.

Answering the question about what visitors would expect to see, do, find out about, and feel in a particular exhibition was a question that visitors could answer based on their personal experience and background as it related to the museum's specific topic and intent. This is a very different question from the more vague, "What would you like to see and do in a history museum?" Or, "What would you like to know about penicillin?" Those questions are not well matched with the exhibit objectives, and are not likely to be answered in ways that give the exhibit planners the visitor-centered direction they need to focus the exhibit topic and communication goals.

The thing I like most about this example from *Manufacturing a Miracle* is the quick and simple way the front-end evaluation was able to reveal how visitors imagined that the exhibition would fit into their intellectual and emotional viewpoints.

SAMPLE SIZES

Often museum practitioners who have not done much of any kind of evaluation ask, "How many people do you need to have in your sample?" The answer depends in part on what you are trying to find out (what your question is), how varied visitors' answers are, and how you plan to use the information or data. For example, consider the question, "Do visitors understand the term 'baroque' and can we use it in our labels without defining it?" This could be answered by testing a large sample (n=200) to enable you to make a generalization, i.e., what percent of the museum's audience understand the word. If that percentage is large enough you might go ahead and use the term, making a decision based on numerical, or quantitative, data. Alternately, a small sample (n=15–25) could be interviewed to get qualitative data about what words visitors associate with "baroque." Developers can then use that information to write sensitively, weighing whether it is necessary for visitors to understand the precise definition on a case-by-case basis when the word is used. Setting up sampling procedures requires some special considerations, but they are not difficult to learn.[4]

Many evaluation decisions are based on qualitative information gathered from small samples of open-ended interviews. This is appropriate and useful, but often the decisions for one exhibit cannot be transferred to a new situation because of the unique set of variables within each specific exhibit situation. Only after doing lots of small evaluation studies and reading about studies done by others can museum practitioners build up a personal base of knowledge that allows them to make informed critical judgments about new situations. Too often, however, there is a tendency to jump to conclusions about all visitors based on one case study or a even single anecdote.

FINDING OUT WHAT VISITORS THINK AND EXPECT

Doing evaluation at the beginning of a project—front-end evaluation—can help shape the exhibit's big idea, communication goals, educational objectives, and the vocabulary and examples that will be familiar to the largest percentage of the audience. Evaluators do not tell curators what the content should be, nor do they tell designers what the exhibit should look like, but together they make decisions based on data from studies that will help shape the content and the design and improve the exhibit's ability to communicate effectively.

The goal of educational exhibitions is to create spaces where people can learn. People learn new things only if they are able to make a connection with the knowledge, attitudes, or skills they already have. Therefore, it is helpful for exhibit developers to know what ways visitors have for connecting with new knowledge. Exhibits also serve to reinforce what visitors already know or help them make new combinations with their existing knowledge—an important function that is often overlooked in favor of offering visitors more and more new information. Front-end evaluation through interviews, questionnaires, and focus groups finds out "where visitors are." From there, exhibit experiences can build bridges to new ways of seeing, feeling, thinking, or being.

Front-end interviews: Brief face-to-face interviews (less than five minutes) with a small, diverse sample (in age, gender, social group, prior experience) of casual visitors about new exhibits in the planning stages can provide useful information. For example, the evaluator can read visitors a sample of text, or show them a series of vocabulary cards or photographs, and ask them, "What comes to mind when you see or think about X?" This will quickly give useful feedback necessary to make plans, adjustments, or edits.

I doubt if the Freer Gallery of Art had to do any systematic evaluation to realize what visitors would associate first with an exhibition about the American artist James McNeill Whistler, called *Whistler & Japan*. The Freer did not disappoint; both the exhibit brochure and wall labels mentioned it:

Whistler was an early and ardent collector of both Chinese and Japanese ceramics. Ignoring the traditional European distinction between "fine" and "decorative" arts, he found inspiration for his work in paintings on porcelain, which according to his mother, he considered the "finest specimens of art."

Exhibit planners were not compelled to use Whistler's mother as the focus of the exhibition, of course, but by including references to her, it showed that the Freer recognized and used what visitors know.[5]

Common sense will get you a long way, but to understand more thoroughly and specifically what visitors think, feel, know, and anticipate requires some form of front-end datagathering.

In some cases, it is desirable to interview people off-site (potential visitors or new audiences) to find out ways to appeal to and relate to their interests and knowledge. This fulfills the objective of looking for the common denominators of knowledge in an audience more diverse than that of on-site visitors. For example, in a front-end evaluation for an exhibit about water in California, four groups of audiences were sampled: visitors to the museum, students on a nearby city college campus, people on a downtown streetcorner at lunchtime, and youth in a local mall. When asked a series of questions about where their drinking water came from, the only word that they all used in common was "reservoir." This concrete, familiar concept could then be made the focal point for the exhibition's discussion of other aspects of the topic, such as: water sources—how water gets into the reservoir in the first place; water transport—how water gets from the reservoir to your house; and water use—the level of reservoir water goes up and down during different times of the year and over the years. Knowing that many visitors would share the concept of "reservoir" gave exhibit planners a focal point from which to work.

Field Museum conducted front-end interviews in front of

American mammal dioramas before their renovations. Visitors' comments became high priority information to include in the different forms of interpretive devices. Notice also in these examples how the type of information and the modality for presenting it were well matched:

> *What visitors said:* How big are that guy's antlers? *What was done:* Label for large moose diorama said, "His antlers measure six-and-a-half feet across!"

> *What visitors said:* Maybe they are going extinct. We don't have them running around North America anymore, do we? *What was done:* Video for bison diorama included footage from *Dances With Wolves* depicting herds being slaughtered, plus historical photographs and narration about the status of bison populations today.

> *What visitors said:* What does it look like inside what they're building? *What was done:* Illustration at beaver dam diorama showed cut-away view of beaver lodge.

> *What visitors said:* The deer are looking at something down the hill, like they hear something, or are startled. *What was done:* Audio label for mule deer diorama said "Maybe they heard a cougar down the canyon. . . ."

> *What visitors said:* They are headed somewhere. Are they migratory? *What was done:* Button-activated electronic label showed yearly migration pattern of caribou at caribou diorama.

These visitor comments and exhibit element responses were above and beyond the most common questions of What is it? and Where does it live? These topics were addressed by maps and labels.

Asking visitors what they think, notice, and want to know did not mean that visitors told the museum what to do or say. There were many things visitors asked about that did not get included in the interpretation. But exhibit developers were sensitive to visitors' questions, assumptions, prior knowledge, and observations, and the developers tailored the exhibit interpretations, when appropriate, to their needs.

Focus groups: Another common method for doing front-end evaluation is focus groups. Focus groups provide a wealth of quotable quotes and anecdotes, and some museum staff can comprehend the findings more easily than the numerical data summarized from surveys or interviews.

Brief interviews take much less time to plan, conduct, and summarize than focus groups, but both techniques require training for the person conducting them. Focus groups have more complicated and expensive requisites: to recruit, follow up, and pay participants (or provide a gift); to rent a room with an observation area and video equipment; to hire a professional facilitator if no one is experienced in conducting a focus group; to provide refreshments; and to transcribe and summarize the results of the feedback.

Visitors in focus groups are often highly motivated (and paid) to talk about their perceptions and expectations. In group discussions participants may even project attitudes and intentions that museum practitioners want to hear. There are no penalties for exaggerating, and participants are under no obligation to tell the truth or actually do what they say. For good advice on how to conduct them, see *Focus Groups: A Practical Guide for Applied Research* by Richard Krueger.[6]

In focus groups, facilitators probe for breadth and depth of qualitative information that can provide rich, detailed data. Nevertheless, focus groups are just one form of evaluation. Like every methodology, they have their limitations. A single focus group provides feedback from eight to 12 people, which is not enough data to represent the majority of any audience. And because they are expensive and time-consuming to conduct, a larger database may be difficult to build unless financial sponsorship is available.

Front-end evaluations of any type that probe for what visitors know are very relevant to label writers. This information will be useful for creating interpretive opportunities for visitors to make new connections and to recollect old ones.

What visitors are concerned about, what knowledge they feel confident about, and what they are less certain of, or what misconceptions they have will help exhibit planners do a better job of formulating appropriate concepts and content. Front-end surveys that ask visitors only to state likes, dislikes, income levels, zip codes, or other target marketing questions are less useful to exhibit designers.

Whatever type of front-end evaluations are done, do them early enough in the planning stages so that relevant information can be incorporated along the way.

FINDING OUT IF IT WILL WORK

Formative evaluation during the development of individual exhibit elements will improve the chances that they will achieve their communication goals. Formative evaluations enable specific ideas to be fleshed out, communication goals refined, texts written and edited, and text and images to be rearranged to go together better. In addition, exhibit developers can attend to a wealth of physical and mechanical details.

The first thing to do is get the label or device to the point where the developers are satisfied with it (in terms of content, not aesthetics) before wasting visitors' time testing it. You should be evaluating something you like and think is good. Visitor feedback helps you make it even better.

Questions such as those below can be used as a checklist, as actual visitors react to inexpensive mock-ups:

- Do they like it?
- Do they think it's fun?
- Do they understand it?
- Do they find it meaningful?
- Does their understanding coincide with (or at least not contradict) the stated communication objectives for the element?
- Does it give the user a sense of discovery, wonder, or "wow"?
- Do visitors have trouble with jargon, unfamiliar technical terms, or words with double meanings?

Other questions deal with text editing and style issues that may have not been worked out in the rough drafts of the label text. Often, these mistakes or edits will only become obvious when the label is made larger and placed in its context.

- Is the text put in "chunks," i.e., one separate thought at a time?
- Is there one phrase per line, or are there natural line breaks?
- Does it look easy to read? (Big enough? Short enough?)

It is always amazing to see what you notice when the label is mocked up that you overlooked while it was on the computer screen.

For interactive exhibit elements, or even just a label that asks visitors to do something, formative evaluation is essential to success. Cueing visitors—asking them to look at the mock-up and talk with you about it—works well in many situations. Visitors have the ability to ignore the crudeness of a paper mock-up, and they are willing to play along with taped-together versions of an interactive (refer again to figure 19). Their reactions predict, but do not give complete assurance of, the exhibit's communication effectiveness.

Formative evaluation of interactives helps to answer questions about mechanics, instructions, content, and visitors' intuitions, including:

- In the label or instructions, are the first things first (i.e., what has to happen first) and are the most familiar things first?
- Does it mechanically function without breaking?
- Does it mechanically function without hurting someone?
- Can visitors correctly figure out how and where to start the activity in two seconds or less?
- Can people follow the directions? Are the directions in three steps or fewer?
- If visitors act intuitively, are they doing the right thing?
- Can visitors figure out what to do without reading anything?

- Do the visitor's actions reflect and/or imitate the phenomena or concept?
- Is the reset or reaction time what it needs to be (fast enough, slow enough)?
- Do the words in the label accurately describe, name, or identify the structures (mechanisms) of the exhibit?
- Do the words in the label match the actions and activities that the visitor engages in?
- Are symbols, graphics, or animation needed to model the actions and structures or mechanisms?
- Does the challenge of doing the activity match most visitors' skill levels while still requiring them to "stretch" a little?
- Is visitors' attention focused and are they absorbed in the experience?
- Do people feel anxious about the content or setting?

Testing and retesting with cheap versions, making improvements at each iteration, is far preferable to sinking big bucks into one glitzy prototype. Although aesthetics are an important component of the total exhibition experience, they are best assessed after the exhibition is completed, during summative evaluations. The main purpose in formative evaluation is to test the exhibit element's ability to communicate.

(In an exception to the guideline above—testing communication goals rather than aesthetics—The Toledo Museum of Art tested the design aesthetics of gallery introduction labels by producing label texts in full-sized mock-ups and placing them on their stanchions in their planned positions in the gallery. Legibility, readability, and more subtle aspects of the type style, color, and design were modified until the design achieved the "feel" the exhibit planners were seeking.)

Formative evaluations of mock-ups of interactive devices can reveal simple things, like the need for changing the position of one object or substituting one word, and can make the difference between comprehension and misunderstanding. For example, formative testing found that visitors could make comparisons between bird feathers more easily when all the feathers were from the same side (e.g., comparing a right wing feather from one bird species with a right wing feather —not a left—from another). In another case, two samples of elephant hide (one real, one fake) had to be dyed the same color, so that visitors could more easily concentrate on texture and pattern as the determining factors.

What happens during formative evaluation when the designers and the visitors have different opinions? In a test of a rotating, six-sided label, visitors were more likely to turn it by pulling it toward them than by pushing it away. The designers had wanted to number the sides one through six as the wheel turned away from the person standing in front of it. This format was intuitive if you think of the label as one piece of paper with number one at the top of the paper, followed by two, etc., that gets wrapped around the wheel. After watching visitors use the rotating label, however, exhibit developers used the design that was consistent with the visitors' actions. It was not an ego contest, however, because everyone had agreed that some decisions would be made by watching, not guessing, what visitors do.

Many ergonomic factors can only be determined by observing visitor behaviors. If visitors are using exhibits in inappropriate ways, careful observations often can reveal why and solutions will present themselves.

Unless there is good communication within the whole exhibit team, findings from formative evaluations might never be seen by the designer, especially if the exhibit is being designed by outside consultants. "I remember that about a pound of paper spit out of our office fax machine every day. Somehow I must have missed some of it," said a designer who read the evaluation reports a year later. The ease of keeping people on track and up to date on a fast-moving design schedule is inversely proportional to the number of people involved and the distance between their desks.

EVALUATION AND ACCESSIBILITY

At the Boston Museum of Science a large reinstallation project involving old dioramas had as a primary purpose the goal of reaching audiences with physical disabilities—the vision- and hearing-impaired, and wheelchair users.[7] New interpretation was added, including things to touch and audio-visuals. Through a series of front-end and formative evaluation stages and comparative testing after improvements were made, developers were able to show marked increases in visitors' use of the hall. They concluded that their efforts to reach audiences with disabilities—by providing a wider range of experiences and shorter labels with larger text—had successfully reached more of the audience as a whole. Everyone benefited from changes that made exhibition elements more accessible to those with disabilities.

For a broader discussion of front-end and formative evaluation and ways to answer many of the questions and issues raised in this chapter, see the books *Try It! Improving Exhibits Through Evaluation, Doing It Right: A Workbook for Improving Exhibit Labels,* and *User-Friendly: Hands-On Exhibits That Work.*[8]

We have seen in this chapter how front-end and formative evaluations during the planning and design phases of making an exhibition give exhibit developers information while there is still flexibility in the plans and time to make changes. Once the exhibition opens, there is usually little or no staff, time, or money available for remedial fixes. Unfortunately, the reverse is true of the evaluation schedule and budget, which is often specified for one big final summative evaluation instead of several shorter responsive studies during development, when visitor studies can do the most good. While evaluations done after opening may have implications for the future, they have less value than front-end or formative studies whose recommendations can also be acted on immediately.

Summative evaluations have the advantages of reviewing visitors' experiences in the context of the whole exhibition, providing an overall look at how well the exhibition achieved its goals and detailing specific areas that need work. In addition, if done with systematic, universally valid tools, collaborative studies can offer opportunities to share data among institutions. These two possibilities will be discussed in chapter 19, but before that, let us consider more of the tasks that go into producing good interpretive labels—images, interactivity, electronics, typography, and fabrication methods that produce durable, attractive products.

NOTES FOR CHAPTER 13:

1. Thomas J. Brennan, "Elements of Social Group Behavior in a Natural Setting," Master's thesis, Texas A&M University, 1977.

2. *Insights: Museums, Visitors, Attitudes, Expectations: A Focus Group Experiment* (Malibu, Calif.: J. Paul Getty Trust and Getty Center for Education in the Arts, 1991), p. 49.

3. Harris Shettel, personal communication. Shettel has had a long and influential career in museum evaluation and has published extensively. An early paper that clearly articulated the issues was "Exhibits: Art Form or Educational Medium?" *Museum News* 52, no. 1 (1973).

4. For advice on small sample procedures, see "Small-sample Techniques in Project Evaluations" by Ross Loomis in Denver Art Museum's interpretive project by McDermott-Lewis.

5. The Freer has made laudable labels for years. See *Washington Post* editorial by Amy E. Schwartz, "The Well-Written Label," June 15, 1993.

6. Richard A. Krueger, *Focus Groups: A Practical Guide for Applied Research* (Newbury Park, Calif.: SAGE Publications, 1988).

7. Betty Davidson, *New Dimensions for Traditional Dioramas: Multisensory Additions for Access, Interest and Learning* (Boston: Museum of Science, 1991).

8. See Samuel Taylor, ed. *Try It! Improving Exhibits Through Formative Evaluation* (Washington, D.C.: Association of Science-Technology Centers, 1991); Barbara Punt, *Doing It Right: A Workbook for Improving Exhibit Labels* (Brooklyn, NY: The Brooklyn Children's Museum, 1989), and Jeff Kennedy, *User-Friendly: Hands-On Exhibits That Work* (Washington, DC: Association of Science-Technology Centers, 1990).

Making Words and Images Work Together

One of the most important and difficult things to achieve with interpretive labels is getting reading and visual, nonverbal experiences to work together—on the label and in the exhibition. Reaching this union is accomplished by an iterative (repeating, cyclical) process of word selection, image selection, word modification, and nonverbal content modification.

Different kinds of nonverbal images, visuals, and experiences accompany labels. They might be illustrations on the label itself, a photo next to the label, the objects or artwork referred to by the label, or a combination of all these. Even though a label may not have any images on it, the things around it are "images" that visitors will see and experience as they read the label—and those things need to be referenced by the label in some way. Label texts should also take account of images produced by image-triggering sources, such as sounds and smells. An image might also be a feeling.

Images created by three-dimensional objects are the most powerful attractors. Labels next to an object will be read more often than labels next to a photo, or a label alone on a wall. But, the visitors' experience will not be complete or memorable if, once attracted by the object, their interests or questions (even just casual curiosity) are not addressed by the label.

Without any references between what the words say and what visitors see, the label is in a vacuum. When there is no connection between what the visitor sees, feels, smells or hears and what the words are about, the label is less likely to be read and comprehended.

CASE STUDY

ENCOUNTER WITH THE TAR PIT LABEL

On a sunny summer Monday in Los Angeles, you decide to take the family to the La Brea Tar Pits Museum, but it turns out to be closed. So you go to the outdoor viewing platform, which overlooks a small, fenced-in lake.

A strong smell of oil or tar pervades the air; the lake is coated with a tarry scum, and large bubbles intermittently break the surface, gurgling and exploding. Three elephants—one in the water, two on the shore, are frozen in desperate poses. Your mind is racing with questions. . . . A-ha, over there, a label! Anticipating finding the answers to your many questions, you excitedly move toward it and begin to read.

The sign says, "This lake fills a quarry where asphalt was mined in the 19th century. After the quarry was abandoned, ground water seepage and rain slowly filled the excavated area." Whaaat? The label takes four paragraphs to get around to mentioning the "thick oil," "tar pools," and "animal death traps" that relate to the concrete images you have just experienced.

Under normal circumstances in an exhibition (lots of labels, lots of objects to see in a little time), if a label took four paragraphs to get to the point, your attention would have quickly wandered.

The label's words and what you are seeing and experiencing must work positively together toward the same objectives because, if they are not working together, they are either competing with or distracting from each other.

In the tar pits example, asphalt mining is not the first concept visitors are seeking to understand in the scene. The label writer probably put it in the first sentence because it was historically logical, but it didn't make sense in the word-image relationship established by the actual setting. Although it may be crucial background material for thinking and knowing about the tar pit, it is not crucial for the immediate experience. The logical, verbal structure of information is rarely appropriate for the actual, experiential exhibit setting where context dictates order. Often, a simple rearrangement of the order of the concepts is all that it takes to make a big difference.

INTEGRATING VERBAL AND VISUAL CONTENT

Everything in an exhibit or on a label has content, whether intended or not. Images that do not support the words are not neutral, or messageless, or without "noise." Superfluous content is distracting. The same goes for adjunct artifacts or props. Exhibit developers should resist the temptation to add visuals and physical structures just for the sake of ambiance, because visitors cannot easily sort out ambiance-only elements from message-bearing elements in exhibitions. When all the content is purposeful and integrated, the exhibit communicates more effectively.

A common mistake in exhibit design is to use an image with text because it is available, not because it is the best one to tell the story. To avoid this problem, exhibit developers should over-research and overcollect the number of images, so when one turns out to be unavailable, another suitable one will fit in its place. If copy has been written first, and the image to be used is not the first choice, make sure that copy is modified to make sure both elements go together.

"Going together" means that the words inspired by the visuals are the same words, in the same logical order, as the written text. For example, in figure 26, what other images would support the text below the picture better than the ones shown? A flying bird or birds would be more appropriate for "migratory species." A picture of a single bird is dissonant with the plural word "species." The mosquito could be replaced with drug vials, or the copy could be edited so that the last sentence, "The anti-malarial drug . . ." comes first, assuming that the audience knows the connection between malaria and mosquitoes.

A quick front-end evaluation could test that assumption: Show 10 different visitors a picture of a mosquito and ask, "Do you know of any diseases carried by mosquitoes?"

PLANNING AHEAD AND EVALUATING

Quick front-end tests like the one above are a good way to try out illustrations or words with visitors so that writers and designers can make choices that will fit with visitors' prior knowledge. If eight out of 10 visitors think of malaria when they see mosquitoes, exhibit planners can feel confident that those two parts (the mosquito image and the word malaria) will resonate in visitors' minds.

You may think that this is being fussy, but average stay-time per unit of space in exhibitions is only one minute for every 300 square feet, which implies that visitors are not focusing on very many things for very long, so every micro-second counts. If something does not make sense to people in the first few moments, it is likely to be ignored, or if only a brief second or two is spent, it is likely to be forgotten. For visitors to make meaningful connections with exhibitions, they must first find something that makes sense to them (in any form, e.g., words, pictures, sounds, smells), then combine that familiar thing with a new piece of information. The right words and images, working together, can forge those links, as seen in figure 27. Another good example is the human body

FIGURE 26
Illustrations, titles, and texts need adjusting in these draft sketches of labels to make each of them work well. In neither case does the illustration make the point in the title.

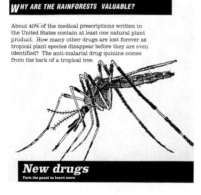

WHY ARE THE RAINFORESTS VALUABLE?

About 40% of the medical prescriptions written in the United States contain at least one natural plant product. How many other drugs are lost forever as tropical plant species disappear before they are even identified? The anti-malarial drug quinine comes from the bark of a tropical tree.

New drugs
Turn the panel to learn more

WHY ARE THE RAINFORESTS VALUABLE?

Many birds that people in the United States think of as North American species migrate to tropical forests for the winter. If their winter homes are destroyed, these birds will disappear no matter how hard we work to protect them here. The Baltimore oriole (renamed the northern oriole recently) is one such species.

Migratory species
Turn the panel to learn more

three rules of the medieval universe

FIGURE 27
This is a good example of how design can resonate with the message. There are "three rules," and each block of copy and its paired object illustrates one of the rules. Resonance is achieved most often when the writer and designer know what the other is thinking about.

slices at the Museum of Science and Industry in Chicago, where one label introduces the exhibit, answers visitors' most common questions, and recognizes their feelings:

Anatomical Sections: Windows into the Body

These unique displays present a rare look inside the human body. They contain actual horizontal sections from a man's body and vertical sections from a woman's body.

These sections were prepared in the 1940s from a man and a woman who died of natural causes. Their bodies were frozen and cut into 1/2 inch sections with a power saw. The sections are preserved in a solution of chloral hydrate, glycerin, potassium acetate, and water.

Although the exhibit may make you feel somewhat uncomfortable, take advantage of this rare opportunity to view at close range the unseen sections of the human body.

The body slices are displayed in multiple windowlike frames that are positioned at right angles to a short wall. The words "windows," "sections," and "anatomical" resonate with the physical layout and content; the words "frozen," "power saw" and "preserved" cut to the heart of the matter. This exhibition appeals to all ages, speaks a universal language and is loaded with affect.

You might think that sometimes dissonance or a lack of resonance is a good thing. It can be, but evaluation will be necessary to make sure that the questions you hope to raise in visitors' minds with the selection of a dissonant combination of words and images are the questions visitors do ask. If the dissonance simply creates confusion, it will hamper communication, not aid it, as in figure 28.

Choosing the right words and images is possible during planning and design, but it only will be complete when you have actual context—when the final placement and the environment of the labels are known. Elevation drawings can show the relative positions of all exhibit elements, as can

FIGURE 28
Design and message should not conflict with each other. "The true story about bats" is the subtitle for this *Masters of the Night* exhibition poster, which suggests a natural history or an ecology theme, not the fictitious or superstitious mood created by the Draculoid typeface, obviously selected for marketing reasons.

detailed dimensional models or computer-based layouts of exhibitions. Throughout the process, check and check again to see:

- If the label directs readers to look "on your right," is the object actually there?
- If the illustration shows the artifact from the front, will visitors see it that way, too?
- If the label makes a comparison with another object, is it clearly visible from where the visitor is standing?
- Would a smaller type size be appropriate for a panel's heading, given the reading distance in a narrow hallway, even though all headings were specified at 72-point type?
- Is a larger type size needed, given that the label ended up in the back of a deep case, even though all captions were specified as 20-point type?
- If one artifact had to be substituted for another at the last minute, does the label copy still match?

While drawings and models can help with planning, only after the exhibit opens to the public can everyone see what things are influencing each other. Time and money allotted for fine-tuning the relationship between words and images after opening will be well spent.

If you cannot wait until after opening, use the semifinal design phase, before the exhibit opens, to review and edit labels in context. At this stage, important last-minute changes to enhance the resonance between words and images can be made. At the very least, label writers should be writing to fit elevation drawings of exhibitions, where they can see what is next to the labels and imagine how visitors will approach the spaces.

EDITING LABELS IN CONTEXT

The Bisbee Mining and Historical Museum was preparing a new permanent gallery and working on a fast schedule and a low budget with a small exhibit team consisting of the director, the curator, a designer, and an evaluator/label editor. The director and curator wrote the labels, and the designer prepared detailed drawings (elevations) of the exhibit floor plan and layout showing where objects and label panels would be placed. Draft text and elevations were given to the editor, who prepared final draft copy to fit the elevations, which became "final" copy after review by the director.

Composed on a computer, using a common word-processing program, several different types of labels (different functions, different sizes) were laser-printed on colored paper and mounted on thin foam backing and installed in the exhibition for the scheduled opening.

After a few weeks of watching visitor behavior—noticing how visitors moved through the new exhibition, what attracted them most, which way they turned, where they were most likely to stop—the team members met. As a group, they reviewed every label in the exhibit, taking into account the total context of the show—physical layout, communication objectives, and visitor reactions.

Mistakes were easy to spot, and solutions were quickly agreed upon. Changes were made in the sizes of some of the larger group labels, e.g., a vertical format replaced a horizontal one that fit better where there was less room than anticipated in the elevation drawings. Line lengths needed to be reformatted for better legibility in some cases. Captions placed too close to dimensional photos, which cast a shadow, were moved down. Minor inconsistencies in style and vocabulary were noted and fixed. A factual error pointed out by a visitor was corrected.

Other labels were fine-tuned. Where there turned out to be more room than expected, two photo captions were rewritten into one text to make the comparisons between the two clearer, and two shorter captions were edited to tie them more closely to the visuals.

In another case, the team could see that simple reformatting a solid paragraph into a bulleted list would make the design and the information read more clearly and quickly:

Three Important Factors

Three factors that set the stage for the development of Bisbee were: 1) containment of hostile Apache Indians, which allowed prospectors and developers safe access to the area, 2) the brief rise of copper prices, and 3) the development of the railroads.

—*original label, all one paragraph*

Three Important Factors

Three factors that set the stage for the development of Bisbee were:
- Apache Indians who had been hostile to outsiders were contained;
- Copper prices were rising;
- Railroads extended to the west.

Prospectors and developers now could have safe access to the area and an incentive to be there.

—*final version, broken up and spread out for easier reading*

Waiting until after the exhibit had opened meant the team did not have to second-guess what would work. There was no argument among team members as to what was wrong or how to fix it, because they all shared the same experience—the exhibit as it was, not how it might be or should be, in their separate visions.

Edits were made and a new set of labels was produced and installed in more permanent materials. Summative evaluation revealed that visitors, children and adults alike, understood the exhibit's big idea: that the town of Bisbee, although located on the frontier, had many of the same problems and issues as other larger urban centers of the same time. As one visitor put it, "It's certainly not just an old burned out mining town."

THE CASE OF THE AMOROUS SNAKES

In an exhibit about a cypress swamp, a label was written to describe how a flat-looking swamp area actually has different subtle elevations that determine where different species live. The animals exhibited next to this label were three kinds of snakes. An illustration showing three snakes using the environment in three different ways was ordered from the artist.

The first sketch arrived (see figure 29). As requested, the snakes had been drawn to look "friendly" by making the snake's pupils round, not oblique. Because the zoo knew that a significant portion of its audience is snake-phobic, the exhibit team wanted to attract visitors to the label's message, not scare them away with a more realistic rendition. Through miscommunication, however, the first version of the illustration had only two snakes—one in the tree, one in the water. A second illustration was needed to include a snake on the land.

The second version of the drawing arrived and was incorporated into the label's design, and, along with the "final" copy, was shown to the zoo director, who exclaimed, "It looks like they're about to engage in an amorous adventure!" Indeed, and because the label text suggested otherwise, the drawing did not jibe with the words. A third illustration was requested, with specific instructions: "Make the snakes look like they are minding their own business." The third illustration was received and approved.

This story shows how illustrations and words can get detached from each other because:
- There can be mistakes in communication between the writer and the artist concerning the point of the illustration.
- Overfamiliarity with the text and topic can numb team members' sensitivity to fine points.
- There might not be enough time (and money) to redo the illustration until it works right.

Many possible forces can derail getting it right. Good communication, clear goals, fresh eyes, and enough time and money are essential. Another ingredient is helpful as well: a sense of humor.

FIGURE 29
Plenty of time and
multiple reviews
are necessary to
get it right.

First version

Revised version

Final version

AN ITERATIVE PROCESS

The old linear process—in which the writer writes the text, hands it over to the designer to design, who then hands it over to the fabricator to produce, who then hands it to the installer to put it all in place—results in multiple missed opportunities to fine-tune all the parts and make them hum together. If only one person is wearing all the hats, the fine-tuning will happen inside that person's head. But most exhibitions are planned and built by more than one person, and the chance to make images and words work together needs to be scheduled in as a series of iterative steps. A back-and-forth series of refinements results in a better product.

THE WONDERFUL WORLD OF CLIP ART

If there is no budget for original art production or for color photographs from a photo stock house, clip art provides an economical alternative.[1] Free, uncopyrighted, black-and-white images reproduce well and come in myriad topics and sources. Cut and pasted from a book, xeroxed or photostated, enlarged or reduced, clip art can enhance a whole system of exhibit labels quickly and cheaply. Images scanned by computers make clip art available directly from a disk. Figure 30 was created on a computer with clip art added.[2]

GENERALIZATIONS REQUIRE MULTIPLE IMAGES

Museums are great places to make generalizations, but we should be helping visitors reach more of their own instead of making them for them. By giving visitors more images to work with, we offer them the experiences they need to come to conclusions that build on what they know already. Too often, exhibit labels provide generalizations or conclusions that are not well supported.

Words and images do not go together when the text makes a generalization and the image or experience provides only one example. To make a generalization requires a set of at least three examples. Visitors tend to see one example as a case study; two examples don't allow the viewer to make enough

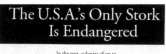

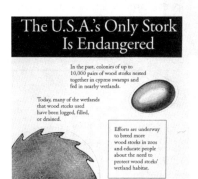

FIGURE 30
No money for illustrations? Free "clip art" complements typography in an affordable and attractive way. Simple and bold, these images reproduce well in black and white. The label sketches here show designs with and without clip art. Even without illustrations, lots of white space can give a label visual breathing room—a rest from solid text.

comparisons to be convinced; but three examples show can enough variability to provide viewers with knowledge that can be used in another situation, and that is the purpose of generalizations. Compare the alternative versions of the label below:

Bulla (Pendant for Holding Charms)

Worn around the neck by adults and children, bullae contained charms to repel evil.

—*text makes a generalization based on only one object*

Pendant for Holding a Charm (Bulla)

The charm held in this pendant, called a bulla, was to repel evil. People of all ages wore bullae.

—*first sentence is specific; second one makes a generalization*

The second version goes from the specific to the general, more in tune with the visitors' experience of a singular object. The text also introduces the unfamiliar term by linking it with a familiar word, and then gives its plural form more in context.

The next example makes a generalization based on one example, but in a way that moves from the specific to the general and makes use of visitors' prior knowledge of the concept of fossils:

Fossil Nautilus

Fossils are our record of ancient days

A hundred million years ago, this nautilus
and its kind swam the seas of northern California,
along with hordes of ammonites.
When the animals died on the seafloor,
their shells filled with mud. Mud turned to stone
and the shells dissolved, leaving these molds.

If the museum does not have three real examples, they can use models or photo supplements. Without three examples for visitors to examine on their own, they must take the label writer's word for it—which creates an information-centered, one-way presentation, not a visitor-centered dialogue.

Making a generalization through multiple experiences with models can be seen in figure 31, showing different sizes, shapes and functions of ancient Greek vases interpreted in *Art Inside Out* in The Art Institute of Chicago's education center. Even without any hands-on interactions, seeing multiple examples is one of the best ways for people to learn something new or have prior knowledge reinforced in a new way, and museum exhibitions can do this really well.

In the best of all possible situations, when images and words are working well with each other, the words and the images together will create a complete experience that neither one could do alone. When visitors read and look, or look and

FIGURE 31
Words and objects work well together in this exhibit. Multiple examples and an interactive experience to communicate the idea that "the shape of the vase determined how it was used and what would be held inside." Questions encourage looking and comparing, and the vases can be rotated to see the answers on the back.

read, the result is a gestalt that leaves the visitor feeling that the effort was worthwhile—they got something more by doing both—even if it only took a total of five seconds.

IMAGES AND WORDS IN THE ENTIRE EXHIBITION CONTEXT

On a broader scale, images and words need to work together in the whole exhibit, not just on individual labels. The graphic look and feel of the exhibition needs to harmonize with the total big idea.

All too often, a discordant situation results when exhibit planners attempt to make a serious subject more "fun," through using such techniques as playful, cartoon-style images to convey complex, scientific information. I believe that this false combination trivializes the information and is misleading to visitors. A "science arcade" or a "circus" setting creates expectations that are not in harmony with the mood and mind-set required of visitors to engage successfully with complex information, experiences, and interpretations of scientific phenomena in a way that will truly lead to increases in science literacy.

We need to pick our metaphors carefully. For example, a

roulette wheel was going to be used as a gambling metaphor for taking risks with unsafe sex and HIV. In a prototype test of the element, a visitor talked about how he did not think roulette was an appropriate metaphor for AIDS risk. He said, "I'm trying to be objective and give you helpful information. My brother died of AIDS, and this isn't doing it for me. It's more than a game—it's a chance, but not a game. You get death, not 40 bucks." Visitors deserve respect, and they will appreciate exhibits that are not trivial. Science museum hype—that you will have so much fun playing with the exhibit that you won't even realize that you are grasping basic scientific principles—is just that, hype.

Other discordant situations occur when the materials or colors are selected for visual impact, rather than as an integrated part of the overall communication goal. For example, in an exhibit about recycling, you would probably expect the paneling of the exhibition structures—including graphics and labels—to be constructed out of recycled materials, not glitzy steel and neon.

More than once I have heard label writers complain that designers sabotaged their words by making poor choices of materials, colors, images, or other factors that affect the mood and atmosphere in ways that contradict and distract from the efficient and effective communication of interpretive messages. In the end, it is the visitors who lose. This situation will continue to occur, unfortunately, as long as the label-writing process is separate from label and exhibition design. Writers and designers must work together and share the same goals.

IMAGES AND ICONS WORKING TOGETHER

In the attempt to reach non-English-speaking audiences in museums, the use of icons or symbols has become more popular, especially with orientation and wayfinding labels. Standard icons are used to identify visitor information, hiking trails, and rest rooms by the Department of Interior for parks, forests, and public property.[3] Only a few icons, however, are truly internationally comprehensible.

Symbols, graphics, and icons invented for specific use in one museum will be unfamiliar to the majority of visitors, not just non-English speakers. An evaluation of a wayfinding system at Brookfield Zoo found that only seven of 40 symbols were clearly unambiguous.[4] Original and unique iconographic labels may win graphic-arts awards from other designers, but they don't win any prizes for clarity from visitors.

Icons should not be used alone. Words are needed to help reinforce, clarify, and decode the image. The best way to find out if an icon works is to test it with a sample of visitors and make changes until it does. For example, what do the icons in figure 32 mean? All three were tested with visitors during development of The Adler Planetarium's new orientation and map system, and they all stand for the same thing, "purchase tickets here."[5]

The first symbol was a mystery to all but a few visitors. The second was misinterpreted as a cash station location. The third one worked well. (The little graphic on the ticket is the Adler Planetarium building.)

Making images and words work together requires knowing what the images and words are going to be far enough in advance so that adjustments and fine-tuning can be done to make sure they match. Waiting until the last minute, or handing the process off in a linear fashion from writer to designer without back-and-forth consultations, can lead to problems. When the images and words also involve some form of interactivity, the job can be even more complicated, as we will see in the next chapter.

FIGURE 32
Graphic symbols or icons must be tested with the public to make sure they communicate effectively. In this instance, the third one worked best for the message about where to get your tickets.

1.

2.

3.

NOTES FOR CHAPTER 14:

1. There are many different kinds of photo agencies. For example, Animals Animals/Earth Scenes specializes in environmental photography and can supply stock photos of mammals, birds, reptiles, rain forests, geology, weather, agriculture, microscopy and environmental degradation.

2. Clip art on the woodstork label sketch are from a historic Montgomery Ward Catalog, *Harter's Picture Archive for Collage and Illustration.*

3. Suzanne Trapp, Michael Gross, and Ron Zimmerman, *Signs, Trails, and Wayside Exhibits: Connecting People and Places,* Interpreter's Handbook Series, no. 4 (University of Wisconsin-Stevens Point).

4. Beverly Serrell and Hannah Jennings, "We are here: Three years of wayfinding studies at Brookfield Zoo," Proceedings of the American Association of Zoological Parks and Aquariums, Oglebay Park, West Virginia, 1985.

5. Britt Raphling, "The Evaluation Process Used to Develop a New Wayfinding System for the Adler Planetarium & Astronomy Museum," Chicago: Adler Planetary & Astronomy Museum, 1995, unpublished report.

Labels for Interactive Exhibits

Labels for interactive exhibits need to be customized so that they respond to and serve the specific design of the interactive and the way visitors use it.

Interactive elements need to be interpreted with more than a simple narrative. Texts for interactives must guide visitors' activities, often in a required sequence, and explain what is going on. Poor label texts will fail to compete with visitors' impulses to do rather than to read.

INFORMAL SCIENCE WRITING VERSUS LABEL WRITING

In a science museum exhibit about imaging, visitors were supposed to look into a tube and see an image of their eye reflected in a magnifying mirror. The label, which contained instructions and explanations, said:

The Peerless, Priceless Imaging Tool

This device is unrivaled for imaging in the visible light spectrum.

Look through this tube to see the most sophisticated imaging tool in existence: the human eye. Much like a camera, the eye adjusts to different light levels and focal distances. When united with the interpretive ability of the brain, the eye far surpasses any imaging machine ever built. However, unaided, it can only see in the narrow visible light portion of the vast electromagnetic spectrum.

This is excellent *science* writing, but it is not good *label* writing, because it lacks resonance with the context in which the interactive device will be used by visitors. It is not responsive to the order of events in which visitors experience the interactive. It tries to dominate, or to be, the visitor's experience by providing lots of important, complex scientific information. The vocabulary is too sophisticated for visitors' needs in the complex exhibition environment. It is more appropriate for writing meant to be read for the sake of the words and ideas themselves, without competition from the noise, distractions, and other concepts surrounding this one interactive device. Interactive exhibits need shorter, more-to-the-point labels, ones that aid and support the visitor's own scientific exploration and thinking, however simple that might be.

THE EXPLORATORIUM MODEL

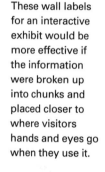

FIGURE 33
These wall labels for an interactive exhibit would be more effective if the information were broken up into chunks and placed closer to where visitors hands and eyes go when they use it.

A format for interactive labels was developed at The Exploratorium in San Francisco. The labels contain four sections, telling visitors "What to do" and "What to notice," and asking the questions "What's going on?" and "So what?" This style and variations of it have been adapted and used by many other museums across the country and around the world (see figure 33). In its longest form, the format provides plenty of room to explain, in detail, the scientific or technological background for the interpretive element, thus fulfilling the exhibit developer's desire to present knowledge.

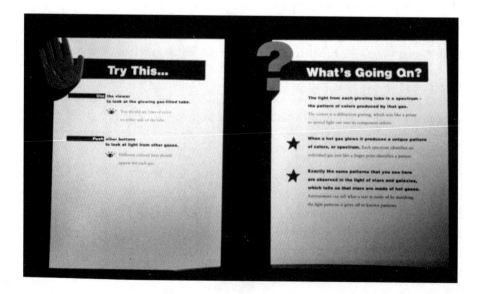

The example below is a very short version of an Exploratorium-style interactive label for the same eye-imaging exhibit mentioned above:

What to do:
Look close up into the tube.

What to notice:
You can see your eye, greatly enlarged in the mirror.

What's going on?
Your eye is the best, most powerful, priceless imaging tool.

So what?
Even though thousands of dollars are spent on high-technology imaging tools, your eye is still the best.

This organization of information is logical, linear, and systematic. It can be applied to any type of interactive exhibit, and provides an easy, "off-the-shelf" design format. Although this format has been widely copied, currently there are not any reports in the visitor studies' literature about the effectiveness of this label style. At the Exploratorium, they are now doing evaluations and are thinking about making extensive revisions to their labels in the near future.[1]

The main criticism of this formulaic style of labeling is that it is typically not responsive to the different physical layouts, components, and conceptual challenges specific to every individual interactive exhibit. It assumes an "empty-headed receiver" role for visitors' participation—visitors are told what to do before they are given any reason to perform the action. In addition, the design format (the four sections) dominates the label content and denies the opportunity to emphasize graphically the information it is meant to convey. The lead-in words (e.g., "What to do") are too prominent and redundant.

BEYOND THE EXPLORATORIUM MODEL

Interactive exhibit instructions, questions, and explanations need to be responsive to the individual design and content of the specific interactive. In certain exhibitions, a formula might work to present the different parts of the label, but in others, a formula might prove to be too rigid. The words, the visitors' actions, the physical mechanisms, and the exhibit developer's intent need to mesh.

This is an evolving area of label writing and design. It is one of the most challenging because of the number of variables involved. Practitioners might come up with several different formulas that could work in most situtations, along with special, flexible cases when they do not. This could avoid both extremes of using one-format-fits-all or having to make each design unique.

In a short paper called "From Hands On To Minds On: Labelling Interactive Exhibits," Minda Borun and Katherine Adams of the Franklin Institute in Philadelphia recommend a promising approach.[2] They tell of a case study of multiple attempts to get visitors to challenge their own assumptions about a commonly held misconception about gravity. They reported, "We learned to look at a label in terms of relationships. The label that worked created a new dynamic between itself, the visitors, and the device." Instead of just telling visitors information, the new label fostered a dialogue that got visitors to think about their own assumptions in a new way.

Borun's approach was used in a formative evaluation to test and improve four mock-ups of interactive exhibits for "Imaging Science" at the Museum of Science and Industry in Chicago. The wording in the prototype labels was changed to promote a more active visitor role, to link the visitor's actions to the device's phenomenon, and to help the visitor anticipate and formulate meanings. The labels asked a question rather than delivering information. By making the interrogative integral to the visitor's experience, using the interactive became synonymous with communicating the exhibit's main message. In other words, doing and understanding the experience became interdependent and mutually reinforcing. For example:

What tool is the best, most powerful, priceless imaging tool?

Look close up into the tube.

When the label invited visitors to try the interactive and to answer an explicit question at the same time, comprehension improved. Visitors' understanding of what the exhibit was about went from 27% (when using the Exploratorium-style label) to 67% (using the one shown above), and visitors' descriptions of the exhibits during evaluation interviews were much more appropriate and accurate when this new style of label was used: "You can have all the machines in the world, but unless you use your eyes to look, you can't tell what it is" and "Technology can see beyond, but you need your eye to understand."

What makes this question strategy work well is that there is something visitors can do other than just reading on to answer the question. The concept brought up in the question encourages the visitor to use the interactive device, and using it answers the question.

Another important advantage to this shorter, more direct style is that it becomes especially easy for parents and teachers to help children use and understand the exhibits by simply reading the question out loud.

Below is another example of a rewrite of an interactive label that eliminates a "why" question and gets rid of the "to do" in favor of a more dynamic question. Notice the difference between what you can imagine just from the question in the second case compared to the first:

Why is a burr so sticky?

What to do:
Look at the piece of burr and wool under the microscope.
Compare them to the hook and loop pieces of Velcro.

—*before, with a dreaded why question*

**What do the burr and wool have in common
with the pieces of Velcro? Look in the microscope.**

—*after, with concept and action incorporated into question*

Although it looks easy, this style of label is much harder to
write, because each label has to be individually crafted to
include the context of the message, the visitor's role and the
action required. The "formula"—a question followed by a
short instruction—is deceivingly simple. As with labeling in
general, the best product, in the end, looks obvious, but it
usually takes more than five drafts, plus formative evaluation
to get there successfully.

Here are some drafts of another interactive question written to get visitors to put their hands on a temperature-sensi-
tive wall and see how the warmth in their hands is imaged by
the material:

- What makes the panel change colors when you touch it?
- How can you make something change color by just
  touching it?
- What do the changing colors on these panels show?
- Can you make these panels change color?
- What does heat look like?
- By touching the wall, what can you see that is usually
  invisible?

Which one do you think works best? The last one contains
the prompt for action (touch) where (the wall), what to
notice (visible), and a clue about the concept (seeing the
invisible). The other five questions lack one or more of these.

PLACEMENT AND PHYSICAL-ACTION WORDS

Besides questions that invite, instruct, and give clues about the nature of the interaction, another important ingredient for labels for interactives is that the label's design and placement must be in the context or proximity of the physical space. Buttons must have labels right next to them, not inches or feet away, and the labels must say more than just "push." Let visitors know what to expect when they push: "Push to hear owl call" or "Push to release gas."

Below are three examples of how words in interactive labels can echo or resonate with the physical action the visitor sees or does, and how graphics support the words and make a bridge from words to actions and consequences:

- A six-sided rotating wheel contained numbered panels with a sequential story about how the forest changes as it is influenced by fire and by moose browsing on the trees. During evaluations, visitors used words such as "cycle," "succession," "progression," and "sequence" to describe the story.
- The label next to a lever said "Generate electricity," and an illustration showed a hand on the lever. Visitors inappropriately and vigorously pumped the lever back and forth. The label was changed to say, "Hold the lever up until the light goes off," and visitors used it correctly.
- A label next to a fake velvet touchable near a diorama asks, "What's the fuzz on the antlers?" After touching it visitors were seen pointing at the mule deer buck in the diorama and overheard saying, "That's what his antlers feel like." (See figure 34.)

Visitors read labels very literally. If the label can be misunderstood, it will be. Here are four examples, all of which involved some form of interactivity, of how things can go wrong, and what was done to correct the mistakes:

- On a gorilla graphics panel at a zoo, visitors were asked a question and told they could find the answer on the back

What's the fuzz on the antlers?

The fuzz is "velvet," a soft skin that covers growing antlers. Velvet is loaded with blood vessels and nerve endings, making the antlers warm to the touch and very sensitive. In a few weeks, this buck's antlers will stop growing, and the velvet will dry up and peel off.

Antler velvet feels a lot like this.

FIGURE 34

The question asked in the label's title is answered right away in the text. In addition, visitors get to touch a facsimile of antler velvet and pretend they are feeling the real thing. Visitors point at the deer's antlers in the diorama and say, "See, that's what they feel like."

of the bench next to the panel. Visitors read as far as "on the back" and walked around to the back of the gorilla graphic panel. Visitors soon created a little pathway through the bushes that reinforced the notion that the answer was back there. The zoo added the answer to the back of the panel in addition to the back of the bench.

- On a panel at an aquarium about how fish hear, a little silhouette graphic showed visitors how they could hear like a fish by putting their hands over their ears and putting their heads against the panel to sense the sound vibrations through their skull bones. The graphic, however, showed a person standing with his head almost touching the panel, with a tiny distance in between. So visitors carefully stood with their heads almost touching the panel. The graphic was redone, showing contact between the person's head and the panel.

- On a zoo mock-up of an interactive about swamps, visitors were instructed to "look among the lily pad roots to find small animals living there." Visitors had no problem pretending that the ropes dangling down from the "lily pad" were "roots," but they told the evaluator who was trying out the mock-up that the label should say, "Look *behind* the roots" because the little animals they were supposed to find were just graphics on the back wall behind the roots. The change was made.

- In an art museum, supplementary information about two paintings was supplied on large laminated sheets tucked vertically in a pocket next to a bench in the center of the room. The label on the wall next to the paintings said, "Pick up the label near the couch." Few visitors made the visual-verbal connection between the laminated sheets and a label and the bench and a couch in the gallery.

- In a science museum, an exhibit invited two people to sit facing each other, looking through a glass, while at the same time adjusting the amount of light shining on them to create a blend of their reflected images. The label told visitors to sit and "line up their noses." Some visitors responded by mushing their noses together against the glass. "Not only did this make doing the activity difficult, it also left lots of nose prints on the glass," reported the exhibit staff. The revised label showed a pictogram of two people sitting with their faces properly aligned and text that read, "Sit so that you and your partner are about the same height." More visitors used it successfully and left far fewer nose prints.

KEEPING IT SIMPLE

As museums incorporate more technology and create complex, in-depth, experiential, or immersion experiences, it is refreshing to think about how effective some of the simpler interactive techniques can be. Labels that encourage visitors to do something with their own low-tech bodies can work in a variety of settings, for example:

Can you find 15 beetles, 7 mushrooms and 2 snakes?

—*next to a natural history diorama*

To make a sound like a whale, hold your nose, close your mouth, and say 'OH!' three times.

—*in a marine mammals exhibit*

ALWAYS EVALUATE

Think ahead and anticipate, then mock it up, and test to see where visitors' hands and eyes go when they approach and manipulate the interactive. When reaching over to grasp a lever or push a button, will a person's arm cover up or cast a shadow on the label, making it difficult to see? Will the handle accommodate a child's arm as well as an adult's? Will visitors' eyes go naturally from what's moving, to the label that explains what's going on? Trying them out, modifying, trying them again, and modifying again will lead to interactive label solutions that get read, used appropriately, and remembered.

The suggestions in this chapter have had to do with making words and actions work together in interactive exhibits. The previous chapter stressed this important relationship between words and images in static exhibitions. Some very similar challenges and solutions are presented by electronic media, as we will see next.

NOTES FOR CHAPTER 15:

1. Kathleen McLean, personal communication. McLean and I worked together on *The Mystery of Things* at the Brooklyn Children's Museum, and she was the exhibit developer for *Darkened Waters*. She has her own business, Independent Exhibitions, and is currently working for the Exploratorium.

2. Minda Borun and Katherine A. Adams, "From Hands On to Minds On: Labelling Interactive Exhibits," in *Visitor Studies: Theory, Research, and Practice,* Volume 4, edited by Arlene Benefield, Stephen Bitgood, and Harris Shettel (Jacksonville, Ala.: Center for Social Design, 1992).

Electronic Labels and Hypermedia

Many of the principles for good exhibitions, good labels, and good typography can be directly applied to electronic media.

Electronic labels include both low-tech devices, such as label texts that light up at the push of a button, or crawl signs (in which text scrolls across a lighted, digital bar), and more high-tech solutions, such as computer-accessed hypertext and videodisc hypermedia (graphics, movies, sound). Whatever the technology, electronic labels should be guided by clearly stated big ideas, visitor-sensitive communication goals, and good principles of typography to enhance legibility and readability. As educator Wendy Aibel-weiss put it after evaluating the sucess of the National Postal Museum's new exhibits, "Technology, as an interpretive tool, is best utilized when totally integrated into the overall interpretation plan of each exhibit story."[1]

Below we will consider three of the most common electronic interpretive devices used in exhibitions: audio tours, videos, and multimedia computers.

AUDIO LABELS

Audio labels are messages or interpretations that you listen to. They can be delivered via single or multiple push buttons at a particular exhibit, or as a carry-along cassette or wand for a tour of the whole exhibition. Linear audio tours prescribe one sequence and, by controlling the order, present a more cohesive, complete narrative with a beginning, middle, and end. Random-access audio programs let visitors choose the order, so sound bite must stand alone.

The two most important advantages of audio labels are allowing visitors to keep their eyes on the objects while listening and making the audio available in multiple languages. The three main disadvantages are that they can isolate visitors from the social aspects of visiting, equipment malfunctions can be common and annoying, and they can cause traffic jams when a large group of audio-users are stopped for a long-playing message. "In the Gauguin exhibition, so many people were using them that it sounded like crickets," reported one evaluator.

Although legibility is not a concern for audio labels, several traits they should share with written words include using appropriate vocabulary, being conversational and friendly, sticking to what can be seen, and limiting the number of different concepts. The style of writing for spoken words can be more personalized and colloquial than text that is read.

Audio labels can be embellished creatively with music, authentic sounds, or realistic accents. At the American Museum of Natural History, a random-access CD audio guide takes visitors on a museumwide tour of 50 treasures selected by the curators of the museum collections. Stories told in different voices (such as Margaret Mead and Indiana Jones) and sound effects make the information more intimate, exciting, and personal. During evaluations, visitors said that they spent more time, appreciated being able to focus their attention on objects instead of labels, and liked being able to choose their own route for the tour. Many commented that "it made the museum come alive."

Although audio tours offer a chance to produce fairly low-cost devices that have the advantage of flexibility, few places have actually experimented with using this technology in multiple ways to creatively interpret permanent exhibitions. As the hardware improves (e.g., adding speed, reliability) and prices go down, audio might be used more for special themes, not just special exhibitions.

VIDEO

Short video programs can serve as another mode for communicating exhibition messages. They function well to show processes, personalities, animations, action, or sequences. They can tell stories visually, without words. Rather than delivering another layer that gives more information, they can serve a more complementary function by presenting a visual form of similar information presented elsewhere in the exhibition. For example, the video in Shedd Aquarium's *Otters and Oil Don't Mix,* omitted a voice-over from the sound track to give visitors a chance to put their own words to a three-minute show. Natural sounds and minimal music accompanied visuals that showed the sequence of otters being rescued from an oil spill, taken to the recovery area, washed and dried, held in captivity until they recuperated, and either released back into the wild or brought to Chicago. Visitors narrated the video to each other from information given in nearby displays or from their own prior experience.

Another example of videos well integrated with other exhibit elements is in the *Spirit of Imagination* gallery at the Autry Museum of Western Heritage. Seven short videos (each one lasted less than five minutes) cover such themes as "B-Westerns," "Women and Minorities in Westerns," and (of course) "Singing Cowboys." Near each of the video stations are cases with artifacts (clothing, props, and movie posters) associated with the cowboys shown in the video. Fans of movie westerns brought more background experience to the displays than visitors who had no idea who the movie heroes were. But cowboy neophytes could, nevertheless, easily follow the themes and relate them to the various actors and artifacts. The gallery was a very good example of appealing to a broad audience through the same, not separate, elements for more or less experienced viewers.

Another powerful example of how a video that can be used to show a process and a personality is in the AIDS exhibit at the Museum of Science and Industry in Chicago. A doctor who became HIV-positive made a video of himself over the course of his disease, right up to the time of his death. He speaks directly into the camera, giving his thoughts and feelings as he progressively shows more debilitating effects. It is a human, touching, empathetic story. It lasts more than 30 minutes, longer than most visitors are willing to spend at a screen, but even a few minutes of viewing communicates the idea and the impact.

All three video examples above strive to present an integrated experience in a different, and very appropriate, modality for a wide range of audience ages and experience levels. None seized on the medium to add more information for the sake of information itself.

COMPUTERS

Computers provide visitors with yet another kind of tool, a different kind of modality. Computers can be used as an element to supplement other parts of an exhibition or they can be an exhibit element unto themselves. Used wisely, computers provide exciting possibilities to combine text, sound, photographs, animation, and video and to make interactive links between subjects. They allow visitors control over the amount and direction of information. A computer that is easily navigated and has an integrated purpose can provide a timely, enjoyable experience in an exhibition for both adults and children.

Just as labels need to be kept short and not too dense, the number of words per computer screen should be kept to less than 50. Legibility of the on-screen type should be a primary consideration. Keep multiple, contrasting colors and shadowing to a minimum in body copy and avoid putting type over images, unless the images are reasonably monochromatic and do not need to be viewed in detail. Unwise designs include hard-to-read on-screen type, text that duplicates what is on the wall labels, text that runs on for several screens (e.g., paragraphs that are broken from screen to screen), slow trackballs or unresponsive mouses, and inconsistent navigation cues.

In science centers, computers often *are* the exhibits, not

supplements to them. As stand-alone devices, they offer visitors an electronic experience that usually takes a longer time commitment than most other exhibits. The guidelines for effective computer writing and design are still the same: have a clear goal and carefully specified communication objectives, and use formative evaluation extensively in the development stages to make sure that visitors can easily and quickly figure out how to navigate through the program.

As exhibits themselves, computers can have the same characteristics and challenges as exhibitions made up of roomfuls of objects and labels: there are *orientation issues*—how and where to get started; *learning style issues*—how to indicate sequence, pace, and choices; *instructional design issues*—how the content is best presented, as open-ended, multiple solutions to a question or problem, or a single-sequence. And, of course, *layers of information issues*—how "layers" are defined and the validity of the assumptions underlying them.

One of the most common scenarios for stand-alone computer programs in exhibitions allows visitors to pretend that they are somebody who has a problem to solve and to follow a sequence or try out a variety of ways to solve it. For example, pretend you are a medical doctor and use the imaging tools; pretend you are the mayor and decide how the water supply will be allocated; pretend you are the inventor and create a new device. This kind of scenario is easy to introduce and has multiple ways to use the program and for varying lengths of time.

During the planning of a new exhibit at Brookfield Zoo, exhibit developers discussed having a computer program that would let visitors pretend they were the "Swamp Manager" and see what the impacts of different decisions were on the swamp. They realized that the cost of making a computer program with complicated graphics would be more than $60,000, but the same concept could be explored by visitors in a simpler program for under $20,000. Anticipating that less than about 25% of the visitors to the exhibition would have the interest or time to use it, the lower-cost version was the best choice. Some of the budget saved on this element could be spent designing and testing more low-tech interactives that would appeal to more visitors.

Evaluations of visitor use of different exhibit elements within a whole exhibition have shown that some high-tech computers and videos are no more popular than simple mechanical devices with short, direct label text.[2] Computers in or as exhibitions often are used by less than one-third of the audience, and even then, only used briefly. This probably relates as much to what visitors like to do in museums as to the quality of the program. Brief, socially oriented encounters are typical visitor behaviors, and some electronic programs are too long or too complicated to be inviting or to share.

If it takes visitors longer than a few seconds to be motivated, and longer than a few minutes to be intrinsically rewarded, a computer will not attract and hold their attention for much of the program's potential length. For example, less than half the visitors who stopped at an interactive computer that offered several scenarios about medical imaging stayed for more than two minutes. But those who did become engaged typically stayed seven to 10 minutes, long enough to explore one full sequence of "solving" a patient's problem.

In light of the considerable expense of developing interactive computer programs and the breadth of experiences and choices they offer, they are clearly justified only when a computer is clearly the best mode to present the desired experience and will appeal to a large enough portion of the museum's audience. Making programs with short sequences and multiple outcomes—to do repeatedly and socially— would seem to fit visitors' normal museum behavior more naturally than the "in-depth" programs often presented.

In the 1980s, when computers first started being used regularly in natural history exhibitions, it seemed to me to be a natural marriage to have new electronic labels with old dioramas. Enhancing those large, historical, valuable, and popular displays with modern technology that could encompass the complex, detailed stories they told in interactive ways could

CASE STUDY

"CLEOPATRA" COMPUTER AT THE ART MUSEUM

At The Art Institute of Chicago, exhibit developers wanted to provide visitors with more information about the newly reinstalled ancient Greek and Roman art collection. A multimedia computer program called "Cleopatra" was planned, after first making a prototype for review and fund-raising purposes. The prototype was tried by staff, multimedia experts, and visitors.

Several changes were made in the original prototype to get a better match between the intentions of the program and the target audience of casual visitors. For example, the number of works of art covered by the program was reduced to 18 from 30 to offer a more reasonable, less overwhelming array of choices. Icons on the touch screen buttons were revised until they were easy to recognize and decode (see figure 35). More graphics and less text were used in the revised version.

The developers recognized that their original version of the program had been more of a static information "dump" that might have appealed to the occasional scholarly, studious person. But the program developers wanted to meet the needs of the majority of visitors—to offer what *they* wanted to know rather than what an expert wanted to tell them. Revisions took advantage of what the computer could uniquely do to make using the program more fun and entertaining to visitors, e.g., provide movement, allowing visitors to zoom in and out for different views, rotate and animate pictures.

"Cleopatra" is located in an exhibit area small enough so that visitors conceivably can move easily between the screen and the real things to use the computer as a truly investigative tool—looking, posing questions, finding answers, looking again, looking more. Summative evaluations will tell.

FIGURE 35

Through formative evaluation, the main navigation screen for "Cleopatra" was simplified and clarified. Fewer choices, more logical groupings, and better icons and illustrations (bottom) improved visitors' ability to use the computer program.

really make them come alive. For example, questions posed on computers and answers from visitors based on their observations could make something else happen electronically in the diorama, such as a spotlight on one specimen, or a sound, or movement. Instead of integrating multiple, low-cost, simple, visitor-centered, computer-assisted interpretations in exhibitions, most museums seem to have opted for computers as high-cost, complex, information-delivery systems.

OVERDOING INFORMATION ELECTRONICALLY

It is far too easy for exhibit developers to use electronic media, especially computers, as an in-depth encyclopedia or library, not another time-limited exhibit element. Hypertext opportunities are good for investigation, tracing through references, hunting down comparisons, and browsing with a purpose. This kind of reading is more strongly associated with research by students or academics than with informal, leisure-time pleasures of family or social groups. It is an inappropriate scenario: "Pretend you are a Ph.D."

By using electronic labels as data dumps, we are making the same mistake we've made with nonelectronic labels for years: overestimating the amount of time and interest most people want to spend looking at information in exhibitions.

Just when some label writers are successfully convincing some curators that labels must be kept short—because most visitors have limited time, are put off by lengthy labels, and are not interested in scholarly questions—along comes the electronic label with its nearly unlimited, encyclopedic opportunity to tell visitors everything. "Five thousand explanatory texts have been created to take advantage of the multimedia possibilities" cheerfully boast the developers of the Micro Gallery at the National Gallery. Considering that exhibit wall texts are currently underused by the majority of visitors in most museums, how can these new, expensive, multimedia technologies be justified, except for the fashion of high tech? Assumptions abound regarding the potential benefits to the public of the on-screen label materials. Perhaps a better use of the technology would be to sell the complete exhibition CD in the museum's gift shop instead of putting it in the gallery.

The promise and popularity of the technology seems sufficient to many museums to justify the presence and cost of computers in exhibits. It is as if a new exhibit is not really new without them. But before investing in or purchasing a program, museum practitioners might be more thoughtful about considering who the users are and what their reasons for being at the museum might be.

Museums need to consider the implications for formative and summative evaluation as well: How will they test with actual visitors and improve the effectiveness of 5,000 entries? What rate of use can be expected or will justify the cost? Are provisions being made for maintenance and updating? The decision to use computers should be for the right reasons.

And then, of course, there is the issue of maintenance. The most common label on electronic interactives is "Sorry, Out of Order."

Printed labels, I believe, will not be superseded by electronic labels in the near future, because words on the wall have several strong advantages. Printed labels are cheaper; they can be made in a wide variety of sizes; they are easier for more people to use at the same time and they are quicker to use—all of which make for a high cost-benefit ratio. "Caught between the page and the screen, I deeply respect the achievements of our book culture, while I simultaneously understand that the screen is our future," says Sharon Poggenpohl, editor of the journal *Visible Language*.[3] How soon the "future" comes to museums remains to be seen.

Printed labels also still have the advantage over screen text of being more aesthetically beautiful as typography, which is the topic for the next chapter.

NOTES FOR CHAPTER 16:

1. Wendy Aibel-weiss, personal communication and a proposal for an AAM panel discussion: "Breaking through Layers of Labels: When Studies Show Your Retired Visitors Touch Screens and Kids Are Reading Labels." Aibel-weiss works for the National Postal Museum.

2. See Serrell and Raphling article, "Computers on the Exhibit Floor," *Curator: The Museum Journal* 35, no. 3 (1992), and "The Relationship Between Exhibit Characteristics and Learning-associated Behaviors in a Science Museum Discovery Space," *Science Education* 79, no. 5 (1995): 503–518.

3. Sharon Helmer Poggenpohl, "More than a Book Review of 'The Electronic Word,'" *Visible Language* 28, no. 2 (Spring 1994).

Typographic Design

Typography affects both the mood and the message; therefore, label writers and designers must agree on how the type will look in the final production.

Typography denotes the style, arrangement, and appearance of the text. Graphic designers, by training, understand the principles of mass, form, shape and line through the use of traditional tools. Although designers are usually the ones who decide about typography, most label writers find themselves confronted with typographic decisions at some point.

Label writers need to understand at least the basics of typography and legibility, because printed words exist as visual and verbal entities to the reader's eye and mind, and the traditions of typography are the basis for creative new ideas.

Composed on a computer—using word processing and desktop publishing programs to compose, edit, and lay out label texts on screen—copy can go from the screen to final production without being typeset by a person trained in typography or graphic design. WYSIWYG ("whizzywig") means "what-you-see-is-what-you-get." Writers, therefore, need some working knowledge about type to give them the skills and tools to communicate their messages most effectively.

Some historical background about printing and composition is helpful to understand the language of typography since many common terms come from older methods of producing type that are not apparent from modern usage.

A BRIEF HISTORY OF PRINTING TYPE

The printed book as most of us know it was preceded by slow and laborious methods of calligraphy (script handwriting), illumination (handmade, illustrated books), and block printing (hand-carved wood blocks).

The invention of movable type in the Western world is usually attributed to Johannes Gutenberg, in about 1450. He used a machine resembling a wine press to print directly from a raised, inked surface of metal type. The mechanical letterform designs were based on calligraphic designs of hand lettering. The speed of the printing process depended on how fast the human typesetter could compose a line of metal letters by hand. The letters could be cleaned, rearranged, and reused. Within 50 years the invention had spread to every major country.

Before 1878, typefaces were not standardized, and different foundries produced type of different sizes. Typefaces sold by one firm were likely to be incompatible with type made somewhere else. With the growth of the printing industry, a more uniform approach was necessary, and printers adopted standard units—points and picas—for measuring the size of type, lines, spaces, and borders. Type styles proliferated. Names such as Garamond, Baskerville, Caslon, and Bodoni recall the men whose early type designs are still popular today.

The invention of automatic typesetting machines, the Linotype in 1886 and the Intertype in 1911, made printing significantly faster. Keyboard-operated machines made "hot type"—words and lines of type cast from molten lead. The typographic term "leading," which today still refers to the amount of space between lines of type, comes from hot type traditions.

In the 1940s, another major change in typesetting took place. Phototypesetting, called "cold type" because no hot metal was used, exposed film to light passed through a template of letter forms. The machine output the type as film or paper developed inside. More typefaces evolved, but the standards of sizing remained constant from the hot type methods that came before.

Another major technological revolution in typography and printing occurred in the 1980s, created by computers, desktop publishing programs, and laser printers that compose letters without any mechanical templates of metal or film. Digital type—shaped by the technology of cathode rays and bit maps—threw out all the rules of the old order. Providing speed, flexibility and economy, computers have changed the face and facts of typography as never before.

Computers quickly took over the traditional methods of graphic design in which graphic designers manipulated letter forms, illustrations, and text blocks by tracing them by hand and repositioning elements on boards until they achieved the desired effects. Now, in nanoseconds, at the touch of a mouse, computers can manipulate those forms. With the new technology, our ability to visualize alternate possibilities of graphic communication is greatly aided and enhanced.

The computer and desktop publishing programs have put powerful and affordable tools into the hands of hordes of amateurs. But just because the computer allows stretching, compressing, slanting, shadowing, and creating new and unfamiliar letterforms, doesn't mean you should. People without knowledge about typography and design—or people born without "designer genes"—can learn about typography and how to use the computer skillfully, but not without time and effort.

THE LANGUAGE AND FUNDAMENTALS OF TYPOGRAPHY

The definitions of typographic terms in the glossary at the end of this book will help a neophyte get started or serve as a refresher for someone who is out of practice with typographic art. If this does not suffice, there are many other helpful books for reference, such as *Stop Stealing Sheep.*[1]

Legibility, readability, appropriateness, design, and effectiveness are all influenced by typography. The elements that make type easy to see (legible) and to read (comprehendable) have been investigated by psychologists, traffic engineers, elementary education specialists, ophthalmologists, researchers for the special needs of the handicapped, graduate students, and the elderly. These researchers have employed a variety of methods in their investigations, ranging from tests on the effects of distance, to counts of eye movements, and measures of the rate of blinking and heart beats when people read, and studies of visual fatigue.

This research—most of which results in common-sense decisions—seems to have not widely influenced museum label practices, judging from the frequency of poor typography, such as tiny print and long line lengths. Do the museums that get awards in the publications category of the American Association of Museum's design competition (involving catalogs, posters, press kits, brochures, newsletters, and books) spend as much time, effort, or money on the words on the walls in their galleries? Not always.

Another frustrating, all-too-common fact is that the label writer's efforts—researching, writing, editing, testing, editing again, testing again, getting approvals, and delivering final copy—can be torpedoed if the designer typesets it on a low-contrast background or puts the label behind the door or in the dark.

Many graphic designers graduate without having a good grasp of typographic design. "It's one of the hardest things to learn, and it takes a long time," says Pasadena Art Center graphic design teacher Rebecca Mendez.

Below are suggestions for an inexperienced or beginning typographer. A more experienced graphic designer will know how to make type legible even while breaking these "rules." Different guidelines apply to body copy (running text, in paragraphs) and titles or headlines (a few words, in one line).

THE LEGIBILITY OF BODY COPY

The ease with which a person can recognize and comprehend words and symbols is called legibility. Good legibility is influenced largely by familiarity—we can recognize something we know more easily than something strange or unfamiliar.

There are many typefaces to choose from that offer excellent legibility for body copy of museum labels. Styles that have been in use for a long time in books, newsprint, and journals include Times Roman, Bodoni, Caslon, Century Old Style, and Clarendon. These faces are easy to read because they are so common.

Times Roman   Bodoni Book   Caslon

Century Old Style   Clarendon   Optima

Redesigning typefaces created for hot and cold type (metal and phototypesetting) for computer bitmaps can change the aesthetics of a typeface's design. Hermann Zapf was the original designer of Optima, which is characterized by delicate curves and near-vertical lines and is difficult to represent digitally. He called the digitizing of his popular typeface "a heartbreaking compromise." "If I had been asked," Zapf wrote in 1985, "I would have done a new design and tailored it to the needs and limitations of today's equipment."[2]

Newer type styles have been created specifically for use with computers and laser printing. These styles were designed to minimize the amount of memory and storage needed by the computer to produce the letters. Type designer Zuzana Licko embraced the early limitations of the first Macintosh's coarse, low-resolution bitmap screens and printers, and invented many typefaces including Emperor, Oakland, Universal, Emigre, Matrix, Senator, and Totally Gothic.

Emigre   Matrix   Modula

Children who have grown up using computers are far more used to reading on-screen text than adults who learned to read before the 1980s. What looks "normal" and legible to them may seem ugly and crude to adults who are accustomed to reading finer resolution print typography. Given the burst of new graphic design capabilities unleashed by computers, legibility issues are changing as we speak.

COMMON QUESTIONS ABOUT TYPOGRAPHY

The context in which the label will be produced and read are important factors to consider when selecting typefaces. Legibility of typefaces will be influenced by type size, word spacing, letterspacing, line spacing, distance, color combinations, and lighting. When all of these factors are known before choices are made, the final result will work better.

Frequently asked questions about legibility for museum labels include: Should the typeface be serif or sans serif? Is bold better? Which is more legible: black on white or white on black? What size should the type be?[3]

The "rules" discussed below are general guidelines that a person skilled in graphic design and typography can ignore, but a person who is not experienced with making type legible should heed them carefully.

Serif or sans serif? The examples shown in figures 36 and 37 represent serif and sans serif typefaces. Neither one is more legible than the other in all situations. The important thing to consider is this: body copy type should allow the reader's eyes to glide smoothly in horizontal sweeps across the lines of type, and to find their way to the beginning of each new line easily. Vertical, compressed, or taller-than-wide typefaces, especially some sans serif fonts, can decrease legibility by overemphasizing verticality. Tight spacing between letters and heavy serif faces with small x-height (see glossary for definitions) can decrease legibility by making the words clump together.

Too tall & tight   Very small x-height

Some serif faces are associated with more classical, sophisticated or traditional looks. Sans serif faces are sometimes called "clean" or "modern." Trends or fads in typefaces, like fashions, can come and go. Helvetica, a face designed in 1957 by Max Miedinger, became popular as a legible body-copy style and was practically an industry and government standard for highways and airport signage. Because of its extensive use, the plea "anything but Helvetica" was the slogan in some graphic design circles by the 1970s.

Serif or sans serif choices have more to do with the appropriate use of style than legibility issues. Serif and sans serif faces can be mixed by the skillful typographer. Some newer typefaces, such as Stone, have been designed with both styles as part of the same family. Other designers have created a serif and a sans serif face to be used together, such as Gerhard Unger's Demos and Praxis.

Boldface or regular? It is not an "or" question, really, because both have appropriate applications. Bold is often used for titles and display type, but it is not often recommended for body copy. Consider making body copy bigger, rather than bolder, for better legibility. Methods for producing label text that only allow for bold styles should be avoided because they will not give you the necessary flexibility for making contrast between titles and body copy, or text and credit lines. Also, boldface type takes up more space than regular.

Black on white or white on black? When using reverse type (light type against a dark background) sans serif may be a better choice in the hands of an inexperienced designer because dark backgrounds can diminish serifs by squeezing them. Figures 36 and 37 show the opposite to this advice, which proves that the "rules" can be broken by designers who know how. If reverses are necessary for design or aesthetic reasons, body copy in paragraphs that are not too dense will help legibility, because reading white or colored type on black backgrounds is more tiring to the eye than the opposite. Although it is a matter of preference, most people prefer to read dark type against a light background.

Regardless of the choice or combination of colors, the most important thing is contrast. Having sufficient contrast between the type color and the background shade is important in all cases. Many museums make the mistake, for aesthetic reasons, of having soft-looking labels, such as white on gray, or brown on tan, which render labels less legible than

FIGURE 36
Typography that
works: light-
colored serif type
against a dark
background, with
the right leading
and wordspacing,
makes this label
inviting and easy
to read. The fact
that it is only 50
words does not
hurt either.

they should be for the reader's sake. The aesthetics of typography (faces, colors, sizes)—the overall look and feel that the type gives to the design—must be balanced with the reader's need for legibility.

With backlit type (clear letters in black film, lighted from behind), sans serif faces are preferred because the light shines out and obscures or "smears" serifs. Backlit labels can be very tiring to read because of the glare. To reduce eye strain, put sheets or strips of colored gels (gray, blue, or combinations) behind the type, which will keep the light from glaring through.

What size type? This question must be answered in the context of how the type will be used—its purpose, position, color and lighting. Is it for a title, a caption, or donor infor-

FIGURE 37
Pleasing typography is achieved through proper contrast, spacing, and margins. Here, dark-colored sans serif type sits against a light background, with the right amount of leading and wordspacing. Flush-left, ragged-right paragraphs of different lengths are balanced with the illustrations and plenty of white space.

mation? How far will the reader be from the label? Is it back-lit? Here are some general guidelines based on what I've heard visitors say:

- For most people, 18 points is the minimum size of body copy type for caption labels that is *comfortably* legible at 20 inches away from a standing reader, with good lighting, using dark type on a well-contrasted light background. Most captions should be printed larger, in 20- to 24-point type, unless visitors are likely to be very close to the label. For text that only contains one or two lines of copy, the minimum can be 12-point type. (For type specifications used in this book, see the colophon on the last page.)

- For introductory copy, group labels, or texts that will nor-mally be read at a distance greater than 18 inches away, type size should be 28 to 48 points, depending on the conditions of lighting, space, color, and typeface and weight.

- Once type is larger than 36 points, however, bigger is not always better. The type needs to "fit" comfortably onto a person's retina.

LETTERS ON YOUR FOVEA

Normal reading distance for a seated reader is 12 to 15 inches and normal book or newspaper type is 8- to 12-point type. At that distance, approximately four letters of type are projected by the lens of the eye onto the fovea of the retina, the place of clearest vision. Around the fovea is the area of peripheral vision, which can encompass about 15 more letters in any direction as our eyes move along a line of type. Peripheral vision helps us anticipate what is coming into focus next—in terms of both legibility and readability.

Normal reading speed is 250 to 300 words per minute, and eye movements consist of alternating sweeps and fixations along a line of type, with a return sweep at the end of one line to the beginning of the next. If a person is reading less legible material, the number of fixations increases and reading speed decreases. When the size of the type is too large for the visitor to stand back from the label until the normal number of letters are in focus on the fovea and in peripheral vision, the reader's eyes have to make more fixations to perceive each word.

With very large, close-up type, you are forced to read letters instead of reading words. This process is both tiring and distracting, because the eyes and the brain are geared to an expected, or normal, perception distance and reading speed. Slowing the eyes down (increasing the number of fixations, or holding each fixation longer than normal) allows time for the brain to wander. The reader has trouble concentrating. (This is why reading electronic, scrolling, digital type is so frustrating: Your eyes are attracted by the moving red dots, but the speed of perception and recognition is far too slow for your brain.) Avoid large type (bigger than 36 to 48 points) if readers are expected to be only two feet away. Testing actual-size labels in context will help resolve many size issues.

Other legibility tips for the novice designer include:

- Use upper and lowercase letters in body copy, not all capital letters. All capital letters in most faces are less legible.
- Use italics sparingly, not for body copy of more than three lines. Italics are less legible in some faces than others.
- Use ragged-right margins (not centered, not justified, not ragged left). Ragged-right margins will not require as much fine-tuning to make word spacing look even and to avoid "rivers" of space running vertically through paragraphs of type. Ragged-left margins make it difficult for the eye to find its way to the beginning of the next line.
- Avoid hyphenating words at the end of lines. It makes for choppy reading. This is especially true for line lengths longer than 50 to 60 characters and larger type sizes.
- The more labels in an exhibition, the more concern there should be about sticking to the guidelines, or taking a conservative approach, and making them easy to read. In exhibitions with very few labels, legibility issues can be of less concern, although I would never recommend creating a situation in which the majority of visitors feel like they have to work hard to read the type.

The guidelines above will help an inexperienced writer get started using type creatively and effectively, but they are no substitute for experience and working with skilled graphic designers. Do not get overconfident at the computer with all those buttons and options for type fonts and sizes if you really do not know what you are doing.

THE READABILITY OF BODY COPY

Readability has more to do with content than typography. It has to do with how difficult or complex the text is, or the ease with which a reader can comprehend the text. Readability is influenced by the reader's familiarity with the subject, by the writing style, by sentence length, and by vocabulary level.

Formulas for determining readability derive a figure according to a set of specifications, such as the number of words per sentence or the average number of syllables per word. Word-processing programs such as Microsoft Word come with built-in applications (measurement and analysis) of these formulas, which convert into readability scores. For example, the Flesch Reading Ease test is based on both words and syllables, and scores range from 0 to 100—the higher the score the greater the number of people who can readily understand the text. The Flesch-Kincaid Grade Level test converts the analysis to a grade level and suggests that standard writing is between sixth and eighth grade.

None of the readability software is able to detect writing with annoying perkiness, pompousness, sappiness, or a casual attitude toward accuracy. These factors affect readability and it takes a human editor to ferret them out.

Label writers working on computers without these tools can do simple mathematical calculations by counting the number of words and the number of syllables per sentence in their texts. Good guidelines are: Sentences should average from 12 to 15 words, and there should be a range of 130 to 150 syllables per 100 words.

According to readability tests, if you decrease the length of sentences and the number of multisyllabic words, you will make the text easier to read. The implication for label writers is clear: review your copy, shorten long sentences, and use shorter words in place of longer ones whenever possible.

TYPEFACES FOR TITLES AND HEADLINES

Guidelines for the use of typefaces in titles and headlines—called display type—are much more relaxed than for body copy. The acceptable variations are greater. Because headlines contain fewer words (e.g., one to six words, not in a full sentence), legibility and readability are not such important issues, while attracting attention is.

For titles and headlines, graphic designers have lots of display typefaces to choose from, or they can make one up.

There are several questions to consider: Does the typeface create the mood or symbolize the meaning in an attention-grabbing header? Will it be legible enough, while still looking interesting and intriguing? Is consistency necessary for all aspects of the graphic look, including the promotional marketing materials? Some museums restrict the choice to one typeface and use it for everything. This decision can be unifying in some cases, but very restricting in others. Consider these questions on a case-by-case basis to decide which is best.

LINE LENGTH AND LAYOUT

Line length (the number of characters per line) and the overall layout of the body copy will affect legibility. In running text, the reader's eyes must be able to find their way from the end of one line back to the beginning of the next line. If it is difficult to find the continuation of the sentence, or readers get lost or confused (e.g., get started at the wrong line), their minds will wander. The size, weight, typeface, leading, and the number of lines can help or hinder this movement. Fifty to 65 characters (including spaces) per line is a reasonable maximum.

To reduce the overall line length in a horizontal layout, texts can be broken into multiple columns of type. But designers should avoid making a common mistake that can discourage reading: columns that begin in the middle of a sentence. In books or magazines this is not a problem because readers of this kind of text are more "dedicated." Readers in museum exhibitions are scanning rapidly, with many things to distract their attention. Writers and designers need to work together to make the text fit into columns without these breaks and make it easy for readers to see the starting points, or jump from one text block to the next. In the following two examples, the first label breaks the second paragraph across two columns. In the second label, the text is written in four paragraphs to fit in two columns without being broken up.

The Ball Game

In Mesoamerican cities, architecture and public ceremony were closely linked. Pyramids, temples, and plazas were settings for various religious ceremonies, while ball courts were specially constructed for the Mesoamerican ball game. A combination of ritual, sport, and celebration, the ball game is a hallmark of Mesoamerican culture and a prominent subject in regional art.

The rules of the ball game varied by locale, but in the best-known version teams of players volleyed a solid rubber ball using only their hips. The object of the game was to send the ball past a goal, sometimes marked by a vertical stone ring on the ball-court wall.

Images of the ball game show clearly its symbolic meaning as a representation of the greater cosmic struggles between life and death, day and night, abundance and scarcity. References to death and human sacrifice are common and indicate that players did not always survive the game.

—paragraphs broken across columns

The Ball Game

A combination of ritual, sport, and celebration, the ball game is a hallmark of Mesoamerican culture.

The rules of the ball game varied by locale, but in the best-known version teams of players volleyed a solid rubber ball using only their hips. The object of the game was to send the ball past a goal, sometimes marked by a vertical stone ring on the ball-court wall.

As a prominent subject in regional art, images of the ball game show clearly its symbolic meaning as a representation of the greater cosmic struggles between life and death, day and night, abundance and scarcity.

References to death and human sacrifice are common and indicate that players did not always survive the game.

—paragraphs not broken across columns

MIXING TYPEFACES AND TYPE DESIGN

Since typefaces were invented, typographers have experimented with combining them, making and breaking various rules. Since digital computer type was invented, some typographers and graphic designers have gone wild with the possibilities. Few rules are sacred, and some designers flaunt the traditional rules of legibility as part of the past. Intertwining, overlapping, stacked, or distorted type explores new aesthetics of tech-expressionistic text. Being radical, crude, unintelligible, angry, and anything-but-traditional is *de rigueur* for those who push the digital possibilities. New designs get copied and instantly mainstreamed, as the field races ahead.

A conservative, yet experimental, approach to typography—one that has positive implications for museum text—can be achieved by loosening up the formal formatting of type. Some ways to break the visual monotone:

- Get away from evenly spaced paragraphs with the same number of words per paragraph for every type of label.
- Break lines where natural phrases end, not by character counts.
- Use smaller chunks, arranged in different places on the page.
- Change spatial arrangements or size to suggest importance or relationships.
- Intertwine text to suggest messages that are being communicated simultaneously.
- Mix text and icons together in body copy, but be sure they are meaningful.
- Mix typefaces to create a variety of different messages within one label or to suggest different voices.
- Design "typewritten" and "handwritten" labels (see figures 38 and 39).

These techniques, easily achieved by the on-screen writer using a digital medium, create new possibilities for words on the wall. But most of this typographic experimentation is taking place among artists and graphic designers, not museum label writers. Museum label texts, especially body copy, is not the place to be too avant garde. My advice is, go ahead and play with wild titles and illustrations, but keep your high tech hands off the body copy.

Museum labels are in a visual communication class by themselves. They are not text-dominant like books or journals, but they use much more text than advertisements in print and electronic media. Compared to most other forms of

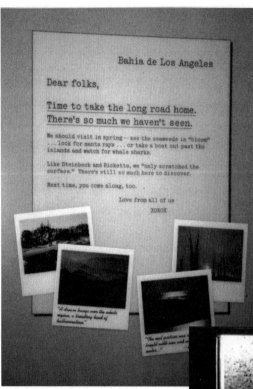

FIGURE 38
Typographic design can add an emotional dimension to a story. The type style on this label, which imitates the look of a letter typewritten to a friend, helps create a "you are there" friendly, casual voice for the text.

FIGURE 39
These "handwritten" labels were intended to look visitor-friendly, informal, and to mimic the field zoologist's notebook style. But some visitors misinterpreted the intent and thought the label looked unfinished.

environmental graphics (e.g., building titles, advertisements, directional signage) labels for outdoor museums such as living history sites, zoos, botanic gardens, and national parks use smaller type sizes, more text and must last longer. More importantly, a museum label's role in communication is more complex than the two part sender-receiver model because there is a third element involved in museums: the object, or thing, or "stuff" the label is about. Labels are not independent entities.

The communication requirements of each label must prevail over the institutional aesthetic or personal style of the designer. This does not mean that the communication intent cannot include a personal look, voice, and point of view, but the experience the label writer is trying to enable for visitors is between the visitor and the object, not the visitor and the label. In my opinion, a label that gets remembered only for its clever style or progressive typography instead of the experience is just as much of a failure as the label that never gets read.

Between getting the words right and getting the label fabricated and installed, there is a big step called design. That step does not have a special chapter in this book because color, layout, sizing, form, balance, and other aesthetic design principles are not my area of expertise. I rely on people with those skills to help me all along the way. Most of the designers I work with will offer suggestions, listen to mine, and create labels that look and work better than I could conceive of on my own. Exhibit designers and writers have the same goals—good communication—but each brings different sensibilities for finding the best solutions to the problems.

The suggestions about typography in this chapter and those offered in earlier chapters about levels of information, chunking text, using bullets, integrating illustrations, and evaluation will improve label design, but they do not actually tell you how to be a graphic designer. For that, my advice is hire a good one. Let us plunge on to production and fabrication issues.

NOTES FOR CHAPTER 17:

1. The title of the book refers to Frederic Goudy (1894–1945), a typographer who had strong opinions about the sanctity of type design, who said, "Anyone who would letterspace lower case would steal sheep," in Erik Spiekermann and E. M. Ginger, *Stop Stealing Sheep & Find Out How Type Works* (Mountain View, Calif,; Adobe Press, 1993). See also type design books by Ronald Labuz and Richard Rubinstein in the bibliography.

2. Hermann Zapf, "Future Tendencies in Type Design: The Scientific Approach to Letterforms," *Visible Language* 19, no. 1 (Winter 1985).

3. Some of these questions were explored in research conducted at the Metropolitian Museum of Art, reported in "What Makes Museum Labels Legible?" by Lisa F. Wolf and Jeffrey K. Smith in *Curator 36*, no. 2 (June 1993).

Production and Fabrication

No easy answers here. Production and fabrication methods and materials for making labels are constantly changing and evolving and are probably all more expensive and time-consuming than you would wish.

Stone cutting, wood block, pen and ink, typewriter, dot-matrix print and Letraset methods of producing letterforms are not commonly used in label production any more. Computers, digital type, and different kinds of laser printers are in because they offer faster speed and lower cost. What will be next?

This chapter is brief because the methods of making labels are changing so quickly. Equipment names and brands come and go; new materials and programs are being developed as we speak. To keep abreast of the newest materials and products, especially for outdoor signage, the Society of Environmental Graphic Designers is a good resource. The National Association of Museum Exhibitors newsletter, *The Exhibitionist,* and the trade magazine *Exhibit Builder* are good sources of information about recent changes in fabrication resources for museums. Zoos and nature centers should consult *Signs, Trails, and Wayside Exhibits* for materials and methods especially suited to out-of-doors. *Identity* magazine has a more corporate design look, but is good for creative ideas.

Today's desktop publishing software, or even simple word processing, gives label writers the opportunity and the tools to be both designers and fabricators as well. Some people may welcome this opportunity, while others might feel confused, unprepared, and overwhelmed by the myriad choices and possibilities. Inexperienced designers can find good examples to follow in the sources mentioned above, and they should probably stick to the basic typographic guidelines.

For many purposes, simple paper labels will suffice. Mock-ups, temporary exhibits, low-traffic areas, or low budgets can get by with practical paper products. For longer lasting labels, permanent installations, and outdoor conditions, most institutions will benefit from establishing a relationship with local fabricators, reputable dealers, and "service bureaus" who can combine their skills with your needs at a reasonable price. Call other museums that have similar budgets, and compare notes on who and what to use. Ask for and check the references of companies you are not familiar with. The lowest bidder is not automatically the best choice. I know of more than one museum that has had a fabricator go out of business in the middle of a project.

SIMPLE LASER PRINTING AND LAMINATION

The simplest label production method is word-processed text, laser printed on paper, and glued to a heavier piece of paper to prevent the paper from curling. Plain, unprotected paper is a good but temporary solution, because sooner or later unprotected paper will be damaged by dirt and humidity.

A cover of clear, rigid plastic over the face of paper labels gives temporary protection from fingerprints and weathering. A simple sandwich of materials creates a space for air, dirt, or moisture to collect and a good place for spiders and cockroaches to hide. Outdoors, plastic covers soon make great displays of condensation and algae.

Lamination is more than making a sandwich. It involves actual adhesive bonding between surfaces. All types of laminations need to be done with equipment that can make the bonds clean, clear, strong, and without wrinkles or air bubbles. Professional equipment is often the best choice over hand-rubbed laminations. Eight- to 10-millimeter thick clear laminate with a ⅛-inch sealed border makes a reasonably durable, inexpensive, but temporary outdoor paper sign.

COMPLEX LASER PRINTING AND LAMINATION

Computer graphics software allows the user to compose text and images on the computer screen with programs such as Adobe Illustrator, Adobe Photoshop and QuarkXpress. Complex detailing with multiple colors can then be printed by production services with larger, more expensive, high-resolution equipment than most museums have. Two such processes are Iris and Scotchprint, which use paper pulp or plastic surfaces.[1] Before installation these are laminated with plastic sheeting front and back for support and protection.

Brilliant colors shown on the computer screen are usually not the same as what you will get from the ink-jet printer, and lamination can further cause colors to change. Keeping designs simple (e.g., using three to five colors instead of 10) can help eliminate some problems. To avoid unpleasant surprises, get samples from each printer and keep them as references. Experimentation, practice, or buying in-house equipment can lead to better predictability for true colors.

The combination of desktop computers and professional printing enables museums to produce large, colorful graphics that are relatively inexpensive compared to silkscreening single or one-of-a-kind pieces.

Care should be taken to work within standard size guidelines. Designers should be aware of the factory-determined sizes of paper, plexiglass, plywood, and frames, so that they do not design custom graphics that are hard to fit, waste materials and money, or require oversized mounting options. The same 4-foot-by-8-foot sheet of material can yield four instead of two pieces, depending on a dimension change of only a few inches. Designers and production crews will get along better when both are willing to consider each other's needs and make compromises for the sake of economics and speed.

DURATRANS AND BACKLIT FILM

Labels made of color or black-and-white film inside dimensional frames with internal lighting are good choices when front lighting is not appropriate. Aquariums use backlit labels with photos and texts extensively in galleries where the fish tanks are brightly lit and the surrounding areas are dark.

A color film product called Duratrans makes the entire image in one single piece of film. It allows for either positive-reading text (dark text against a light background) or negative (light text over a dark background), and text can be mixed with images. Because the finished piece of film is greatly enlarged from a small negative, text will be a little fuzzy, not crisp. The most common mistake with Duratrans is allowing type to run over images and make reading difficult. Ideally, text and images are kept distinct, and both are legible.

Labels made with plain black film negatives, called Kodalith, have the advantage of being inexpensive, but the disadvantage of being less legible, because transparent type glaring out of a dark background can be hard on the eyes. To cut glare and improve legibility, place transparent color gels or a diffuser panel of white acrylic between the light source and the back of the film. Kodalith should not be used without gels or diffusers.

As an alternative to the more expensive Duratrans, Koda-lith film can be patched together with photographs and film negatives of line art illustrations to produce a relatively low-cost, attractive product. Figure 12 was produced in this manner. The patched film can be hidden from view by using a "solar gray" acrylic front piece instead of clear acrylic.

HEADLINER

Computerized vinyl-cutting machines, sometimes called headliners, are popular for making durable, indoor or outdoor signs. Vinyl comes in a wide variety of colors, has a strong adhesive bond, and can be put onto a variety of smooth surfaces. Headliners can cut prespaced letters, words, and sentences. By selecting typefaces that do not have fine serifs, the job of peeling letters off the carrier sheet will be easier if they do not come prepeeled, or "weeded."

Simple graphics, such as silhouettes, geometric shapes, or a collage effect, can also be made on a headliner. Skillfully combined text and illustrations can make colorful, relatively inexpensive and attractive labels for museums.

There are, however, several inappropriate applications of vinyl letters having to do with size and location:

- The machines can cut letters in sizes down to about ½- or ¼-inch tall, but, body copy at that size does not look good in the bold faces made by headliners. Running text in small sizes is also very difficult to lift off the carrier sheets. Some sign makers have devised ingenious ways of "weeding" (removing the tiny insides of letters like "e" or "a"), but for the inexperienced person it can be a messy, tedious headache, and the results are not often worth it. Use the headliner for what it does best: making headlines in large type with few words.

- Avoid applying vinyl letters on surfaces where visitors can reach them easily. As soon as one little corner of the vinyl gets lifted away, people are invariably attracted, almost unconsciously, to peel them away more. Missing letters make reading difficult, not to mention making the sign look miserable. Use vinyl letters on surfaces far from people's hands.

The *Exhibitionist* has a good article about using vinyl type called "A Beginner's Guide to Vinyl Lettering Systems."[2] You can often pick up other production tips there and at occasional regional workshops (see section on Resources at end of book) offered by NAME.

DRY-TRANSFER LETTERS

Dry-transfer, prespaced letters, typeset in lines and paragraphs in almost any size, typeface, and color, can be rubbed onto smooth, rigid surfaces such as paper, panels, or walls. Dry-transfer letters are a less expensive alternative to silkscreening letters directly on walls, but they are also less durable and can be rubbed off, even accidentally.

LABELS THAT WILL LAST OUTDOORS

Because of their one-of-a-kind, text-heavy, small-typography requirements, the production of outdoor museum interpretive labels poses exceptional challenges, compared to that of directional signs, logos, or name-only ID placards.

For outdoor labels, there are three desirable characteristics:

Colorful, Durable, and **Inexpensive**
Pick any two.

Colorful, durable signs that are silkscreened, fiberglass embedded or made of porcelain enamel are not cheap. Durable, less expensive photographically processed metal products, typically used for botanic garden plant name labels, lack color choices. Colorful, inexpensive paper products (such as color xerox) will not last long outside. Even when laminated, they will need to be replaced often due to fading or humidity. But frequent replacement might be worthwhile, especially if updating information is necessary or desirable.

SILKSCREENING

For outdoor labels, silkscreening provides color and durability. Two-part acrylic polyurethane paints are extremely weatherproof and resistant to fading. The surface of a silkscreened sign can be treated with a matte finish to reduce glare and provide a graffiti-resistant covering that can be cleaned.

To reduce the amount of set-up time and help keep costs low, one-of-a-kind labels can be designed in similar sizes so that the screener can "gang" them during production. Borders, background colors, headline rules (underlining) or logos used repeatedly can be printed from one screen, with customized text and illustrations added from others set up as one-of-a-kind. Limiting the number of different sizes, using fewer colors, having no overlapping colors, and turning all of the artwork in at one time or in batches of like pieces can help reduce expensive labor costs for silkscreening.

Certain types of base or substrate materials for silk-screened labels can be repaired if they get damaged or an error is noticed. Screens, artwork, and all documentation about color specifications should be kept for reference when making repairs. It is much less expensive when you do not have to start over from scratch.

Silkscreening on clear plexiglass is simple, but very problematic:

- If text is screened on the face of the plastic, the letters will cast shadows on the wall behind them.
- When type is screened on the reverse surface of clear plexiglass to avoid shadows and protect the letters, you may still get annoying shadows and decreased legibility if the labels are not mounted absolutely flush with the wall surface.
- When clear plexiglass labels are placed in cases or on top of graphics, what is visible behind them can and will cause distraction and decrease legibility.
- Plexiglass labels, front or reverse-screened have highly reflective surfaces. Glare decreases legibility and is annoying and tiring.

Only when type is screened on the reverse and then back-painted—usually to match the color of the wall—is clear plexiglass recommended as a substrate. Textured nonglare Lexan is a much better choice.

"Floating" text by silkscreening directly onto the transparent surface of an exhibit case can be attractive when the background color in or beyond the case contrasts sufficiently with the color of the type (refer again to figure 27).

Labels silkscreened on Formica surfaces often get rubbed off because of the inability of certain kinds of paint or inks to adhere permanently. Mechanical and chemical adhesions need to be strong enough to resist normal wear and tear. Check this requirement with your fabricator ahead of time, and specify it explicitly in your bid documents before production begins. Putting a plexiglass sheet on top of the label is not the most attractive, best, or only solution.

I like labels to be touchable. When labels are on reading rails outside cases, visitors can interact with them more directly. I am always happy to see visitors running their hands along text as they read, or touching parts of a label as they call a friend over to see what they have read. The slight surface texture of painted, front-screened labels adds a warmth and friendliness to labels, unlike a clear, flat, cold, reflective surface or the uniform surfaces of back printing on Lexan. Rubbed-off letters indicate that visitors have been using them. Why not replace them with materials that can withstand and invite their use?

Labels on accessible reading rails have an added benefit of letting exhibit teams test texts as mock-ups before final installation because the labels are not out of reach inside cases.

Silkscreening labels directly on the wall, in larger letters, above paintings in an art exhibition makes the text easier to see while standing back from the pictures. This solution eliminates the "dance" that visitors typically do in art museums—two steps up and squint at the tiny label on the wall, three steps back to view the painting, five steps to the left and repeat.

FIBERGLASS EMBEDMENT

Embedding silkscreened labels in clear fiberglass makes a very durable, lightweight outdoor sign that can include color photographs. The National Park Service has used this technique extensively.

Some of the earlier products were subject to fading, as are photos, and fiberglass can be fractured or gouged. Replacement costs can be lower if multiples are screened at one time and stored for later use, but that raises initial costs.

PORCELAIN ENAMEL

Advances in enameling techniques now provide excellent quality and durability for text and four-color-process photographs. Initial costs may be very high, depending on the manufacturer and number of signs produced at one time.

Porcelain enamel is weather- and ultraviolet-light resistant, and it is a good choice for outdoor labels, as in figure 22 (bottom). But, because it is a form of glass, it can be shattered by intentional or accidental impact.

I have worked with the same fabrication companies in the Chicago area for more than a decade to produce graphics for indoor and outdoor installations. We have tried a variety of materials and found advantages and disadvantages to them all. With Proto Productions, Inc., an exhibits fabricator, our favorite is the clean-looking, almost bullet-proof PVC (polyvinylchloride) panel with colorful, fade-resistant acrylic polyurethane paints and screen inks that form chemically-bonded adhesions. Clear finishes protect the face from graffiti. These panels do not require special framing or covers and can be fabricated in any shape. PVC panels with acrylic polyurethane screen printing are less expensive than porcelain enamel signs and have a warmer look and feel than plexiglass, porcelain, or fiberglass.

PHOTOMETAL AND ENGRAVED PLASTIC

Photosensitive metal plates are commonly used by botanic gardens for small plant labels. Larger plates can be used for interpretive labels that last well out-of-doors and are relatively inexpensive to produce. During production the metal plates are exposed to light and the label's image is transferred from a negative film of the text, line drawings, and half-tone photographs. Photometal is available in limited color combinations. Most common are black with silver or gold.

Figure 40 shows an example of engraved plastic labels that are also common in botanic gardens, and they have the same advantages and disadvantages as photometal. They are relatively inexpensive and durable, but come in limited colors and have limited capacity to show illustrations.

CAST METAL

Historical markers have typically been made out of heavy, long-lasting metal with cast letters and sparse graphics. This

FIGURE 40
Engraved plastic, often used for botanic labels, offers a durable, relatively inexpensive option for outdoor labels, but it comes with the disadvantage of limited typefaces and fonts.

product offers a limited range of choices of typefaces and type sizes, and its cost, which is high, makes it less suitable for an exhibition consisting of many different interpretive signs. Harsh outdoor environments might make bronze or aluminum the material of choice, as in figure 22 (top).

Donor plaques are often made of cast metal, probably because this material conveys a permanent, historically significant reverence.

Theft might be a problem with certain materials that are valuable when melted down and reused.

NO SUCH THING AS VANDAL-PROOF

Nothing has been invented yet that is vandal-proof, but some materials are more resistant to intentional damage than others. Plexiglass covers over signs may keep vandals from marring the original surface, but scratched or graffiti-covered plexi looks just as bad.

RECYCLED MATERIALS AND HAZARDOUS MATERIAL

The use of recycled materials has not gained wide acceptance, but with time they may become more common and practical. In the meantime, refer to the Fall 1995 *Exhibitionist* article on environmental correctness, and the Appendix on "Environmental Considerations" in McLean's book *Planning for People in Exhibitions.*[3] Among companies that manufacture paint, plastics, and adhesives and the Environmental Protection Agency (EPA) and the Occupational Safety and Health Agency (OSHA), there is a continual striving to produce safe, economical, long-lasting materials.

DON'T FORGET TO EVALUATE

After production, fabrication, and installation have been accomplished, it is time to step back and evaluate. Too often, time and money have already been used up, and the exhibition team has collapsed from exhaustion. The last thing they want to know is if something is not right (see figure 41). To avoid this pessimistic attitude, think of evaluation as yet another good opportunity to improve the exhibition's communication ability and then to bask in the praise of satisfied visitors and admiring peers. To learn more about ways to find out if your visitors and peers are admiring your efforts, see the next chapter about summative evalution.

FIGURE 41
A shadow cast across the label is a common problem often not anticipated in the design phase. If enough time—and space—is available, designers could modify layouts to fix this problem during installation.

NOTES FOR CHAPTER 18:

1. These are brand names for photo processes.

2. Ed Mastro, "A Beginner's Guide to Vinyl Lettering Systems," *Exhibitionist* 14, no. 1 (Spring 1995).

3. Jonathan Jager, "Environmental Correctness (EC) for Designers," *Exhibitionist* 14, no. 2 (Fall 1995).

Evaluation After Opening

Summative evaluation of exhibitions tells you what actually did work as expected, what unexpected but appropriate outcomes are occurring, what did not work, and (maybe) what to do about it.

No matter how hard you try or how experienced you are, there is no way to know how the whole exhibition will look and work until you have the whole thing up and running. It will not take a professional evaluator to tell you what the exhibition's major strengths and weakness are, since many of them will be obvious. But finding out how well it is working, in more introspective detail, requires some form of analysis.

Summative evaluation of labels is done within the context of the whole exhibition, and, therefore, does not have a special strategy separate from summative evaluation in general.

SUMMATIVE EVALUATION FOR REMEDIATION PURPOSES

Evaluations after opening will reveal mistaken assumptions or expectations by the exhibit team and weaknesses or omissions that can often be fixed with relative ease. Minor changes in label copy can sometimes make a dramatic difference, providing that the labels were produced in a modular or correctable format (e.g., computer-printed, laminated, or dry-mounted paper labels). Labels silkscreened on the walls or inside cases are more difficult to fix—a good argument for making and placing labels in more accessible, modular, repairable formats. Computer-generated labels allowed the California Museum of Science and Industry to make minor, fine-tuning changes to more than 50% of the texts and graphics in their *Molecules in Motion* exhibit to improve directions for interactives and interpretations of the chemistry for younger visitors, who were clearly attracted to the exhibition and spent lots of time interacting with it but were not grasping some of the intended messages.

Problems with orientation and traffic flow or circulation can be rectified by the addition of banners, introductory labels, arrows, maps and floor plans, baffles, lighting, or directional signage. New illustrations or photographs can be added to supplement texts, and labels can be repositioned to make conceptual relationships stronger. Over the years of remodeling exhibitions at the Field Museum in Chicago, the clarity of floor plans and interactive instruction labels improved as exhibit developers responded to the results of summative evaluations of their phased projects in the animal halls.

Leaving money in the budget to evaluate and fix what needs fixing after the exhibit is open—remedial evaluation—is a very good idea because it carries the iterative process of exhibit development to its logical and complete conclusion. Although you can never fix everything that needs it, whatever is made better will benefit everyone. "If you think the graphics are bad now, you should have seen them before we made the changes" may seem like a futile lament, but any evaluation and repair is better than none.

Fixable things should be fixed sooner, not later, because with every day that passes there are more visitors being confused or disappointed and exhibits being ignored that otherwise could be successful. Even fixes that look temporary are better than none because they say to visitors, "We care about making this work better for you."

THE BENEFITS OF SUMMATIVE EVALUATION, BEYOND REMEDIATION

There are several things that you can do with summative evaluation that are not possible with front-end or formative evaluation in which the time schedule is usually rushed, sample sizes are usually small, and there is no exhibition context to work within. With more time, larger sample sizes, the completed exhibition context (and maybe even a larger evaluation budget, if money was set aside and reserved for it) summative evaluation allows:

- Use of multiple-method approaches to look at the same exhibition from several different aspects.
- Development of more sensitive, thorough and authentic measurement tools and strategies.
- Comparisons between audiences in the same exhibition during different seasons or at different sites.
- Collaborative studies that compare exhibitions to create new hypothesis about visitor behavior and museum learning, or to confirm existing assumptions.

Each of these benefits is discussed below. The direct connections between what follows and label writing are not always obvious, but keep in mind that interpretive labels contribute to the overall impact and effectiveness of exhibitions.

MULTIPLE METHOD APPROACHES

Summative studies are a good time to use more than one technique to find out how well the exhibition is working. Using several strategies to look at the same exhibition will enable stakeholders (e.g., exhibit developers, funders, administrators) to gain a more thorough perspective about how the exhibit is being used and what visitors are taking away with them.

Many evaluators use exit surveys or interviews to provide feedback about what visitors found memorable, enjoyable, and meaningful. Unobtrusive observations of visitors as they use exhibitions can answer other questions that cannot be self-reported as fully or accurately. For example, few visitors would be able to recall the names of all the exhibit elements they stopped at in an exhibition or which labels they read. But although they may not recall or be able to articulate every experience, they may be taking away some tacit knowledge, even based on brief exposures. By observing the number of visitors who stop at each exhibit element and engage in certain learning-related behaviors (e.g., reading labels, talking, pointing), information important for constructing a picture of total exhibit use can be obtained. Data from questionnaires

FIGURE 42
A section of
*Darkened Waters:
Profile of an Oil
Spill* shows a
well-integrated
variety of visitor
experiences:
layers of labels,
photographs,
real specimens,
otter pelt to touch,
and microscope.
Other parts of the
exhibition included
audio, computer
program, and low-
tech interactive
devices.

or interviews—what visitors said—can be analyzed along with data about visitors who were observed—what visitors did.

A comprehensive, multimethod summative evaluation was done by Harris Shettel in 1976 on *Man in His Environment*. Drawing on his experience in social science and psychology, he used questionnaires, oral interviews and observations to gather feedback from visitors.[1] Pre- and post-test groups of visitors were queried for their knowledge, attitudes, and "personal commitment to change," and results were compared and correlated with demographic information, such as age, sex, education, and residence. Based on Shettel's three-factor model of exhibit effectiveness (attracting power, holding power, teaching power), the study was exemplary in its thoroughness—detailed, quantitative and qualitative, and statistically valid.[2]

For the 1990s traveling exhibition *Darkened Waters: Profile of an Oil Spill* (see figure 42), a combination of data was gathered from visitor comment cards, unobtrusive tracking and timing, structured exit interviews, open-ended interviews at specific exhibit elements, and questionnaires filled out by cued visitors.[3] In addition to the visitor feedback from the variety of methods listed above, peer review and critical appraisals were obtained at the exhibit's original venue, and from subsequent reviews as it traveled. While the study covered factors similar to those given in Shettel's model, the sample sizes were smaller, the research questions were broader, and the data were not subgrouped for comparisons (e.g., between age or gender group types) or subjected to detailed statistical analysis.

Evaluations showed that people responded to *Darkened Waters* positively and appropriately:

- Visitors moved through the exhibit slowly and thoroughly.
- They read many of the labels, and they used the interactive devices repeatedly (e.g., a U.S. map with a movable overlay of the spill, the "petroleum game" flip labels and oil products, audio tapes of Native Americans talking about the impact of the spill on them, an otter pelt to touch).
- On exiting the exhibition, visitors could remember general ideas (the main communication goals) from the exhibition, and they reported learning specific new concepts, making new connections, and finding personally relevant meanings in specific elements of the exhibit.

Drawing on, but altering Shettel's model, the *Darkened Waters* evaluation was my inspiration to devise ways to gather data (through observations and questionnaires) with simplified, standardized, museum-practitioner-friendly methods and to compare data across a wide range of exhibit types. This will be discussed more in the upcoming section on collaboration.

NEW MEASUREMENT TOOLS

Museums are moving away from traditional education models of summative evaluation that use questioning techniques with yes-no, right-wrong, fact-based, multiple-choice or closed-ended questions. The informal nature of museum learning calls for new measures that challenge evaluators and educators to define learning broadly and to ask visitors more holistic, contextual, and open-ended questions. Rating scales and bipolar adjectives get visitor feedback about likes and dislikes and other affective and motivational indicators, but these formats often do not provide descriptive information about learning. What is needed are better ways to tell what visitors understood and found memorable and meaningful.

We want to know how visitors rearrange information to fit into their preexisting knowledge and what kinds of emotional associations they make with the exhibits. One method is to record visitors' conversations in exhibitions. Research studies have shown that verbatim label text, paraphrasing and values (such as historical and financial importance) are incorporated into the language and ideas of visitors as they use exhibits.[4] Another strategy is through extended open-ended visitor interviews during and after looking at the exhibits. But content analysis of hours of visitor conversations can be a cumbersome and expensive way to hear what visitors have to say.

Another way to capture rich, verbal indicators of meaning-making in more practical yet still personal terms is through the use of an open-ended questionnaire described in "Capturing Affective Learning."[5] It asks visitors to briefly tell in their own words what they think the purpose of the exhibition is, and to write about something they didn't know or never realized before, and what they were reminded of in the exhibition.

Content of visitors' written feedback can be analyzed qualitatively or in quantitative goal-referenced ways.[6] By tallying the percent of the comments that are specifically related to the communication objectives and the big idea and by assigning a rank (e.g., high, medium, low) to each person's sheet overall, the degree to which visitors "got" the communication objectives can be assessed. This open-ended questionnaire captures memorable "exhibit echoes"—instances in which visitors remember what they read, did, found out, or saw, and report it so clearly that you can tell where in the exhibit they probably had the encounter.

SEASONAL AND MULTISITE AUDIENCE COMPARISONS

One of the questions that comes up regarding summative evaluation is, Will the audience sampled at one time of the year be representative of other times as well? This question has implications for both marketing and evaluation of effectiveness. Evaluators and stake holders want to know if the results are the same regardless of the time of year or where the exhibition is on display.

At the Old South Meeting House in Boston, a summative evaluation included two separate studies at different times of the year (summer and fall) to see if visitors during those two seasons had different demographic characteristics and if they used the exhibition differently.[7] The study showed that they indeed were demographically different: the summer audience was made up of more out-of-town visitors, a higher proportion of family visitors, and more young visitors. In exit interviews, the older fall audience made more references to "time," "history," and "long ago" than the summer visitors. The differences between the two seasonal audiences, however, did not seem to have an impact on what they did in the exhibition—where they went, whether they used audio and low-tech interactive devices, and how many labels they read. They used the exhibits in almost exactly the same ways. The amount of time spent by summer and fall visitors was the same. The most popular and least popular exhibits were the same. This unexpected uniformity of visitor behavior suggested that the assumption that the fall audience always consists of more "serious visitors" may be misguided.

In a multisite summative evaluation of the American Museum of Natural History's traveling exhibition *Global Warming*, the same measurement techniques were used with different audiences as they viewed the exhibit in its various locations. Provocative questions, such as the impact of variations in the way the exhibition was installed (e.g., different layout of elements), the type of museum (e.g., natural history, science center), and the demographics of the cities from which visitors came (e.g., average education level) are being addressed in this study.[8] Knowing more about how exhibits work in diverse situations will aid the development of better traveling exhibitions.[9]

COLLABORATIVE RESEARCH STUDIES

Besides the *Global Warming* study mentioned above, only a few research studies have looked at visitors in different museums, asked the same kinds of questions, and used the same research methods and strategies, so that the results could be compared. In the past, no set of standards for judging the excellence of exhibits has been accepted or widely used. Even the suggestion that exhibit standards be set is annoying to many museum practitioners. But without some form of guidelines, goals, or even a basic understanding of what is normative, we are adrift, with little means of measuring our progress or direction. Not-for-profit organizations like museums are accountable for leadership, mission fulfillment, and high standards of quality.

Large-scale, collaborative research and evaluation projects and shared criteria for success can help us move closer toward the goal of making good educational exhibitions. The five projects discussed below have asked broad questions about visitors, museums, and exhibitions; looking within those issues we often find important implications for interpretive labels.

1. The Getty Insights Project used the research technique of focus groups in a large, well-funded, collaborative project conducted for the Getty Center for Education in the Arts and The J. Paul Getty Museum in 1987–1990. Eleven large American art museums conducted focus groups with staff, visitors, and nonvisitors (people who had not visited the museum before). Sessions were videotaped, and museum staff observed the group from behind a one-way mirror, as visitors

and nonvisitors discussed their expectations and impressions before and after visiting the museum. It was the first time some staff had the opportunity to listen carefully to what people thought about the exhibitions, labels, visitor services, and other aspects of the museum.

The findings had remarkable consistency across all 11 participating museums. Getty focus group participants said that their contact with art in museums created emotional, exhilarating, habit-forming experiences. The museum experience was meaningful and rewarding for first-time visitors and repeat visitors. First-time and repeat visitors wanted information about the art, especially in contemporary collections and art from non-Western cultures. There were implications for labeling in many aspects of the report, including these findings:

- Orientation, layout, and organization were a problem at all 11 museums.
- Intimidation and inaccessible information were concerns of nonvisitors.
- Visitors wanted "those little signs on the wall" to be larger, more informative, legible, and written in language people can understand.

It was an eye-opening experience for art museum staff to hear intelligent, caring, well-intentioned museumgoers say things like, "Many times [labels] would use terms that, if you were really into history or really into art, you would probably recognize, but which I didn't know. They would use the term and not explain it enough. It would leave me hanging." Many staff had their prior assumptions about visitors challenged and revised in ways that made them more sympathetic to visitors' concerns.

A final report, *Insights: Museums, Visitors, Attitudes, Expectations*, summarized the findings, individual museum projects, and the presentations and discussions of a colloquium for all participants and invited speakers. It is recommended reading for practitioners of all types of museums.[10]

2. The Museum Impact and Evaluation Study (MIES) was a two-and-a-half-year collaborative project (1990–1992) that involved eight science museums and one children's museum. No one type of research methodology was used at all the sites, and the questions raised varied from one place to another, with only a very broad common theme: how visitors related to science museum exhibits.

Like the Getty project, this one was also well-endowed (by the Joyce Foundation of Chicago), but unlike the Getty report, the final publication broke little new ground. The MIES report, published as three volumes (a summary, composite report, individual site reports) is titled *The Museum Impact and Evaluation Study: Roles of Affect in the Museum Visit and Ways of Assessing Them.*[11]

The benefits of this project were probably more for the participants than the museum field at large. "The most powerful outcome of this enterprise was the act of participating in a research collaborative for two and a half years . . . and (participants) grew professionally."[12]

Productive research collaborations obviously take more than adequate funding. They are aided by working together, cooperation, commitment to shared strategies, systematic endeavors, and follow-through, all of which have been informed by prior research, so that the collaboration produces findings that have as many external benefits as internal ones.

3. The Annapolis Conference got support from the National Science Foundation to help Science Learning, inc. organize and convene a conference of 48 participants from museums, academia and funding agencies. Entitled "Public Institutions for Personal Learning: Understanding the Long-Term Impact of Museums," the purpose was to develop a plan of action for conducting research on learning in museums.

The American Association of Museums published the results of the conference as part of their Technical Information Service series. The book includes seven background papers, a synthesis of the conference deliberations, and a summary of the learning outcomes and research strategies developed at the meeting, and presents suggestions for establishing a national museum learning research agenda. As yet, no new collaborative research program has been established, but an important step has been taken in that direction.

4. In the search for generalizable and transferable data, I have been working on a research project that grew out of the 1992 summative evaluation of *Darkened Waters* (discussed earlier) to address the issue of the comparability of summative evaluation data.

Darkened Waters was called a successful exhibition, but what did that success really mean, and would it be possible to compare "goodness" across exhibitions in some fair way? "The 51% Solution" employs a methodology that combines a systematic, summative evaluation strategy with criteria for assessing and comparing the effectiveness of a broad range of educational exhibitions.[13]

The data compared are from unobtrusive tracking and timing studies, a well-used method for looking at the process by which visitors interact with the various elements that make up the total exhibition experience. Visitor tracking and timing studies measure the relative thoroughness with which visitors use exhibitions. Time spent—allocation (where) and duration (how much)—in an exhibition is a means for learning to take place. This study is looking for answers to questions about normative trends and exceptional data on visitor time and use of all types of exhibitions.

Started with the help of 24 museum practitioners at the 1993 Visitor Studies Association conference, the number of exhibitions in the database is growing. A goal of 100 is sought, and a summary report is due in 1997. The final year of this research project is being supported by the National Science Foundation.

5. Initiated in 1982 at the Field Museum of Natural History and supported by the W. K. Kellogg Foundation, a project

called "Museums: Agents for Public Education" took place over a six-year period. Five hundred museum professionals, from more than 300 institutions, attended workshops held in Chicago for educators and exhibit development teams. Although this was not specifically a research collaborative, it was definitely a collaboration and it had many implications for exhibitions, interpretation, and evaluation. The final publication is a synthesis of the interactions, explorations, and discoveries shared by the participants. Called *Open Conversations: Strategies for Professional Development in Museums,* the report also contains activities that museum practitioners can conduct for themselves in their own institutions.

These types of collaborative studies will help us reach a time when all types of evaluation will be standard practice in museums. Raising the priority of educational effectiveness, recognizing the importance of labels as primary communicators in exhibitions, and allocating more of the resources toward this objective will help get us there. Research, evaluation, and visitor studies—regardless of the methodology—that challenge entrenched views by institutional staff will take time to have an impact on overall policymaking or the specifics of exhibition development. We're getting closer, and there's no reason to stop trying.

NOTES FOR CHAPTER 19:

1. Harris Shettel, *An Evaluation of Visitor Response to "Man in His Environment,"* Report no. AIR-43200-7/76-FR, Washington, D.C.: American Institutes of Research, 1976. This is also available as a technical report from the Center for Social Design, Jacksonville, Ala.

2 Harris Shettel et al., *Strategies for Determining Exhibit Effectiveness,* Report no. AIR E95-4/68-FR, Washington, D.C.: American Institutes for Research, 1968.

3. "Profile of an Exhibit: Evaluation Report" is a 1992 unpublished study done by Serrell & Associates for the Pratt Museum in Homer, Alaska. Data were gathered while the exhibition was at the Oakland Museum in California.

4. Paulette McManus, "It's the company you keep . . . The social determination of learning-related behavior in a science museum," *The
International Journal of Museum Management and Curatorship* 6
(1987): 263–270, and Lois H. Silverman, "Visitor Meaning-Making in
Museums for a New Age," *Curator: The Museum Journal* 38, no. 3
(1995).

5. Britt Raphling and Beverly Serrell, "Capturing Affective Learning,"
in *Current Trends in Audience Research and Evaluation*, Vol. 7, AAM
Committee on Audience Research and Evaluation, 1993.

6. Harris Shettel's paper cited in note 1 above also contains a discussion about how to analyze open-ended responses.

7. "1992 Visitor-Use Survey at Old South Meeting House" is an
unpublished report done by Serrell & Associates in conjunction with
Stahl Associates Architects, the National Park Service, and American
History Workshop.

8. Ellen Giusti, evaluator for the American Museum of Natural
History, has presented information from this on-going project at the
AAM and VSA meetings.

9. Randi Korn, "An Analysis of Differences Between Visitors at
Natural History Museums and Science Centers," *Curator: The
Museum Journal* 38, no. 3 (1995).

10. *Insights: Museums, Visitors, Attitudes, Expectations: A Focus Group
Experiment* (Malibu, Calif.: J. Paul Getty Trust and Getty Center for
Education in the Arts, 1991).

11. P. A. Anderson, *The Museum Impact and Evaluation Study: Roles of
Affect in the Museum Visit and Ways of Assessing Them* (Chicago:
Museum of Science and Industry, 1993).

12. Deborah L. Perry, "The Museum Impact and Evaluation Study:
How Visitors Relate to Science and Technology Museums," in *Visitor
Studies: Theory, Research, and Practice*, Vol. 5, edited by Don Thomp-
son, Arlene Benefield, Stephen Bitgood, Harris Shettel, and Ridgeley
Williams (Jacksonville, Ala.: Visitor Studies Association, 1993).

13. Beverly Serrell, "Using Behavior to Define the Effectiveness of Exhi-
bitions" in Bicknell and "The 51% Solution Research Project: A Meta-
Analysis of Visitor Time/Use in Museum Exhibitions," *Visitor
Behavior* 10, no. 3 (Fall 1995), plus a response by Harris Shettel.

Ten Deadly Sins and 14 Helpful Research Findings

Many common mistakes are avoidable, and some findings from visitor studies guide the way.

In *Making Exhibit Labels,* I listed eight deadly sins that fell mainly in the categories of poor writing, poor editing, bad typographic design, and poor placement that rendered labels uninteresting or illegible or both.[1] Steve Bitgood extended the list to include two more: the use of unintelligible codes, such as color coding, time lines or charts, and icons—usually on maps, but sometimes used to "signal" a type of information; and excessive density of label copy and graphics, where the sheer number of objects and labels makes it difficult for visitors to select and focus on any one thing.[2]

Here is a revised and updated list of the common sins that label makers commit. Prescriptions for ways to avoid them have been given elsewhere in this book, but a brief summary will remind you again of what to avoid:

10 DEADLY SINS

1. Labels that are not related to a big idea, that ramble without focus or objectives.
2. Labels that have too much emphasis on instruction (presenting information) instead of interpretation (offering provocation).
3. Labels that do not address visitors' prior knowledge, interests and/or misconceptions—that don't know who the audience is.

4. Labels with no apparent system of design and content to organize the messages, codes, or context.
5. Labels written with a vocabulary that is out of reach for the majority of visitors.
6. Labels that are too long and wordy.
7. Labels that ask questions that are not visitors' questions.
8. Labels for interactives that do not have instructions or interpretations located in integrated, logical ways.
9. Labels that do not begin with concrete, visual references.
10. Labels that are hard to read because of poor typography (bad choice of typeface, design, colors, lighting, materials, or placement).

Research and evaluation of labels in exhibitions tells us that there are things that tend to decrease visitor reading and comprehension, and there are things that tend to increase it. The list above deals with the bad stuff.

Below, we will summarize some of the good stuff—findings that can help us make better decisions about exhibition design so that we can raise the number of visitors who read—an important activity in educational exhibitions.

14 HELPFUL RESEARCH AND EVALUATION FINDINGS

Effective labels and effective exhibitions are unique combinations of variables that together can enhance or deter communication. The 14 points below are based on unpublished evaluation studies, published empirical research data, and the collected wisdom of label writers, designers, exhibit developers, and evaluators who have been working to improve labels for years.[3]

1. When visitors have good conceptual and spatial orientation in exhibitions, they are more likely to spend more time and learn more.
2. When visitors spend more time, they tend to use more parts of the exhibition, and are more likely to understand what it was about.

3. More visitors read shorter labels, and read them more thoroughly than longer labels.

4. The most popular parts of a good exhibition will attract a broad cross section of the audience, not a special sub-group.

5. Among adults, those who read labels and those who use interactive devices are not two separate audiences.

6. Labels placed higher than six or seven feet off the ground are often not seen by visitors. Labels placed directly next to what they are about will be read more than labels keyed by a number on the text and placed at a greater distance away.

7. Labels next to dimensional elements in exhibits get read more than flat label panels on the wall, without objects nearby. This includes introductory and orientation information.

8. Chunking information into short paragraphs, 25 to 75 words long, increases the likelihood of reading.

9. Labels that contain concrete, visually referenced information will increase visitors' tendencies to read-look-read-look, pointing and talking.

10. Labels that visitors find interesting will be read aloud more than others. Reading aloud increases social, intra-group behaviors.

11. Visitors who read labels spend more time and do more things in exhibitions overall than nonreaders of any age.

12. More adults will read label text to children when labels are easy to read out loud without the need to paraphrase or translate unfamiliar vocabulary words (for themselves or their children).

13. Children will read labels if the labels provide them with easily accessible and useful information. Adults, who are accustomed to receiving information through the written word, will work harder to get it than children.

14. Labels with images and words working together are meaningful and memorable to more visitors than all-text labels.

The scope of these guidelines clearly takes us beyond writing interesting, short, well-crafted, visitor-comprehensible, legible labels. It makes effective communication of the whole exhibition a goal. "Our eyes are on another professional guideline—creating integrated presentations of well-written words with objects, illustrations, and interactives—that really work, and to do this requires extraordinary teamwork and lots of formative evaluation."[4] It takes more than increased knowledge and improved skills of individual professionals. But if all eyes are on the same prize, it's sure to be within reach.

The guidelines listed here will not guarantee success, but they will help you avoid problems that prevent effective interpretation. The glossary and the resource lists that follow will help label writers communicate with each other more efficiently and effectively and accomplish their task of communicating with visitors more successfully. Good luck!

NOTES FOR CHAPTER 20:

1. Beverly Serrell, *Making Exhibit Labels: A Step-by-Step Guide* (Nashville, Tenn.: American Association for State and Local History Press, 1983).

2. Stephen Bitgood, "Deadly Sins Revisited: A Review of the Exhibit Label Literature," *Visitor Behavior* 4, no. 3 (Fall 1989).

3. The most comprehesive bibliography of published studies can be found in C. G. Screven, ed. *Visitor Studies Bibliography and Abstracts*, 3d. ed. (Shorewood, Wis.: Exhibit Communications, Research, Inc., 1993).

4. Frances Kruger, former interpretive specialist, Denver Museum of Natural History, personal communication. Kruger is now doing exhibit development, writing, and editing on a free-lance basis and running a used bookstore, "Old Friends."

Glossary

As a profession, museum exhibit practitioners are a relatively young group with few agreed-upon standards, no basic training manuals, and an unclear shared vocabulary. We need to be more careful in defining our terms and using them consistently.

In 1993, while I was working on a poster for the AAM's Current Trends session involving a questionnaire for museum practitioners, I discovered that some of the words I had used meant different things to different people. This normally would not have been surprising, but these were very basic words, like "visitor," "museum," and "exhibit." I wondered how, if we did not agree on definitions of such fundamental terms, could we ever hope to communicate to our visitors. So, here are mine.

The glossary has three parts: **General Terms, Evaluation Terms,** and **Typographic Terms.** Some terms do not fall neatly into one particular category. For example, "accountability" might refer to a general museum mission issue, or educational efforts, or evaluation.

GENERAL TERMS

Accountability: The responsibilities of the museum to show that their educational intentions, mission, objectives, etc., are having the intended impact. Evidence for impact can be gathered by systematic techniques that include visitor surveys, open-ended interviews, observations of visitor behavior, or other forms of feedback from visitors. Comment books are not considered systematic, valid forms of feedback for documenting impact, but they often do gather interesting and useful anecdotal information.

Broad audiences: Audiences that include a diversity of demographic characteristics—i.e., ages, social groups, races or cultural backgrounds, economic and education levels, and prior museum visitation habits. To be thought of as a pluralistic whole, not segmented into separate groups.

Communication goals: Unifying themes, stated in language that a visitor might use, that you hope visitors receive and integrate from the exhibition. Used in this book interchangeably with learning objectives, although the term "goals" is typically broader than "objectives."

Educational exhibit: An exhibition with stated and specific learning goals, communication objectives, and intended teaching impacts. It has a self-proclaimed didactic purpose from which the exhibit planners work.

Effectiveness: The degree to which the exhibition achieves its stated objectives with its intended audience.

Exhibit, or exhibit elements: Discrete, conceptual units, experiences, or components within the exhibition layout, planned by the exhibit developers as separate experiences for visitors. They may vary widely in size and type, such as, a panel, a case, a diorama, a set of artifacts, a video theater, a computer, an interactive device.

Exhibit developers: Individuals or teams who have the responsibility of conceiving, researching, designing, writing, fabricating, installing, and evaluating exhibitions.

Exhibition: A defined room or space, with a given title, containing elements that together make up a coherent entity that is conceptually recognizable as a display of objects, animals, interactives, and phenomena.

Exhibition objectives: A variety of intentions stated by exhibit developers to identify what they hope the exhibit will accomplish. Some have to do with *presentation*—what the exhibits will present or show. Others are related to *impact*—what the results will be, either for educational, economic, public-relations, or professional recognition. Exhibition objectives related to impact on visitors' learning are also called learning objectives and communication goals. Each of these different kinds of objectives should be defined completely, separately, and clearly.

Impact: A change in visitors' beliefs, attitudes, behaviors, skills, or understanding that occurs as a result of experiencing the museum exhibit. Immediate impact becomes the basis for additional and long-term impacts.

Informal evaluation: Unsystematic methods used to gather data. See systematic evaluation.

Iterative: An action or process that is repeated, with modifications, several times.

Label: Written words used alone or with illustrations in museum exhibitions to provide information for visitors, presented as text on exhibit graphic panels or computer screens. Known to visitors as captions, descriptions, titles, blurbs, explanations, placards, plaques, legends, cards, labels, and "those little words on the wall."

Layer: One quantity, factor, or purpose that has a hierarchy over or under another. Implies some order, such as first-to-last, top-to-bottom.

Learning: A change, small or large, that happens in a person's cognitive structure as a result of a new integration—new information, attitudes, feelings, or skills; new connections between prior knowledge and new information, and a new reflection of something already known (another kind of new connection).

Learning objectives: Defined as intended, measurable changes in visitors' knowledge, memories, feelings, or other cognitive events specified by the museum. Can be stated broadly: "Visitors will find out about or realize something new about X"; "Visitors will make a personal connection with Y"; "Visitors will be inspired to wonder 'what if . . . ,' about Z as a result of experiencing this exhibition." Or as more focused statements: "Visitors will comprehend the purpose of the exhibition"; "Visitors will be able to identify the main theme of the exhibit." This statement—"The exhibit will present the current thinking about A and B and will explore the contrasts and similarities of C and D"—is not a learning objective because it only says what the museum will *present,* not what the visitors (the learners) themselves can *do* as a result. (See also: educational exhibits, exhibition objectives, and communication goals.)

Learning styles: Learners' preferences for how they like to receive and process information and solve problems. Not to be confused with modalities, which refers more to forms of instructional design, not learners.

Level: One quantity, factor, or purpose that has a hierarchy over or under another. Implies some order, such as first-to-last, top-to-bottom. See layers. I use these two terms interchangeably.

Modalities: Different methods, modes, or forms of communication used in exhibitions, or the manner in which interpretation is presented, such as labels, AV, demonstrations, or graphics.

Museum: An institution open to the public, with professional staff, that collects and displays "stuff"—real objects and facsimiles, living and dead organisms, organic and inorganic materials, and phenomena—and usually serves the multiple functions of education, conservation, research, and recreation.

Museum practitioners: The people who work in the museum or who are well-versed in the skills, background knowledge and functions of a museum. Examples include directors, curators (or subject matter experts), educators, evaluators, exhibit and graphic designers, administrators, fund-raisers.

Novice: A person who is inexperienced, new to the subject, a beginner who is interested in learning; a person who has no special knowledge, interest, training, or vocabulary about a particular topic. Opposite of an expert.

Outcomes: A change in visitors' beliefs, attitudes, behaviors, skills, or understanding that occurs as a result of experiencing the museum exhibit. Learning. Also called impacts. Immediate outcomes become the basis for additional and long-term impacts.

Systematic evaluation: Using the same definitions and techniques in the same ways at different times or in a variety of settings so that the data will be comparable. Systematic is a more precise term than the more commonly used "formal evaluation," and is the opposite of "informal" or unsystematic.

Visitor studies: A broad term for a variety of evaluation or research studies on museum visitors. Examples: Demographic and psychographic visitor surveys; formative evaluation of mock-ups; focus groups with target audiences or advisory groups; visitor behavior research.

Visitors: The self-selected people who come to the museum voluntarily, alone, or with a social group of family or peers. Unless stated otherwise, I will use the term to refer to adults who are casual, free-ranging visitors, not school groups, people in tour groups, or those using audio-headsets.

Voice: A point of view, expressed through a variety of exhibit techniques in an exhibition, that usually speaks to visitors as an unseen figure.

EVALUATION TERMS

Average time (in exhibitions): Average time is calculated as the sum of the total times spent by all visitors in a random sample, divided by the number of visitors in the sample. It is the amount of time the majority of visitors did not exceed in an exhibition. For example, if the average time was 10 minutes, then it is highly likely that half the visitors stayed less than 10 minutes in the exhibit.

Formative evaluation: Evaluation done on mock-ups or prototypes of exhibit elements to test their effectiveness before making a final version. Usually related to parts of the exhibition, not the whole thing.

Front-end evaluation: Evaluation done before exhibition plans are firm to help shape exhibition content, goals, and vocabulary. Also called status-quo evaluation. Usually related to overall conceptual plans, not just one particular element.

Informal evaluation: Unsystematic methods used to gather data. See *systematic evaluation.*

Majority: More than half (over 50%) of a sample of visitors or elements in an exhibition. It does not refer to the majority of the general population (e.g., city residents or census figures).

Randomly selected: Selected without bias for gender, age, race, or social group. Subjects are selected by a specified mechanism (e.g., every fifth visitor) over representative periods of days of the week and time of day. In museums, true random sampling is rarely used because it is impractical to select samples during all times of the day/week/season/year.

Summative evaluation: A type of evaluation conducted on the whole exhibition with all its parts in context with actual visiting public after the exhibition is open.

Systematic evaluation: Using the same definitions and techniques in the same ways at different times or in a variety of settings so that the data will be comparable. Systematic is a more precise term than the more commonly used "formal evaluation," and is the opposite of "informal" or unsystematic.

Visitor studies: A broad term for a variety of evaluation or research studies on museum visitors. *Examples:* Demographic and psychographic visitor surveys, formative evaluation of mock-ups, focus groups with target audiences or advisory groups, visitor behavior research.

BASIC VOCABULARY OF TYPOGRAPHY

Body text: Running copy, or text that is written and read in sentences and in paragraphs.

Bold face: A thicker version of a typeface to add emphasis.

Characters per line: The number of letters in one line of type, or the number of letters that will fit in a line of type.

Display type: Larger typefaces designed for special emphasis, often elaborate or unusual designs, not appropriate for body copy, but good for titles.

Fonts: A display of all the characters within a typeface, including punctuation, accents, and symbols. The font lets you see all the choices all at once for that face.

Italics: A slanted version of a typeface to create emphasis or separation between words or lines of words, or to signify a quotation, title, or a scientific name.

Justification: The spacing and alignment of lines of type to fit equally between the right and left margins. When type is flush left and right, it is justified.

Kerning: Adjusting the amount of space between letters for the most attractive fit, especially when a slanting letter is next to a round one, as in WOW.

Kiss: Three definitions: 1) a typographic term for letters without letterspace, touching; 2) a printer's term for touching the paper lightly to the printing press; 3) an abbreviation for the advice, Keep It Simple, Stupid.

Lead, Leading (pronounced "ledding"): Refers to the amount of space between the lines of type.

Letterspace: The distance between the letters. For example, tight, touching, wide, or extra wide letterspace. In computers, it is called tracking, and is incremented by points, from a zero reference, e.g., "plus two" or "minus one."

Line space: The vertical distance between the baselines of type, also called leading after metal typesetting when adding space was done by adding a solid bar of lead between lines of type. Measured in points.

Picas: In typography, a unit of measure that equals one-sixth of an inch (6 picas equals one inch).

Point: A measure of the size of type, based on one point equals 1/72 of an inch.

Ragged: The spacing and alignment of lines of type set to be flush to the left or right margin, with equal space between each word, allowing uneven line lengths.

Serif and sans serif type: Serifs are the small end strokes on letters, and serif type usually has varying widths within the letterforms. Sans serif mean without serifs, and usually means letters that have the same weight to all their lines. The two groups traditionally were easy to distinguish and serif fonts were not mixed with sans serif. Some newer typeface designs have combined serif and sans serif into one family.

Typeface or face: The particular design of type, the shape and look of the letters, which are named by or after their designers, such as Garamond, Optima, Matrix.

Type family: A range of variations designed within one typeface. The family shows the names of the choices of styles (regular, bold, italic, small capitals) for that face.

Type size: Determined in one of two standard methods: the distance between the top of the tallest ascender and the lowest descender of a lowercase typeface, measured in points ("This is 12-point type); or the height of a capital letter, called key size, and measured in picas, centimeters, or inches. "It was set in 36-point type" refers to the overall size of text.

Word space: The distance between words. In computer page-layout programs, it is called "standard," and can be adjusted in increments of "-1," "-2," or "+1," "+2" (etc.) A -5 wordspace makes the letters touch, or "kiss."

x-height: The size of type measured by the height of a lower case letter from the baseline to the top of the letters, not including ascenders or descenders. The x-height of a typeface will influence the look of its overall size.

Resources

There are lots of interesting papers about the effectiveness of labels and how to write them, many of which can be found in publications available through the Visitor Studies Association, and the Center for Social Design. Since 1986, the quarterly newsletter *Visitor Behavior* has provided reviews, summaries and research reports on exhibit labels and many other aspects of exhibitions.

Steve Bitgood, founder and editor of *Visitor Behavior,* has provided two issues that focus exclusively on labels, including one that presented summaries of research on labels (Volume 4, Number 3, Fall 1989). Studies on label length, vertical placement, letter size, relational placement, graphic elements, and cueing visitors to read were summarized, and the studies were related to some of the common precepts of "deadly sins" of labeling. In addition, there is an alphabetical listing of many articles by author. To join the Visitor Studies Association and/or subscribe to the newsletter, contact:

Department of Psychology
Colorado State University
Ft. Collins, CO 80523-1876

Current Trends in Audience Research and Evaluation has been published each year since 1987 by CARE (Committee on Audience Research and Evaluation, a standing professional committee of the American Association of Museums) in conjunction with the AAM's annual conference. *Current Trends* is a compilation of each year's poster sessions. CARE also has an occasional newsletter called the *Gage.* To join CARE or receive back issues of *Current Trends,* contact:

American Association of Museums
1225 Eye Street NW
Washington, DC 20005
or

CARE
c/o Mary Beth Mobley
St. Louis Science Center
5050 Oakland Avenue
St. Louis, MO 63110

Curator, a journal published by the American Museum of Natural History, often carries articles with frequent references to exhibitions and evaluation. To subscribe to this quarterly magazine, contact:

Curator: The Museum Journal
American Museum of Natural History
Central Park West at 79th Street
New York, NY 10024

The extensive *Visitor Studies Bibliography and Abstracts* is an essential resource for label writers. The third edition is available from:

ILVS Review
P.O. Box 11827
Shorewood, WI 53211

Another standing professional committee of the AAM is NAME, which has a handy and provocative newsletter called *The Exhibitionist.* To join and receive it, contact:

National Association of Museum Exhibition (NAME)
c/o Exhibitionist Newsletter editor Diana F. Cohen
MRC 808,
Washington, DC 20560

The sources mentioned above, for the most part, are available, readable, and very useful for writers and exhibit developers. Other organizations that hold conferences and/or have publications available include:

The Association of Science-Technology Centers (ASTC)
1413 K Street, NW, Tenth floor
Washington, DC 20005

American Zoo and Aquarium Association
Oglebay Park
Wheeling, WV 26003

The Interpretation Publications and Resource Center
P.O. Box 398
North Stonington, CT 06359

Journal of Museum Education
Museum Education Roundtable
P.O. Box 23664
Washington, DC 20026

Society of Environmental Graphic Designers
47 Third Street
Cambridge, MA 02141

Two other magazines available by subscription are:
Identity
407 Gilbert Avenue
Cincinnati, OH 45273

Exhibit Builder
P.O. Box 4144
Woodland Hills, CA 91365

Bibliography

Alt, M. B., and K. M. Shaw. "Characteristics of Ideal Museum Exhibits." *British Journal of Psychology* 75 (1984).

Anderson, P. A. *The Museum Impact and Evaluation Study: Roles of Affect in the Museum Visit and Ways of Assessing Them.* Chicago: Museum of Science and Industry, 1993.

Bicknell, Sandra, and Graham Farmelo, eds. *Museum Visitor Studies in the 90s.* London: Science Museum, 1993.

Bitgood, Stephen. *Knowing When Exhibit Labels Work: A Standardized Guide for Evaluating and Improving Labels.* Technical Report No. 87-90. Jacksonville, Ala.: Center for Social Design, 1987.

―――. "Deadly Sins Revisited: A Review of the Exhibit Label Literature." *Visitor Behavior* 4, no. 3 (Fall 1989).

―――. "The ABCs of Label Design." In *Visitor Studies: Theory, Research, and Practice, Volume 3,* edited by Stephen Bitgood, Arlene Benefield, and Donald Patterson. Jacksonville, Ala.: Center for Social Design, 1991.

―――, ed. "Special Issue: Labels, Signs, & Graphics." *Visitor Behavior* 1, no. 3 (October 1986).

―――, ed. "Special Issue: Orientation and Circulation." *Visitor Behavior* 1, no. 4 (January 1987).

―――, ed. "Special Issue: Exhibit Labeling." *Visitor Behavior* 4, no. 3 (Fall 1989).

Bitgood, Stephen et al. *Effects of Label Characteristics on Visitor Behavior.* Technical Report No. 86-55. Jacksonville, Ala.: Jacksonville State University, Psychology Institute, 1986.

Black, Linda A. "Applying Learning Theory in the Development of a Museum Learning Environment." In *What Research Says about Learning in Science Museums.* Washington, D.C.: Association of Science-Technology Centers, 1990.

Blackmon, Carolyn P., Teresa K. LaMaster, Lisa C. Roberts, and Beverly Serrell. *Open Conversations: Strategies for Professional Development in Museums.* Chicago: Field Museum of Natural History, 1988.

Borun, Minda, and Katherine A. Adams. "From Hands On to Minds On: Labelling Interactive Exhibits." In *Visitor Studies: Theory, Research, and Practice, Volume 4,* edited by Arlene Benefield, Stephen Bitgood, and Harris Shettel. Jacksonville, Ala.: Center for Social Design, 1992.

Boisvert, Dorothy L, and Brenda J. Slez. "The Relationship between Exhibit Characteristics and Learning-Associated Behaviors in a Science Museum Discovery Space." *Science Education* 79 (5) 1995.

Brennan, Thomas J. "Elements of Social Group Behavior in a Natural Setting." Master's thesis, Texas A&M University, 1977.

Chambers, Marlene. "Is Anyone Out There? Audience and Communication." *Museum News,* June 1984.

———. "Beyond 'Aha!': Motivating Museum Visitors." In *What Research Says about Learning in Science Museums.* Washington, D.C.: Association of Science-Technology Centers, 1990.

———. "After Legibility, What?" *Curator: The Museum Journal* 36, no. 3, 1993.

Crane, Valerie et al. *Informal Science Learning: What the Research Says about Television, Science, Museums, and Community-based Projects.* Dedham, Mass.: Research Communications Ltd., 1994.

Critiquing Museum Exhibitions: The Sequel. The AAM 87th Annual Meeting. Videocassette. Eldridge, Md.: Chesapeake Audio/Video Communications, Inc., 1995.

Csikszentmihalyi, Mihaly. *Beyond Boredom and Anxiety: The Experience of Play in Work and Games.* San Francisco: Jossey-Bass Publishers, 1985.

Csikszentmihalyi, Mihaly, and Kim Hermanson. "Intrinsic Motivation in Museums: What Makes Visitors Want to Learn?" *Museum News* 74, no. 3 (May/June 1995).

Csikszentmihalyi, Mihaly, and Rick E. Robinson. *The Art of Seeing: An Interpretation of the Aesthetic Encounter.* Malibu, Calif.: J. Paul Getty Museum and Getty Center for Education in the Arts, 1990.

Davidson, Betty. *New Dimensions for Traditional Dioramas: Multi-sensory Additions for Access, Interest and Learning.* Boston: Museum of Science, 1991.

Diamond, J. "The Behavior of Family Groups in Science Museums." *Curator: The Museum Journal* 29, no. 2. 1986.

Dillenburg, Eugene. "Turning Multiculturalism on Its Head." *Exhibitionist* 14, no. 2 (Fall 1995).

Falk, John H., and Lynn D. Dierking. *The Museum Experience.* Washington, D.C.: Whalesback Books, 1992.

———, eds. *Public Institutions for Personal Learning: Understanding the Long-term Impact of Museums.* Profession Practice Series. AAM Technical Information Service.

Gardner, Howard. *Frames of Mind: The Theory of Multiple Intelligences.* New York: Basic Books, 1985.

Harris, Neil. "Exhibiting Controversy." *Museum News* 74, no. 5 (September/October, 1995).

Harter, Jim. *Animals: 1419 Copyright-Free Illustrations of Mammals, Birds, Fish, Insects, etc.* New York: Dover Publications, 1979.

Insights: Museums, Visitors, Attitudes, Expectations: A Focus Group Experiment. Malibu, Calif.: J. Paul Getty Trust and Getty Center for Education in the Arts, 1991.

Jager, Jonathan. "Environmental Correctness (EC) for Designers." *Exhibitionist* 14, no. 2 (Fall 1995).

Kennedy, Jeff. *User-Friendly: Hands-On Exhibits That Work.* Washington, DC: Association of Science-Technology Centers, 1990.

Korn, Randi. "An Analysis of Differences Between Visitors at Natural History Museums and Science Centers." *Curator: The Museum Journal* 38, no. 3 (1995).

Kroeger, Otto. "Exhibiting Our Differences." *Exhibitionist* 14, no. 1 (Spring 1995).

Krueger, Richard A. *Focus Groups: A Practical Guide for Applied Research.* Newbury Park, Calif.: SAGE Publications, 1988.

Labuz, Ronald. *The Computer in Graphic Design.* New York: Van Nostrand Reinhold, 1993.

Lankford, Sherri, Stephen Bitgood, and Amy Cota, eds. "Special Issue: Orientation and Circulation." *Visitor Behavior* 10, no. 2 (Summer 1995).

Layton, Jennifer. *Writing for Novice Visitors: The Minneapolis Institute of Arts Handbook of Style.* Minneapolis: Minneapolis Institute of Arts, 1991.

Litwak, Jane Marie. "Another Measurement Tool for Exhibit Evaluators: The Time/Activity Matrix." In *Visitor Studies: Theory, Research, and Practice.* Vol. 8, edited by S. Lankford. Jacksonville, Ala.: Visitor Studies Association (in press).

Mackinney, Lisa Hubbell. "What Visitors Want to Know: The Use of Front-end and Formative Evaluation in Determining Label Content in an Art Museum." Master's thesis, John F. Kennedy University, 1993.

Mastro, Ed. "A Beginner's Guide to Vinyl Lettering Systems." *Exhibitionist,* 14, no. 1 (Spring 1995).

McCarthy, Bernice. *The 4MAT System: Teaching to Learning Styles with Right/Left Mode Techniques.* Barrington, Ill.: EXCEL. Inc., 1987.

McDermott-Lewis, Melora. *The Denver Art Museum Interpretive Project.* Denver: Denver Art Museum, Winter 1990.

McLean, Kathleen. *Planning for People in Museum Exhibitions.* Washington, D.C.: Association of Science-Technology Centers, 1993.

McManus, Paulette. "It's the company you keep . . . The social determination of learning-related behavior in a science museum." *The International Journal of Museum Management and Curatorship* 6:263–270. 1987

———. "Watch Your Language! People Do Read Labels." In *What Research Says about Learning in Science Museums.* Washington, D.C.: Association of Science-Technology Centers, 1990.

Miles, Roger S. "Lessons in 'Human Biology': Testing a Theory of Exhibition Design." *The International Journal of Museum Management and Curatorship* 5 (1986).

Minneapolis Institute of Arts, The Interdivisional Committee on Interpretation. *Interpretation at the Minneapolis Institute of Arts: Policy and Practice.* Minneapolis: Minneapolis Institute of Arts, 1993.

Perkins, D. N. "What Constructivism Demands of the Learner." *Educational Technology,* Vol. XXXI, No. 9. September 1991.

Perry, Deborah L. "The Museum Impact and Evaluation Study: How Visitors Relate to Science and Technology Museums." In *Visitor Studies: Theory, Research, and Practice, Volume 5,* edited by Don Thompson, Arlene Benefield, Stephen Bitgood, Harris Shettel, and Ridgeley Williams. Jacksonville, Ala.: Visitor Studies Association, 1993.

Poggenpohl, Sharon H. "More than a Book Review of 'The Electronic Word.'" *Visible Language* 28, no. 2 (Spring 1994).

Postman, Neil. *The End of Education: Redefining the Value of School.* New York: Alfred A. Knopf, Borzoi Books, 1995.

Punt, Barbara. *Doing It Right: A Workbook for Improving Exhibit Labels.* Brooklyn: The Brooklyn Children's Museum, 1989.

Rand, Judy. *Fish Stories that Hook Readers.* Technical Report No. 90-30. Jacksonville, Ala.: Center for Social Design, 1985.

Raphling, Britt, and Beverly Serrell. "Capturing Affective Learning." In *Current Trends in Audience Research and Evaluation, Volume 7.* AAM Committee on Audience Research and Evaluation, 1993.

Roberts, Lisa Carrole. "From Knowledge to Narrative: Educators and the Changing Museum." Ph.D. dissertation, University of Chicago, 1992. To be published by Smithsonian Press (in press).

Rorimer, Anne. "Michael Asher and James Coleman at Artists Space." In *Michael Asher / James Coleman, June 2 – July 2, 1988.* New York: Artists Space, 1988.

Rubinstein, Richard. *Digital Typography.* Addison-Wesley, 1988.

Schloder, John E., Marjorie Williams, and C. Griffith Mann. *The Visitor's Voice: Visitor Studies in the Renaissance–Baroque Galleries of The Cleveland Museum of Art 1990–1993.* Cleveland: The Cleveland Museum of Art, 1993.

Schwartz, Amy E. "The Well-Written Label." *Washington Post,* June 15, 1993.

Screven, C. G. "Computers in Museum Settings." In *Visitor Studies: Theory, Research, and Practice, Volume 3*, edited by Stephen Bitgood, Arlene Benefield, and Donald Patterson. Jacksonville, Ala.: Center for Social Design, 1991.

———. "Motivating Visitors to Read Labels." *ILVS Review: A Journal of Visitor Behavior* 2 no. 2, 1992.

———, ed. *Visitor Studies Bibliography and Abstracts,* Third edition. Shorewood, Wis.: Exhibit Communications, Research, Inc., 1993.

Seagram, Belinda Crawford, Leslie H. Patten, and Christine W. Lockett. "Audience Research and Exhibit Development: A Framework. *Museum Management and Curatorship* 12 (1993).

Serrell, Beverly. *Making Exhibit Labels: A Step-by-Step Guide.* Nashville, Tenn.: American Association for State and Local History Press, 1983.

———. Introduction to *What Research Says about Learning in Science Museums.* Washington, D.C.: Association of Science-Technology Centers, 1990.

———. "Learning Styles and Museum Visitors." In *What Research Says about Learning in Science Museums.* Washington, D.C.: Association of Science-Technology Centers, 1990.

———. "Characteristics of a Positive Museum Experience (PME)." In *Visitor Studies: Theory, Research, and Practice, Volume 5*, edited by Don Thompson, Arlene Benefield, Stephen Bitgood, Harris Shettel, and Ridgeley Williams. Jacksonville, Ala.: Visitor Studies Association, 1993.

———. "The 51% Solution Research Project: A Meta-Analysis of Visitor Time/Use in Museum Exhibitions." *Visitor Behavior* 10, no. 3 (Fall 1995).

Serrell, Beverly, and Hannah Jennings. "We are here: Three years of wayfinding studies at Brookfield Zoo." Proceedings of the American Association of Zoological Parks and Aquariums. Oglebay Park, West Virginia, 1985.

Serrell, Beverly, and Britt Raphling. "Computers on the Exhibit Floor." *Curator: The Museum Journal* 35, no. 3 (1992).

Serrell & Associates. "From Stuffed Birds on Sticks to Vivid Feathers, Gleaming Talons and Sparkling Beaks: A Summative Evaluation of the Bird Halls at Field Museum of Natural History." Unpublished.

Shettel, Harris. "Exhibits: Art Form or Educational Medium?" *Museum News* 52, no. 1, 1973.

———. *An Evaluation of Visitor Response to "Man and His Environment."* Report no. AIR-43200-7/76-FR. Washington, D.C.: American Institutes of Research, 1976.

Shettel, Harris, et al. *Strategies for Determining Exhibit Effectiveness.* Report no. AIR E95-4/68-FR. Washington, D.C.: American Institutes for Research, 1968.

Silverman, Lois H. "Of Us and Other 'Things': The Content and Functions of Talk by Adult Visitor Pairs in an Art and a History Museum." Ph.D. dissertation, University of Pennsylvania, 1990.

———. "Visitor Meaning-Making in Museums for a New Age." *Curator: The Museum Journal* 38, no. 3 (1995).

Spiekermann, Erik, and E.M. Ginger. *Stop Stealing Sheep & Find Out How Type Works.* Mountain View, Calif.: Adobe Press, 1993.

Taylor, Samuel, ed. *Try It! Improving Exhibits Through Formative Evaluation.* Washington, D.C.: Association of Science-Technology Centers, 1991.

Tilden, Freeman. *Interpreting Our Heritage,* Third edition. Chapel Hill, N.C.: University of North Carolina Press, 1977.

Trapp, Suzanne, Michael Gross, and Ron Zimmerman. *Signs, Trails, and Wayside Exhibits: Connecting People and Places.* Interpreter's Handbook Series, no. 4. University of Wisconsin-Stevens Point.

Vance, Cynthia L., and Daniel A. Schroeder. "Matching Visitor Learning Style with Exhibit Type: Implications for Learning in Informal Settings." In *Visitor Studies: Theory, Research, and Practice, Volume 4,* edited by Arlene Benefield, Stephen Bitgood, and Harris Shettel. Jacksonville, Ala.: Center for Social Design, 1992.

Wallace, Mike. "The Battle of the Enola Gay." *Museum News* 74, no. 4 (July/August 1995).

Williams, Joseph M. *Style: Ten Lessons in Clarity and Grace,* Third edition. Chicago: University of Chicago Press, 1990.

Winn, William D. "The Assumptions of Constructivism and Instructional Design." *Educational Technology,* September 1991.

Wolf, Lisa F., and Jeffrey K. Smith, "What Makes Museum Labels Legible?" *Curator* 36, no. 2 (June 1993).

Zapf, Hermann. "Future Tendencies in Type Design: The Scientific Approach to Letterforms." *Visible Language* 19, no. 1 (Winter 1985).

Figure Credits

FIGURE 1, page 2, "Otters and Oil" at Shedd Aquarium, photo by
author; FIGURE 2, page 3, "Light! Spectra! Action!" photo by author,
courtesy of The Adler Planetarium & Astronomy Museum,
FIGURE 3, page 13 "Anchovies" © 1994 Monterey Bay Aquarium,
All Rights Reserved; FIGURE 4, page 13, "Bison" © 1995 All rights
reserved, Photo Archives, Denver Museum of Natural History,
Photographer Rick Wicker; FIGURE 5, page 23, "Messages from the
Wilderness" photo by author, courtesy of The Field Museum,
Chicago; FIGURE 6, page 25, "The Civil War" photo by author,
reproduced with the permission of the Chicago Historical Society;
FIGURE 7, page 29, "Six Plants" photo by author, courtesy of The
Field Museum; FIGURE 8, page 32, "Please don't touch" at Cleveland
Art Museum, photo by author; FIGURE 9, page 38, "Gator Bellow" at
Shedd Aquarium, photo by author; FIGURE 10, page 45, potential
label readers, photos by author; FIGURE 11, page 69, "Spanning the
River" photo by author, reproduced with the permission of the
Chicago Historical Society; FIGURE 12, page 73, "Catfish Farm" at
Shedd Aquarium, photo by author; FIGURE 13, page 74, "Electric
Fishes" at Belle Isle Aquarium, Detroit Zoo, photo by author;
FIGURE 14, page 76, "Jade" photo by author, courtesy of The Field
Museum; FIGURE 15, page 76, "Shore Patrol" at Michigan Maritime
Museum, photo by author; FIGURE 16, page 81, "Maya" in *Art Inside
Out: Kraft General Foods Education Center,* © 1995, The Art Institute
of Chicago, All Rights Reserved; FIGURE 17, page 86, "Sievers,
Graspers" at Natural History Museum, London, photo by author;
FIGURE 18, page 87, "Why Stripes?" at Toledo Zoo, photo by author;
FIGURE 19, page 89, "Post Contact" at British Columbia Provincial
Museum, photo by author; FIGURE 20, page 93, "Two Girls" photo
courtesy of The Denver Art Museum; FIGURE 21, page 99, "Mrs.
O'Leary" photo by author, reproduced with the permission of the
Chicago Historical Society; FIGURE 22, page 103, "Glacial Goop" at
Banff National Park and "Sam Nail Ranch" at Big Bend National
Park, photos by author; FIGURE 23, page 108, lift labels at the
Brooklyn Children's Museum, photo by author; FIGURE 24, page
118, "Key Clock Post" at Michigan Maritime Museum, photo by
author; FIGURE 25, page 126, "The Butterfly Connection" © John G.
Shedd Aquarium, Photographer Edward G. Lines, Jr.; FIGURE 26,
page 150, mosquito and bird draft sketches courtesy of National
Aquarium in Baltimore; FIGURE 27, page 151, "three rules" photo by

author, courtesy of The Adler Planetarium & Astronomy Museum; FIGURE 28, page 152, "Masters of the Night" photo by author, courtesy of The Field Museum; FIGURE 29, page 157, snake illustrations courtesy of Steve Stratakos for Brookfield Zoo; FIGURE 30, page 159, clip art sketches courtesy of Susan Sanvidge for Brookfield Zoo; FIGURE 31, page 160, vases in *Art Inside Out: Kraft General Foods Education Center,* © 1995, The Art Institute of Chicago, All Rights Reserved; FIGURE 32, page 163, wayfinding symbols courtesy of The Adler Planetarium & Astronomy Museum; FIGURE 33, page 166, "Try This" photo by author, courtesy of the Adler Planetarium & Astronomy Museum; FIGURE 34, page 172, "Antlers" © 1995 All rights reserved, Photo Archives, Denver Museum of Natural History, Photographer Rick Wicke; FIGURE 35, page 184, "Cleopatra" © 1995, The Art Institute of Chicago, All Rights Reserved; FIGURE 36, page 196, "Mash House" at the Macallan Distillery Visitor Center, photo by author; FIGURE 37, page 197, "Red Panda" at Bronx Zoo, Wildlife Conservation Park, photo by author; FIGURE 38, page 204, "typewritten label" photo courtesy of Monterey Bay Aquarium; FIGURE 39, page 204, "handwritten label" photo by author, courtesy of The Field Museum; FIGURE 40, page 216, engraved plastic label at Arizona Sonora Desert Museum, photo by author; FIGURE 41, page 217, shadow photo by author, reproduced with the permission of the Chicago Historical Society; FIGURE 42, page 222, "Darkened Waters" at Oakland Museum, photo by author. COVER PHOTO by Alan Teller and Beverly Serrell.

Index

COLOPHON

This book was designed and composed in QuarkXPress 3.3 for Macintosh. Primary specifications: Body text is printed in 10.5-point Minion regular, justified. Chapter titles are in 27-point Minion; introductions are in 13-point Minion italics. Univers 55 was used for the figure captions and case studies in 8- and 9-point type, ragged right.